Routledge Revivals

The Chains Are Broken

Originally published in 1964, this further volume in Poul Borchsenius' history of the Jewish people, is the story of the emancipation from the time when the Jews lived a segregated life in the ghetto, until the Age of Enlightenment they achieved equality. This was the time of Moses Mendelssohn, the famous philosopher and of the poet Heinrich Heine who gave expression to contemporary thought in his lyrical poetry. It was also the time when the Rothschild dynasty became an economic and political factor in contemporary Europe, and the Dreyfus Affair promoted a new wave of antisemitism. In Eastern Europe, particularly, antisemitism took a violent turn, and it was this that made the founder of Israel, Theodor Herzl, begin to agitate for the establishment of a Jewish national state.

The Chains Are Broken
The Story of Jewish Emancipation

Poul Borchsenius

First published in English in 1964 by George Allen & Unwin Ltd.
This edition first published in 2024 by Routledge
4 Park Square, Milton Park, Abingdon, Oxon, OX14 4RN
and by Routledge
605 Third Avenue, New York, NY 10158.

Routledge is an imprint of the Taylor & Francis Group, an informa business

© 1964 English Translation George Allen & Unwin Ltd.

The right of Poul Borchsenius to be identified as the author of this work has been asserted by him in accordance with sections 77 and 78 of the Copyright, Designs and Patents Act 1988.

All rights reserved. No part of this book may be reprinted or reproduced or utilised in any form or by any electronic, mechanical, or other means, now known or hereafter invented, including photocopying and recording, or in any information storage or retrieval system, without permission in writing from the publishers.

ISBN 13: 978-1-032-91137-3 (hbk)
ISBN 13: 978-1-003-56154-5 (ebk)
ISBN 13: 978-1-032-91143-4 (pbk)
Book DOI 10.4324/9781003561545

THE CHAINS ARE BROKEN

THE STORY OF
JEWISH EMANCIPATION

POUL BORCHSENIUS

TRANSLATED BY MICHAEL HERON

Ruskin House
GEORGE ALLEN & UNWIN LTD
MUSEUM STREET LONDON

FIRST PUBLISHED IN 1964

This book is copyright under the Berne Convention. Apart from any fair dealing for the purposes of private study, research, criticism or review, as permitted under the Copyright Act, 1956, no portion may be reproduced by any process without written permission. Enquiry should be made to the publishers.

This Translation © George Allen & Unwin Ltd, 1964

Translated from the Danish

LØSTE LAENKER

© H. Hirschsprungs Forlag, Copenhagen 1958

PRINTED IN GREAT BRITAIN
in 11 on 12 point *Juliana* type
by EAST MIDLAND PRINTING CO. LTD.
BURY ST. EDMUNDS

CONTENTS

I	The Road	9
II	The Chains are Broken	40
III	Reaction	63
IV	Judenschmerz	79
V	Heinrich Heine	93
VI	Reform	110
VII	The Fruits of Peace	127
VIII	Hep! Hep!	149
IX	Pogrom	177
X	Exodus	202
XI	Zion	212

I

THE ROAD

A SPORTIVE October wind was blowing in great gusts across the road to Berlin. The tall elm trees lining the roadside had already felt its effect. Great gaps had been torn in their luxuriant foliage, yellow and copper-coloured leaves danced away over the stubble and the freshly ploughed grey sandy soil. The sun was low in the heavens and could only cast fitful golden shafts of light on the flat Brandenburg countryside because blue-black cloud banks kept piling up and sailing in front of it. Suddenly the weather took a turn for the worse and the scudding clouds emptied themselves in a fierce cold downpour which swept over horsemen and pedestrians alike. When the rainstorm came hissing up they wrapped their capes tighter round themselves and pulled their hats down over their faces as protection against the cold and wet. There was no relief until the road entered a pine-wood which gave a little warmth and shelter.

The road from Dessau to Berlin was a long one, almost fifty miles. Nowadays, a gleaming asphalted straight line, it seems short. It stretches away to the horizon as if drawn by a ruler; a car can cover the distance in less than an hour. But it was very different 200 years ago. It was five days' march on foot. Like all German roads it was in a wretched state. It was full of pot-holes and deeply rutted with wheel marks; a carriage was hopelessly stuck once the wheels sank up to the hub caps.

In rainy weather the road was a bottomless morass, while in dry sunny weather grey clouds of dust hung over it like fog. If a wayfarer finally reached a town or a rickety bridge, he was stopped dead by a barrier where travellers had to pay

THE CHAINS ARE BROKEN

a toll. The King of Prussia raised a considerable part of his income from such dues on men and merchandise. Special high rates were in force for the Jews. If they were on their way to the cemetery in a funeral procession they had to pay the same rate for the dead as for the living, and a pregnant woman had to pay double, the same as a cow with young.

But in spite of all the difficulties the traffic on the road was heavy. Royal express messengers from Sans Souci thundered along on their heavy horses, on their way to the Imperial Court at Vienna. It was easy for them to keep up their pace, for fresh horses awaited them at every post station. It was a much slower business for a heavy awkward diligence. It lumbered laboriously along the uneven road drawn by four steaming horses. As its wheels bumped down into a pot-hole and lurched out again, the passengers were jerked backwards and forwards on its uncomfortable seats. If an exhausted passenger tried to doze off, he was likely to bang his head against his neighbour's a moment later. At times an elegant carriage came up, drawn by four or six horses. The outriders ordered everyone to move to the side of the road in the ringing tones of the sergeant-major. Braided lackeys stood erect at the front and back of the carriage. Through the window it was possible to catch a glimpse of His Excellency's gold-braided frock coat and his aristocratic arrogant face. At night in the inn mine host was ordered to turn his guests out of the best rooms so that His Highness would not be cramped and could rest in comfort.

But most of the people using the road were pedestrians. They advanced in droves. With bundles on their shoulders and staffs in their hands they stumped on, striding over pot-holes and ruts. Journeymen on the move, singing and whistling students on their way from one university to another, with an eye open for a pretty girl at a roadside inn. They were not averse to an affair if the opportunity occurred. Here a Jewish pedlar waded through the mud, laboriously carrying his trashy wares on his back. A long grey caftan which was drenched through flapped round his skinny figure; he was dirty and long-bearded with elaborate corkscrew curls dangling at his ears. Then followed two Dominican friars, a chattering group of strolling players and some travelling

THE ROAD

salesmen. The wet busy road was the stage for a stream of changing human destinies, some bad, some good, some banal, some extraordinary. It was like an artery in which the blood sometimes courses vigorously and sometimes flows sluggishly.

But something special happened on this blustery showery day in 1743 on the road from Dessau to Berlin. All the other travellers have long been forgotten, but one of them, merely by walking from one town to another, changed the course of history. No one would have believed it to look at him, he was neither rich nor handsome. On the contrary he was an insignificant grey anonymous particle in the crowd, poor into the bargain and so flagrantly ugly that other pedestrians were startled at the sight of him. It was really unusual to see so much ugliness concentrated in one person. Involuntarily they increased their pace to pass him, but afterwards they kept looking back to make sure that it was really true.

The target for these bewildered looks was a fourteen-year-old youth with a skinny deformed body. At times he swayed dangerously because his weak spindly legs found it hard to carry a massive lopsided hump which made him look like a hideous gnome. His neck was far too short. His head looked as if it was set right down between his shoulders. But worst of all was his face; it was a classical example of the traditional caricature of the ugly Jew—the man who is 'different', with full lips, an abnormally long hooked nose, fleshy cheeks and hair in thick tight curls behind his ears.

But the first impression was misleading, for if anyone caught his eye, their impression rapidly changed. The ugliness dwindled into insignificance like the scarred cracked clay soil which bears a colourful exotic fruit. Everything else was forgotten as soon as people saw those eyes, which shone with strength not passion; they had a calm fire, a glint of spiritual and intellectual power, which forced the observer to discover hidden beauties in his ill-starred face. And they were indeed beauties: a lofty thinker's brow, a good-natured twist to his mouth and a melancholy yearning. People immediately realized that here were both intelligence and goodness.

The youth had decided to call himself Moses Dessau when he was away from home; it was a Jewish custom to use one's home town as a surname. But Moses' father was the scribe Mendel, so his name finally became Mendelssohn and he is known to posterity as Moses Mendelssohn. He was a precocious lad. Illness and suffering had made him more mature than other boys of his age. Diligent studies, often until late into the night, endless discussions and debates with his father and the teacher he idolized, rabbi David Hirschel Fränkel, about life's ultimate riddles of the kind Jews find in the Torah, the Talmud and the works of the philosophers, had given young Moses a vast fund of knowledge and sharpened his sense of logic and his dialectical faculties.

He was well aware of his own worth, realizing that he was one of the rare chosen spirits. Not that it made him arrogant or swollen-headed, it was simply a fact. Already he had developed the characteristics of friendliness and lack of pretension which he kept throughout his life. If a brutal pedestrian in a hurry jostled him on the road to Berlin, making him stagger, he did not turn and abuse him, but moved aside politely. And if anyone was kind to Moses, gave him a helping hand across big puddles or shared his bread with the hungry lad in the shelter of an outhouse he rewarded them with a warm smile which showed that he was genuinely grateful. Moses Mendelssohn never—either then or later in life—accepted help or consideration as a right or a matter of course.

It was just as well that someone helped him, for the road was long, too long for a weakly, deformed lad. And the October gale never stopped blowing during the five days it took him to reach his goal. The rain clouds went on sailing over the Brandenburg heath and made the wet travellers even wetter; the days were short, it got dark early and the travellers had to seek shelter for the night. Only once was Moses able to knock on the door of a synagogue and spend the night in the wing reserved for guests; it was the only place between Dessau and Berlin where Jews lived, for in the kingdom of Prussia they were few and far between outside the capital. Otherwise he sought out a roadside farmhouse and asked for permission to sleep in the barn. His poor family had done the little that was in their power to equip him for the adventurous journey. It amounted to a few loaves of bread

THE ROAD

which lasted him the first couple of days and a single guilder. Moses changed it into groschen pieces which he used to pay the dues at toll-gates and octroi houses. His luggage presented no problem, it was limited to his *tallit*, prayer shawl, his *tefilin*, the small capsules containing Biblical texts that are attached to the arm and forehead, and a couple of Hebrew prayer-books. The cloak he had wrapped round him was old and patched. It was the same one his father had given him one cold winter morning when he went to school for the first time, at the age of five. It was the only one he had and fortunately it still fitted his stunted figure.

On the fourth and fifth days of the journey it was all Moses could do to keep going. He was using up the last ounce of his feeble forces and it was a frozen, wet and hungry lad who slowly and laboriously struggled on; his feet were sore and there were tears of pain and fatigue in his eyes. But he was determined to go on. He literally willed himself. His fertile powerful brain made up for the strength his body lacked. And his will forced his weak body to hold out and keep going forward, ever forward. He must, he had to get to Berlin.

Moses Mendelssohn had said a momentous goodbye to the town of his childhood. His beloved parents, his brother Saul and sister Jente had blessed him when they parted. The big decision to make the journey had actually been taken a month before, but Moses had mastered his impatience to leave. He made up his mind to wait so that once again he could share in the celebrations of the important autumn holidays in the synagogue of his childhood. And as he walked along the muddy road the voices which had chanted and prayed in Dessau's low-ceilinged synagogue on *Rosh Hashanah*, New Year's Day, *Yom Kippur*, the great Day of Atonement and *Sukkoth*, The Feast of the Tabernacles, still rang in his ears.

But they were voices from the past. Long before Moses' stumbling feet had carried him from Dessau, he had left the town of his childhood. On wings of thought he had flown away from the stuffy cramping atmosphere of the ghetto to something new and free of which he had only a vague presentiment. But out there the future must lie, not only for him, but also for his people. It had something to do with his beloved rabbi David Hirschel Fränkel, that much he did know. The rabbi had left Dessau a couple of months previously and now lived in Berlin. Therefore Moses Mendelssohn, too, felt he had to go to Berlin.

At last he arrived. On the fifth day of the journey the towers of the great city appeared beyond the last hill top. There lay Berlin which ranked as the intellectual capital of Germany, after Leipzig. It was unbelievable that the exhausted lad could do it, but he almost ran along the last few miles of road. Out of breath, he neared the city's big west gate, but when he reached it he was ruthlessly stopped by a drawn bayonet. He looked up at two fierce eyes above a bristling moustache. It was the sentry, a tall Prussian grenadier.

Where did he think he was going, barked a gruff voice. Didn't he know that Jews could not pass through this gate? He had to apply to the Rosenthaler Gate. For that was the entrance to Berlin for cattle and Jews.

Trembling, Moses stammeringly asked where the Rosenthaler Gate might be. And in a brusque tone the sentry explained that it was on the east side of Berlin, in other words the opposite end of the city from where he was.

So the scared despondent lad summoned up the very last of his energies and made the long detour round the whole city. At last he found the Rosenthaler Gate, the door to paradise on earth. But it, too, had a guardian angel. It was not a Prussian sentry but a Jew who controlled the traffic through the side door in the Rosenthaler Gate, which was the only way Jews could enter the capital of the kingdom. But even if one was a Jew like Moses, it could still be quite difficult to pass through—rather like the camel going through the eye of a needle. The guard posts had strict instructions and rejected everyone who did not satisfy the regulations to the letter. The examination began.

What was his name?

Moses.

With great punctiliousness, as if to show the importance of his office, the sentry took down a heavy ledger, opened it and noted down the answer in the appropriate column.

THE ROAD

Where did he come from?
Dessau.
That too was written down with the scratching goose quill.
Whom did he intend to visit?
Rabbi David Hirschel Fränkel.
What did he want with him?
The trembling lad knew exactly what he wanted and he managed to get the word out, one of the few German words he knew.
Lernen, to study.
The sentry inspected the lad. Yes, he knew the type. One of those harmless youngsters who gathered round a favourite rabbi. This deformed youth certainly looked like one of these types who willingly starved during his youth in order to 'study'. He gave a last searching look at Moses' face and peered into the big dark intelligent eyes. Then he opened the gate, but Moses, like all Jews, had to pay *Leibzoll* (a toll on his person), before he passed through it. He groped in his pocket for his last two groschen and handed them over. Then at last the sentry let him pass and Moses entered Berlin.

In the official record for this October day at the Rosenthaler Gate one can still read:

'Today six oxen, seven pigs and one Jew passed through the Rosenthaler Gate.'

Seventy-three years before this day an event took place which we must know about if we are to understand why Moses Mendelssohn was so intent on reaching Berlin. On Monday, March 1, 1670, imperial heralds, in stately procession accompanied by fanfares, stopped in the marketplaces and squares of Vienna and all the towns of Upper and Lower Austria and solemnly read a proclamation in which the Emperor of the Holy Roman Empire, Leopold I, announced that 'for the sake of God's honour' all Jews were banished and must leave the country before Corpus Christi 'never to return'. For centuries the primitive idea had prevailed that the Jews alone were responsible for all the misfortunes which befell a people. Whether it was plague, war, fire or defeat, it could be traced back to evil Jewish influences; for the Jews were 'outsiders', they were quite defenceless and

THE CHAINS ARE BROKEN

there was often rich booty to be taken from their houses.

It was true that strange things had happened in Vienna. An imperial castle had burnt down, a newly born prince had died and worst of all it looked as if the Empress Margaretha, an ultra-Catholic Spanish Infanta, would not be able to bear any more children. The Emperor himself was in the power of his Jesuit advisers and they assured him constantly that Her Majesty's ill-fated unfertility would last as long as the heathen Jews were allowed to live in the country. The merchants of the capital were only too glad to be free of Jewish competition. They seized the opportunity, organized processions and demonstrations, and supported the church's claim. So the blow fell and 1,346 Jews, men, women and children, had to leave everything behind and go into exile. But this intrinsically banal and everyday occurrence brought lasting consequences in its train which introduced a turning point in Jewish history.

A few decades ago, the ravaging tornado of the Thirty Years' War had died away; the storm had left the country and its towns in such a state of devastation that we have to look to modern times to find its equal. The numerous small German states were busy on the work of reconstruction. A veritable race began between the princely courts to reach the winning post a neck ahead of their competitors. The race was decisively won by the Electorate of Brandenburg, the kernel of the subsequent kingdom of Prussia. It was a poor country, full of barren heaths, and had always been isolated from the rest of Europe, receiving none of the money flowing from big business. But at this moment there was a sudden reversal of fortune. The old Hohenzollern princely family produced one of its proudest scions in 'the great Elector', Frederick William.

Like other farsighted princes of the age—the greatest of them all was the *roi soleil* at Versailles—the Elector was in favour of the mercantile system. His problem was to make his country economically strong and independent of others; to this end commerce and industry would help. So the state took a hand in every kind of trade and profession. One of the Elector's measures was to summon colonists to the numerous abandoned farms or almost depopulated towns, for

THE ROAD

the war had wiped out whole families. The Elector enticed them with tax reliefs and trade facilities. It worked as he had intended; many Dutch and especially French exiled Huguenots came to Brandenburg. But the far-seeing Elector did even more, in 1671 he issued an official edict which astonished Europe. It contained an invitation to fifty exiled Viennese Jewish families to come and live in his kingdom with the promise of good living conditions.

Jews had lived in Brandenburg before. We know that the plague, the Black Death, brandished its fatal scourge in every country in Europe and that it also smote the little township which Berlin was in the Middle Ages and decimated its modest population. Whose fault was it? The Jews', of course. They had poisoned the wells. In senseless fear the Margrave of Brandenburg had them slaughtered like mad dogs or driven out of the country. Not until long after did they dare to return and appear again in Brandenburg. But in the century exactly preceding the great Elector's reign the country had been *judenrein*, i.e. free of Jews. The story of how it happened, like another brush stroke, forms part of the picture of Jewish life 3-400 years ago.

The Elector Joachim died unexpectedly in 1571. He had had a *Hofjude*, a court Jew, called Lippold, one of many contemporary examples of a talented Jew who ended up as his prince's confidential and appreciated servant owing to his intelligence and energy. Like everyone else who rises high in the world, Lippold excited the envy of others. Suddenly they saw their chance to get at the Jew. Lippold was accused of having caused the Elector's death. A search of his home brought some suspicious volumes to light. With sufficient ill-will his accusers were able to find indications in them that the Jew had been addicted to magic. The death sentence followed immediately. In an exceptionally barbaric way the sentence was carried out by quartering the man alive. All the remaining Jews were banished from the country.

But in 1671 the air was clearing for the Jews. Holland provided a shining example of how useful Jewish merchants could be to their host country. And the great Elector learnt the lesson, he opened the door of the kingdom, or rather half-opened it, to Jewish immigrants. The edict he issued breathes a spirit of tolerance almost totally unknown at the time. A limited number of Jews were even given permission to settle in Berlin, primarily certain specialist workers who were in short supply. They were assigned a *Judengasse* (Jews' Street) behind the Rosenthaler Gate and they were given permission to build synagogues.

Time was to show that Frederick William was right. For the next 262 years Jewish citizens worked in Prussia. Within their field of activity they made a contribution which made itself felt throughout the whole body politic and one could safely claim that without them Prussia would never have become the power it did. The Star of David's light in Berlin was only extinguished in 1933 by the Nazi's *Machtübernahme* (taking over the power).

I do not want to give the impression that the Jews found idyllic easy conditions in Prussia. Far from it. Only the few who were lucky enough to acquire a *Schutzbrief* or *Geleitbrief*, had permission to live there; they were known as 'protected' or 'tolerated' Jews. They were immediately the object of suspicion, had to pay sky-high special taxes, the product of downright malicious ingenuity; they were subject to restrictions of all kinds; they were forbidden to have more than a certain number of children, and only one child in each family inherited his father's letter of safe-conduct. Statistics of the Jews' breeding were actually kept, as if they were in a stud. And they came into perpetual conflict with their Christian neighbours. For the Jews brought modern methods to business dealings; they promptly clashed with the stiff inflexible guild system which had hitherto confined Prussian trade within a narrow framework lacking initiative and drive. And those Jews who sneaked into the city without permission to live with their friends, the so-called *unvergleiteten* (people without a safe-conduct) who lived 'underground', were in constant danger of being discovered and ejected through the Rosenthaler Gate.

But in spite of everything the Jews had won a bridgehead in Berlin. Later generations were able to see how they managed both to use and develop it. This was the Berlin to which Moses Mendelssohn walked; it was to become the second centre in his life. The first was Dessau, the town of

THE ROAD

his childhood, which he said goodbye to and left.

The great Elector's example incited others to follow him. It became quite the fashion among German princes to summon Jews to their kingdoms. And one of these countries has a place in this story. Wedged in between Prussia and Saxony lay a typical Lilliputian state, one of those the country was full of, which made the map of Germany like a mosaic. This particular state was Anhalt-Dessau with its capital of Dessau. Here too Jews found shelter, both Viennese and Polish refugees.

As a matter of fact the princes of Anhalt-Dessau did not have much idea of how to promote trade. First and foremost they were stalwart warriors. Not in their own army, for the country was far too small to have any military influence. But for three generations in succession they had been at the head of the Prussian army as field-marshals. One of them was called Leopold; even for the baroque period he was an unusually strapping fellow, robust and vital. In his younger days he had provided all the courts of Germany with splendid material for gossip by his love affair with a quite ordinary middle-class girl, Anna Luise Föhse, the daughter of an apothecary. Without the least regard for royal convention he elevated her to the throne and forced through a marriage with her. She put the gossips to shame and ended up as her people's 'liebe Landesmutter', the beloved mother of her people.

This did not imply that Leopold was by any means democratic. On the contrary he ruled the country with a firm hand, caroused royally and expensively and his only friends were his soldiers and drinking companions. With one exception: the court Jew Moses Benjamin Wulff. Leopold had inherited Wulff from his father, together with a small Jewish colony newly founded in Dessau. He has a place in Moses Mendelssohn's family tree, so we shall stop for a moment and take a look at the family's history. One of his ancestors was Moses Isserles, the celebrated scholar I have written about in another book. Isserles' name will long be remembered by the Jews. His great achievement was the preparation of the Polish edition of *Shulhan Aruk* which rapidly helped the European circulation of a book which set its stamp

THE CHAINS ARE BROKEN

on Jewry for centuries. The afterglow of fame continued to shine on the family. For example it made Isserles' great-grandson Simon Wulff a distinguished rabbi in Vilna.

In old Jewish families there were always generations when lightning struck and the family chronicle has to tell of drama and catastrophe. In the Mendelssohn family they lowered their voices and trembled when the conversation turned to Simon Wulff. For his time came within 'The Black Decade', the decade after 1648 when Europe breathed freely after the Thirty Years' War, but the Polish Jews underwent their period of horror. The Cossacks ravaged Vilna; Simon Wulff was only able to save his life by headlong flight. After many adventures he reached Hamburg, where Glueckel von Hamelen mentions him in his reminiscences. Simon Wulff had a son, who was also destined to experience many vicissitudes, far more than there is space to describe here. But his story ended happily; at last he found a peaceful corner of Europe where he could settle and had the opportunity to develop his unusual talents. For he was the Moses Benjamin Wulff already mentioned, whom the monarchs of Anhalt-Dessau took in their service from father to son.

Wulff is one more example of what a Jew could achieve in government service. As Court Agent he was at the head of many branches of the country's administration. Wulff reorganized the monetary system; he was proud of minting 'hard rix-dollar pieces' whose gold content matched their face value. He also reorganized the postal system and it became a rich source of revenue for the little state. He was a pioneer in this sphere. But first and foremost Wulff was imbued with the theory of the mercantile system and devoted his energies to developing trade and industry; he established salt works and started factories. The little kingdom's potentialities were exploited and Wulff's activities produced rich results for both prince and country. We possess letters from the princes which give us some idea of the intimate terms on which Wulff was with his masters, indeed we realize that they were actually fond of their court Jew. He taught them to trust in Jewish ability, so that they summoned many more Jewish colonists to the country.

Dessau was a small town with only a few thousand in-

THE ROAD

habitants. As in hundreds of other German miniature states the seat of the ruler had a quite idyllic appearance. It lay on the river Mulde, a tributary of the Elbe; the town had been recently rebuilt after the Thirty Years' War; it had handsome new houses, a sleepy square with a purling fountain in the centre and parks which did their best to imitate the French landscape gardening of the grand chateaux.

In comparison with the size of the town the Jewish colony was a large one, numbering several hundred souls. The Dessau Jews were enterprising people who owned the stocking factory, tobacco works, distillery and glass factory. But the majority were in business, especially drapery. Naturally the Jews lived cut off from the Christians; the Judengasse was in a suburb. Most of them were Polish refugees, they spoke Yiddish with an admixture of Polish; their Christian fellow citizens did not understand much of their gibberish. Life was organized according to strict religious principles, just as the Jews had lived in Poland's Jewish golden age, the days of the Third Temple. Intellectual interests occupied a central position; the Torah and the Talmud were read and studied assiduously. Wulff was even able to establish a printing-house in the town. After Wulff's death the family's prosperity declined. Their home was a cramped room in some back premises opening onto an alley behind the Judengasse. And in it was Moses Mendelssohn's cradle. On the twelfth day of the month of Elul in the year 5849 after the creation of the world, September 6, 1729, according to the Christian calendar, he saw the light of day as his parents' first-born. There was nothing to indicate the great future which awaited the child. The family's greatness lay in the past. But his parents had not forgotten it. That is why they called the boy Moses after the greatest of his ancestors, Moses Isserles.

His father's main occupation was copying the Torah on parchment for use in the synagogue. It was badly paid work and the family was one of the poorest in the town; there were times when they did not have enough food to satisfy their hunger. But people looked up to Mendel in spite of this; after all he was a scholar and came of a distinguished family. The boy was weakly; his back had been damaged at birth, as a baby he had an attack of infantile paralysis, he never had a really sound diet or even enough to eat. All this left its mark. Moses grew up as a little lopsided hunchback. But in spite of difficult circumstances, at times amounting to want, Moses grew up in a home which was good in the real sense of the word. His parents were affectionate; they gave their son the best they could, their faith and piety. From the age of five onwards his father took him to school every day. On cold blustery winter days he wrapped the boy's slight body in the patched cloak which later went to Berlin with him. He did not eat breakfast every day. On the other hand he learnt Hebrew at school, studied passages in the Bible and the Talmud, and learnt long passages from the scriptures and their commentaries by heart. And as has always been the way with Jewish boys, Moses' intellect was sharpened, he was delighted with the rapier play of discussion and learnt dialectic's flexible methods, while the sure impregnable defences of the Torah and the Talmud watched over his mind and kept it vigilant and suspicious of every alien system. The precociously mature, alert and clever Moses Mendelssohn grew up safely in a typical time-honoured Jewish background which was self-contained and had no religious doubts.

Moses reached the age of thirteen and was *bar mitzwah*, or as we would say a candidate for confirmation. His sole delight was books and he had an insatiable thirst for knowledge. The boy only wanted to 'learn'; he always sat with a book in his hand. And his abilities matched his keenness, so that his father did not hesitate to take him from the Heder, the primary school, and put him into the Beth Hamidrash, the higher school. It was there that he had rabbi David Hirschel Fränkel, an eminently learned and exceptional pedagogue, as a teacher. He showed the last-named quality at once, by setting his new pupil, whose unusual talents he rapidly spotted, to study Maimonides' famous book *Moreh Nebukim*, the Guide to the Perplexed, which had just been brought out by a printing-house in the neighbourhood of Dessau.

It was undeniably a bold step. I am not thinking so much that by modern standards it was a bad thing to give a thirteen-year-old boy a difficult mediaeval philosophical work to study. But it was *forbidden* to read Maimonides before the age of twenty-five. The rabbis had learnt from bitter experi-

THE ROAD

ence that the old, undeniably rationalist Spanish philosopher could be dangerous to the faith. Nevertheless, rabbi Fränkel acted as I have said. He knew his young pupil, saw his vigilant delight in questioning, his sharp intelligence and knew that he was both diligent and pious. And with his audacious methods Fränkel set forces in motion which were to bring lasting consequences in their train.

The lad sat in a poky cold garret and read the long nights through. By the tallow candle's flickering light he worked laboriously through the massive tome, reading and re-reading it until he had penetrated every single one of its lines of thought. This concentrated study almost cost Moses his life. He caught a dangerous nervous fever and was bedridden for a long time. When he started to get out of bed again his back was even more humped than before. Later in life he used to say:

'Maimonides ruined my body and wrecked my digestion. Nevertheless I love him, because he sweetened many bitter hours for me and indemnified me tenfold for what my body has had to suffer.'

The old Spanish Jew opened the windows wide for his young German pupil. Moses breathed the stuffy air of the ghetto, like all Jews 200 years ago. Not only the ghetto in which the Christian citizens imprisoned the Jews. No, he was confined to Jewry's inner mental ghetto which locked Christianity out. Jewry had become a hermetically sealed building, defended by the Torah and the Talmud, safe against all dangers. But only against dangers from *without*. Within the ghetto lurked doubt and uncertainty. And the study of Maimonides had precipitated the boy into a crisis far ahead of his years, the dilemma between faith and doubt.

Gradually it dawned on Moses Mendelssohn that both he and his people were bogged down, spiritually speaking, and that the way out could only be found if the wall behind which the Jews had hidden themselves was knocked down. There was a life outside which they did not know, but had to reach. A bridge had to be built over the abyss between doubt and faith, between Jewry and modern culture, such as Maimonides had tried to erect 5-600 years earlier. While Moses struggled with these thoughts which were stimulated

THE CHAINS ARE BROKEN

by *Moreh Nebukim* in the stillness of the night, his pale cheeks began to glow. Was it going to be his mission to be a new guide to the perplexed? Could he find the way himself and lead his people out of the ghetto's narrow alleys and rigid ideas to the vigorous life of the new age?

That was as far as Moses Mendelssohn had got when catastrophe overtook him. Rabbi Fränkel was appointed chief rabbi in Berlin and left Dessau. He said goodbye and went. Many years later Moses Mendelssohn told the story of the sad morning when Fränkel walked out through Dessau's gates on the road to Berlin. The little deformed boy stood on a hill top and waved goodbye, as bitter tears streamed down over his pale cheeks. The kind-hearted rabbi recognized his favourite pupil in the dejected figure, went over to him, stroked his hair and said something like 'one fine day a favourable destiny may take you to Berlin as well. Don't forget to come to me'.

Then he was off. But a torch had been lit in the boy's mind. He began to broach the subject of following Fränkel to his parents. They shook their heads. How would he cover the long road? And anyway he had no safe-conduct with permission to live in the capital; he could not even speak German. Where would he get the money for food and lodging and books? But when his father and mother looked down into the eager eyes and at the pale face marked by sickness and nocturnal studies they began to weaken. After all the boy was the descendant of Moses Isserles, they remembered. Finally they gave in. They scraped the bottom of their empty money-box. The result was one guilder, all they had. With it in his pocket and the patched cloak over his shoulders he kissed the four who stayed behind goodbye. He received their blessing and began the walk to Berlin, towards the great future he imagined lay waiting for him.

And Moses Mendelssohn actually covered the long road to Berlin.

Berlin had been the city of his dreams. He wanted to find freedom there, and also a new outlook, activity, modern thinking—all the things Moses Mendelssohn thirsted after. But the actuality did not live up to his expectations. The

THE ROAD

Judengasse behind the Rosenthaler gate was no different from the street he knew at home in Dessau; it was just as narrow and cramped, teeming with men with long beards, tired women and noisy children. It was easy enough to find rabbi Fränkel's house, there was only one street with a few dark alleys behind it. The rabbi's residence looked quite small in it, poor and spartan. Could the famous man really live here? Moses knocked cautiously on the door and ventured inside.

The worthy rabbi opened his eyes in astonishment when he saw his visitor, a weary dirty lad who slipped shyly into the room and did not dare to sit down. What on earth did he want in Berlin? Fränkel's first irritable impulse was to send Moses home again. But the rabbi was a warm-hearted man. And he could not resist those big eyes, so pleading and confident. He gave the boy his hand and listened to his story. Moses claimed that if he could make the long journey to Berlin he could do more. And rabbi Fränkel decided to do the little that lay in his power to enable Moses to stay in Berlin and 'study'.

Poverty. The word is synonymous with Moses Mendelssohn's long early years in Berlin. A devout man called Heimann Bamberger who made a practice of giving aspiring youth a hand lent him a cold narrow attic; the *yeshive*, or Talmudic school, where Moses registered as a disciple, gave him a loaf of bread every weekday; rabbi Fränkel promised him a free lunch on the sabbath and found him some copying work. Moses had inherited beautiful handwriting from his father and he carefully copied Hebrew parchments. It earned him a groschen once in a while. That was all he got out of it, but he managed to make a precarious livelihood.

No one can give more than they have. And the Jewish community in Berlin was poor. Naturally there were a couple of eminent court agents and rich merchants, but the great majority lived close to subsistence level. Three years before Moses Mendelssohn arrived in the capital, Frederick II, later called the Great, became king. Even as crown prince he had had the reputation of being open-minded and enlightened. The Jews greeted his accession to the throne expectantly, but King Frederick disappointed them. In contradistinction to his father and grandfather he looked on the Jews with a jaundiced eye and imposed more restrictions on them. And for the time being the king thought only about war. War costs money, and new taxes were imposed. Naturally the thick end of the stick fell on the Jews. One of Frederick II's Jewish taxes is still remembered; it forms a good example of malicious ingenuity.

In accordance with the principles of the mercantile system the Prussian state had set up a procelain factory. To provide a market it was prescribed that every Jewish bridegroom had to buy a certain number of porcelain articles. He was not asked what he fancied, but had to buy unsaleable goods which the factory was finding it difficult to get rid of. Later, when Mendelssohn married, twenty life-size porcelain monkeys were delivered to his home. I might add that many of these discarded *objets d'art* from Frederick's period have a reputation as valuable antiques today and fetch high prices.

Moses Mendelssohn bore his poverty without complaining, he had had enough practice at home. And the community's intellectual poverty, its isolation and stuffiness oppressed him much more than material want. There was an abyss between the old Spanish Jews' towering culture and the Berliners' ghetto mentality, stamped with the mark of Polish Jewry. Here people were on their guard against everything new and looked on alien trends with the deepest suspicion. The wall between the ghetto and the world outside was as insurmountable as ever. Moses had walked from Dessau to Berlin, but he now realized that the road led from one form of obscurantism to another. But he would not be shut in, he kept his eyes open and finally found the way out.

The way was learning German. From his home he only knew the sacred Hebrew language and Yiddish. The people of the ghetto did not understand German, and no one outside understood the two foreign languages, there was no bridge to be built with them. A hundred years before Mendelssohn Spinoza had been faced with the same dilemma. But Spinoza had one thing to help him; he spoke a universal language, Spanish, which became his point of departure. Moses Mendelssohn had nothing to begin with; with indescribable toil he had to put one stone on another, starting from ground level, pick up one word after another, compare

THE ROAD

them and laboriously guess his way forward. The work lasted three years.

He had ventured on a dangerous path; he had to pursue his German studies in the greatest secrecy. If any Jewish authority got wind of what he was doing, he ran the risk of the severest punishment known to Jewry, excommunication and banishment from Berlin. For German was the language of 'the others' and it was treachery to learn it. A boy the same age as Moses was carrying a German book under his arm when he was met by a relieving officer. The punishment followed immediately and the lad was driven out of the city. Moses was lucky. No one discovered what he was up to. And the German the indefatigable autodidact taught himself was so pure that when he wrote his books in it later it was regarded as an expression of the German language in its classical form.

His knowledge of German made the first breach in the ghetto wall for Mendelssohn. Outside lay an alien world which summoned him—enticing, exciting, new. He ventured out into it with stumbling steps and looked around in amazement. One day Moses plucked up the courage to go into a German bookshop; he stood leafing through the pages of the books and later became a frequent visitor. If he found a book which promised to be particularly useful, he asked cautiously what it cost. During the weeks that followed he saved up his few groschen, each of which was a capital sum costing want and hunger to put by. Moses seldom bought food for himself, he made do with his free meals and the bread he received every week in the *yeshiva*. When he had taken it home, he made seven cuts in it indicating each day's ration. In that way there was no need for him to go to bed on any day without having eaten a slice of bread at least. His savings were put aside. When at last they reached the price of the book he coveted, he hastened off and bought it. Moses hid his German books in a hole in the wall and no one discovered his hiding-place. He made the most of his spare time in the same way. When he was alone and ran no risk of being surprised, he read the new books eagerly and greedily.

The new world was a labyrinth; questions and problems piled up for the young man who only knew the ghetto's

27

school and ways of thinking. Gradually Moses Mendelssohn discovered that he was not the only one in the Judengasse who was groping his way out. For instance he heard of Abraham Posner who had the presumption to shave his beard off! Naturally he was forced to let it grow again. The authorities were so watchful that the king was persuaded to issue an edict ordering Jews to wear long beards. Nevertheless it was like a tiny spring flower; it gave warning of something new that was in the air.

Moses Mendelssohn must have had a special gift for winning friends. One after another he found like-minded companions. They could help him and vice versa. One of them taught him Latin, another gave him a grounding in Euclidean mathematics. We get some idea of the difficulties these young ghetto Jews experienced when we learn that Isaac Samosz, a Polish school teacher who knew a little mathematics, could not speak a word of German. He had to translate the mathematical doctrines into classical Hebrew before Mendelssohn could understand them. In return Mendelssohn taught his friend German.

Once Mendelssohn had started, he worked on tirelessly. First and foremost on the scholar's discipline, philosophy. And he steadily broadened his horizon. He began to teach himself English and French in order to continue his endless exploration of the strange world outside the wall.

He spent seven long years like this. People began to take notice of him, his gentle nature, his modesty and industry. Then came the turning point in his life. A prosperous silk merchant, Isaac Bernhardt, offered him a position as tutor to his children. Mendelssohn moved into Bernhardt's house where he set about his new task with his usual care. Suddenly he was in comfortable circumstances; he could eat his fill every day, he had warmth and light in his room, and plenty of time to attend the *yeshiva* and pursue his private studies as well. Bernhardt was very satisfied with him. When the children grew up he did not want to part with their tutor. Mendelssohn's beautiful handwriting had made an impression; the merchant suggested that he become the firm's bookkeeper. Moses accepted and stayed with Bernhardt. Later he made him a director of the business and a partner in the

THE ROAD

firm. Now Mendelssohn had no more financial worries and was delighted that he could often send a handsome present home to his parents in Dessau.

But most important of all Mendelssohn was at long last given the opportunity of broadening his culture rationally. And he did so with all his accustomed energy. Naturally the ancient Hispano-Jewish thinkers were not forgotten. Maimonides', Abraham ibn Ezra's and Jehuda Halevi's books were always to the fore. But their German pupil was primarily engrossed with the thinking of his own time. He had learnt English so that he could read the English deists; Locke was one of his favourites. He soon became an enthusiastic disciple of the German school of philosophy headed by Leibniz and Wulff, that rather dull reflection of the great French encyclopaedists, and the dry rationalist thinking (as we look on it) of the whole epoch. Mendelssohn never became a philosopher in his own right, he was content to express the trends of his day. He was not keen on the French philosophers; 'Frenchmen philosophise with wit, the English with their emotions', he used to say.

Mendelssohn had already gone a long way before he won real recognition. It came through his friendship with Lessing.

Gotthold Ephraim Lessing came from a Protestant vicarage. The year of his birth was 1729; the fact that he shared it with his dearest friend Mendelssohn was almost like an omen. His father was a rigid upholder of joyless orthodoxy and did his best to persuade his gifted son to become a divine as well. But young Lessing never felt the least inclination to follow in his father's footsteps. A restless busy mind like his could not be locked up in the pietism of the age. On the contrary he was attracted by the theatre, threw himself into the study of the drama, cultivated friendship with actors and was on intimate terms with beautiful actresses. In short Lessing broke with the background of his home; he became not a priest but a writer. He also rapidly freed himself from Christianity's dogmas; all his life he entered the lists against formalism and religious thinking which were contrary to reason. Lessing did not deny religion in itself, but he was perpetually critical of its forms of expression. He compared

himself to Euripides' Ion, the man who daily sweeps the steps outside the temple of Phoebus and says:
'I am not inside the temple, but connected with the temple. I sweep the steps, but am proud of this humble task and I know best in whose honour I do it.'

Lessing created an epoch for Germany's Jews with his liberalism. It hurt him to see a whole people cut off from European culture for narrow-minded religious reasons. It never took him long to move from thought to action. He threw himself boldly into the fight to win human rights for the Jews. When he settled in Berlin in 1751, his name was already made by the comedy *Die Juden* (The Jews). It is still worth taking a look at this work written with a playfully light hand.

The play follows a traveller who saves a baron from mortal danger. The distinguished man naturally wants to reward his saviour, but he refuses all offers, even marriage to the baron's lovely daughter, whom he is already in love with, of course. But why? It is madness to refuse. The baron presses him for an explanation. At last it comes. The traveller stammers out:

'I am a Jew.'

This comes as a shock and it takes a few minutes for the baron to get over it. But then he breaks out:

'How we could respect them, if all Jews were like you!'

And the saviour replies:

'Yes, and if all Christians were like you, how lovable they would be.'

At this moment his own servant learns of his master's race and religion for the first time. In his confusion he bursts out:

'It really looks as if there are some Jews who aren't Jews at all.'

In this way Lessing wittily and elegantly stamps hereditary prejudice against the Jews as stupidity. One phrase in the play caused a special stir and was constantly quoted:

'The Jews have already produced so many prophets and saints—yet people still doubt whether an honourable soul can be found among them.'

Lessing and Mendelssohn met for the first time in 1754.

THE ROAD

At the time the writer lived in a tall narrow house near the Nicolai Church. His home was a meeting place for Berlin's young intellectual bohemians, actors and men of letters. One of Mendelssohn's friends, Dr Gumperz, of a rich Jewish family, was a regular visitor. One evening, as usual, the circle played music, drank and argued. Lessing sat in a corner of the room playing chess with Dr Gumperz. He won one game after another from the young Jew. Late at night Gumperz stood up, knocked the pieces over and burst out:

'That's enough. Instead let me introduce you to a better chess player than me. Come to my house tomorrow and you'll have an opponent who is worthy of you. '

Lessing went. Moses Mendelssohn sat waiting at the chess-board. That evening started a friendship which was to last for life and have far-reaching consequences both for themselves and German culture.

As long as Lessing lived in Berlin, the two saw each other daily; they were on the most intimate terms and exchanged their innermost thoughts. People saw them walking up and down the avenues around the Nicolai Church discussing philosophy. Perfectly natural, we would think; but Jews and Christians had not done the like since Renaissance days. This sight foretold a new day for Germany and its Jews. Lessing raised the monument to their friendship with his famous drama *Nathan der Weise* (Nathan the Wise), that milestone in Jewish history.

The drama is based on the legend of the three rings in the *Decameron*; I retold it in my book *The Three Rings* which was named after it. The great religions, Judaism, Christianity and Islam are represented by three brothers, each of whom contends that *he* owns the original ring. This is the contention of the three religions that each is the one true faith. And the point of the play is that men struggle towards God by different roads; no confession is entitled to say that theirs is the only right one. On the contrary true humanity and morals can be found in all religions and stand above any rigidly formulated faith.

Lessing hoisted the flag of tolerance right in the middle of the stage. In an age when Catholicism and Judaism were fiendish heresies to the Protestants, and the Catholics for

THE CHAINS ARE BROKEN

their part consigned both Protestants and Jews to eternal perdition, it was literally heroic to speak as openly as Lessing did.

Even more epoch-making is the daring with which Lessing makes the Jew Nathan the play's central figure and a shining counterpart to the Shakespearean Shylock. A Jew as the writer's mouthpiece. Such a thing had never been seen before and it set people's minds in a whirl. On top of which the model for Nathan was Mendelssohn.

That was how a Jewish philosopher inspired a Christian writer. But a friendship is always mutual and Lessing had something to give as well. He was the first person in the outside world who aroused Mendelssohn to see his real calling in life: to break the chains which had made the Jew a prisoner for centuries. Not only the iron fetters Christianity had forged round his hands and feet, but also the self-elected ties of isolation and narrow-mindedness in which the Jews had bound themselves of their own free will.

Lessing first started his friend on an author's career. Mendelssohn had given him a philosophical paper to read through. To his surprise he received the book soon afterwards in proof, together with an advance from the publisher. It was the first of a long series of books and treatises.

Mendelssohn rapidly caused a stir as a writer; the thought in his books is clear, the language and style simple and elegant. And he was fortunate enough to have his name cause a sensation on many occasions. Two hundred years ago, as today, some things give a man the publicity necessary for success. For example, there was the time when he trod on the king's toes. King Frederick was not only a warrior king, he also won fame as 'the philosopher of Sans Souci', Voltaire's friend and protector. He wrote poems as well. Mendelssohn reviewed one of them and permitted himself a cautious critical remark. He was immediately summoned to Sans Souci to answer to it before the king. But Mendelssohn won the king's favour by his quick reply:

'When playing bowls, even a king may find that the pin-boy calls out how many skittles have been knocked over.'

King Frederick granted Mendelssohn a permit to stay in Berlin. Until then his position had been vague. At any moment, as an *unvergleitete Jude* (a Jew without a safe-conduct) he had been in danger of an expulsion order. Besides he was never at home in the frivolous atmosphere of the court where a smart answer or a double-edged reply rapidly counted as 'genius'. It was a courtier who once made the condescending remark:

'All that Herr Mendelssohn lacks to become a great man is a little foreskin.'

Mendelssohn's fame rose steeply, when he won the first prize of the Academy in open competition. The second prize was awarded to an unknown man from the East Prussian provinces. His name was Immanuel Kant and later he was to become well enough known. But no one had ever seen a Jew beat his Christian competitors before. And Immanuel Kant's later fame naturally also put Mendelssohn's name in relief.

Time went by. Mendelssohn was in his thirties when he decided to marry. The story of his engagement is a new variation on an old theme. A Hamburg Jew discreetly allowed news to reach Mendelssohn that he had a virtuous blue-eyed daughter who read his books and was enthusiastic about them. Perhaps she could be an affectionate and useful wife to him? Mendelssohn went to Hamburg, was welcomed in friendly fashion by the father and introduced to Frommel, as the girl was called, a common diminutive of *fromm* (pious). She looked at him with her blue eyes, then lowered them modestly over her needlework while she listened to what he had to say.

The next day he went to her father to discuss the arrangements for the marriage. To his surprise he found him hesitant and stiff. At long last the father stammered out that it was not he who objected to Mendelssohn as a son-in-law. Suddenly Moses realized what was the matter.

'Of course, it's Frommel who's against it, probably because of my hump.'

'You're right,' admitted the ashamed father.

Mendelssohn asked his permission to see the girl once more and say goodbye. And again he sat in front of the blue-eyed maiden bent shyly over her needlework. Again Mendelssohn spoke and as before the spell of his books began to steal into the girl's mind. There is no need for the road from philosophy to love to be long. It is the Talmud which says that 'marriages are made in heaven'. He cleverly found an opportunity to say so. She looked up quickly at him.

'Do you really believe that?'

He seized his chance and answered:

'I certainly do. Strangely enough that old saying played a part in my life. At the time when it was decided in heaven whom I should marry, I learnt that the girl was blue-eyed and beautiful, but that alas she had a hump. The angels lamented and pitied the poor girl. What use were all her other virtues when they were united with a hump? If she had been a man, the misfortune would not have been so great. Then I jumped up and asked for the girl's hump to be put on my shoulders. And that is what happened.'

He stopped. A strange silence filled the room. The girl's needlework had fallen into her lap, big tears filled the blue eyes. Suddenly she stood up, went to her hunchbacked suitor, put both arms round his neck and looked him in the eyes. There is no need for me to tell the rest.

It was a harmonious and secure marriage. The newly-weds settled in a small house with a garden on the outskirts of Berlin. To be sure they had to find place for the twenty porcelain apes which were not at all to their taste. But when the children came, six in all, they looked on them as silent playmates. The shadow over the otherwise happy childhood the two parents gave their children was other people's contempt. When the modest, learned father walked down the street with one of his children, the other children nearly always shouted insults after them and grown-ups made a detour round the Jews. Sometimes Mendelssohn had to listen to his child's wondering question:

'Daddy, is it sinful to be a Jew?'

His heart was heavy when the words came. And later in life the feeling of being outsiders had momentous consequences for Mendelssohn's children.

Vulgar anti-Semitism could not stop Mendelssohn's entrée to the cultural élite. The world was small in those days, European culture only stretched from the banks of the Seine to the Spree, with a branch as far as the Neva; it was a refined intellectual culture, strongly biassed by the ideas of the encyclopaedists and only accessible to the chosen few. It is Mendelssohn's achievement that he, the boy from the dark alleys of the Dessau ghetto, made his way into this brilliant world and with his wit, personal charm and quiet modest behaviour forced its habitués to accept him as one of themselves. His *Phädon*, a book in which he upholds the immortality of the soul, was hailed as a model of purity and beauty. The book was translated into every European language and became the best-seller of the age. The cultural world thronged round the author; it was an honour to have shaken his hand. Herder praised Mendelssohn as 'the German Socrates', with a subtle allusion not only to Socrates' mental powers, but also to his appearance. For Socrates was certainly no beauty.

But in the midst of all the honour and praise from Christianity Moses Mendelssohn remained true to Jewry. He observed the traditional precepts with scrupulous care and had his permanent seat in the synagogue. There was no dichotomy between thought and faith as far as he was concerned, his whole personality was characterized by harmony. Mendelssohn never sought to put himself forward, on the contrary he preferred to stay in the background.

'I have always lived in solitude,' he said, 'and have never wanted to enter the world's hurly-burly. A small circle of friends is my sole company; they go the same way as I do.'

However, he was not allowed to stay in his quiet corner. Instead he was whirled into a discussion which the whole of Europe followed on tenterhooks. Johann Caspar Lavater, the strange clergyman from Zürich, the Christian counterpart of the *Sturm und Drang* writers, admired Mendelssohn and could not imagine that so noble a man could stay outside Christianity. Impulsively he issued a public challenge to Mendelssohn to refute the doctrine of Christianity or be baptized.

Mendelssohn was so badly upset by this not particularly tasteful form of intellectual dispute that he fell ill. He had never believed in the value of polemics and it was against his peace-loving nature to offend those who thought otherwise. But he accepted the challenge and answered. His answer gave rise to new contributions, a swarm of articles and pamphlets flooded the country. The battle lasted for years. Mendelssohn did not budge an inch from his convictions. He said:

'If our Jewish faith brings us so much sorrow, why do we stay Jews? I do not understand what would tie me to such a strict and despised a religion if I was not convinced in my heart of its truth. I bear witness before the God of truth, before your and my creator and protector, that I will cling to my principles until my soul acquires a new nature.'

But it was not defence against attacks from outside which made Mendelssohn a pioneer in Jewish history. We now look at the internal content of his work, the special quality which inaugurated the modern epoch for the Jewish people. When he had lived in Berlin for twenty years, a change had taken place in the ghetto mentality, at first slight and almost imperceptible, but later more obvious. The first hint of it was when a man so highly thought of in the community as Isaac Bernhardt chose Mendelssohn as a tutor instead of one of the usual Polish *yeshiva* students. Naturally the Judengasse was not unaffected by Mendelssohn's rising fame. A reflection of it shone right into the dark alleys, although there were inevitably many who cried out in dismay when they saw how freely Mendelssohn mixed with the outsiders.

The time was ripe for Mendelssohn's decisive contribution. It came when he published his translation of the Bible into German, with a Hebrew commentary—first the Pentateuch, later the Psalms and the Song of Solomon. He had been engaged on this task for many years, but only so that his children could read the Bible in German. Now he published the book so that everyone was able to read it. Of course Luther's translation of the Bible had been available to the Jews for centuries. But what Jew could think of reading a Christian Bible? The Jewish one was not nearly so frightening. Mendelssohn's translation of the Bible was read assiduously in every German Judengasse.

And reading the holy book, which had created Israel and was its very soul, reading it no longer in the ancient Hebrew language, but in modern German, introduced an entirely new and unknown feature into the ghetto. The biblical text was in German, the commentary in Hebrew. Thereby Mendelssohn split the Yiddish jargon into its two component parts. Every Jew knew the Bible from childhood and could repeat it by heart. So it was a natural consequence that reading Mendelssohn's Bible taught the Jews German. And just as knowledge of German had made a breach in the wall for Mendelssohn, it did the same thing now for thousands of Jews. It was the magic 'Open Sesame' of the door to the world's spiritual treasure chest. The wall crumbled, the chains were broken. The German Jews saw the way into the world open up before them. And Mendelssohn's fantastic dream in the garret at home in Dessau came true; he had become the guide to the perplexed.

It did not happen without protests. It is possible for a prisoner to have been in prison so long that he refuses to put the key in the lock even when it is offered him. There were rabbis who reproached Mendelssohn with harsh words for lowering the beloved Torah to the status of a handmaiden when he used it to teach people German. Others asserted that the Torah should not be read as literature but solely as a holy revelation. The translation was condemned and anathematized in Prague, Hamburg and Posen. There were also serious gentle Jews who warned against Mendelssohn's way. It would lead to unbelief and apostasy. They were not entirely wrong.

Jewry has always housed two conflicting tendencies, the narrow national religious one and the broad universal one. Like Philo in the olden days Mendelssohn was an adherent of the latter. He subscribed completely to his friend Lessing's theory that religion is not dogma, but life. In one of his main works, *Jerusalem*, he expresses himself as follows:

'There is not a single one of the Mosaic law's countless precepts and doctrines that says: "Thou shalt believe this or thou shalt not believe this." They all say: "Thou shalt do and thou shalt not do." For faith cannot be commanded, it accepts no orders. Doctrines change, but what the Lord requires of you is "to do justly and to love mercy, and to walk humbly with thy God" as the prophet Micah puts it.'

Aufklärung, enlightenment. That is the title of the epoch

THE CHAINS ARE BROKEN

in the development of culture to which Moses Mendelssohn belongs. He was its legitimate child, a confirmed rationalist, like it and his first master Maimonides. He never tried to immerse himself in Jewry's profound mysticism. He wanted to expound his own and his people's faith so that it was reasonable and sensible in the eyes of free-thinkers and critics. He continued his work indefatigably until his scanty forces finally gave out. He died in 1786.

But long before his death Mendelssohn had acquired a large following. A new generation grew up in the ghetto, who, like him, looked out through the holes which had been made in the wall. These youngsters translated *Aufklärung* into Hebrew; it was called *Haskalah*. The word was a banner, it waved over them and many successors. At first they gathered round the periodical *Hameassef*, which means the collector, and called themselves *Meassefim*. As the title implies, they wrote in Hebrew. They developed their native tongue so that it could express modern ideas in prose, poetry and drama. They did not isolate themselves, nor did they keep their ideas to the few but tried to get everyone to hear, including the next generation, the children. In 1778 they set up the first German children's school run by modern methods.

That is how Moses Mendelssohn initiated the emancipation of the Jews. The weak cripple dared to make his way along the rutted windswept road from Dessau to Berlin. He did it because in his heart he longed for emancipation. Not only for himself but also for all his people. Unconsciously the fourteen-year-old lad carried the ghetto with him on his weak crooked back. He came at an hour when the fruit was ready to ripen. That is why he succeeded in breaking a hole in the wall from within, where others had tried in vain.

But outside the wall still stood, massive and threatening. And yet no, outside there were also free spirits who worked to remove the blot on Christianity's escutcheon which the ghetto wall had been for centuries. And just as tunnel workers advance from both sides of a mountain and meet at last, the road was slowly built for the Jewish people. The chains were broken.

THE ROAD

But it did not begin in the old world. We shall move over to the new world, far beyond the sea, to find out how it happened.

II

THE CHAINS ARE BROKEN

THE three small ships dropped their anchors when they came close enough to the flat coast of San Salvador. The adventurous voyage had succeeded; Columbus had found the way to America. Aboard the flagship *San Salvador* the crew lowered the longboat and manned it. A few minutes later it left the ship's side and covered the last short stretch of the journey from the old world to the new. Columbus himself stood in the stern of the boat, clad in shining armour with a scarlet cloak over it. He held the Spanish royal banner in his right hand. Strong fists plied the oars, the boat shot smoothly through the surf and onto the shore. It was Friday, October 12, 1492, according to the Julian Calendar (October 21st by our Gregorian Calendar).

The first man to jump out of the boat and set foot on American soil was the interpreter Luis de Torres. He was Jewish, one of the unfortunate *marranos*. Just before the departure from Spain he underwent forced baptism. But we know the names of many other Jews on board the expedition's ships. There are even strong grounds for believing that Columbus himself was of Jewish origin. In any case it is certain that the charts and instruments he navigated by were drawn or constructed by Jewish astronomers in Spain.

However, 1492 is not only the year when America was discovered. The day before Columbus sailed away from the bay of Cadiz, the 'Catholic kings', Ferdinand and Isabella, issued the edict banishing from the country all Jews who refused to be baptized. Perhaps it was the dream of finding a haven beyond the sea, out of the reach of the bloody Inquisition, that drove Luis de Torres and many others to leave

THE CHAINS ARE BROKEN

Spain. It was in the Spanish Jews' blood to look out for distant places where they would have a chance to breathe freely. That is why we find large numbers of *marranos* and Jews travelling to Mexico, Peru and Brazil. But the Inquisition had long arms which stretched over the sea as well. As early as 1520 'Jewish heretics' were burnt in New Spain, as Mexico was called at the time.

For a long time it looked as if there were great possibilities for Jewish colonists in Brazil. They brought the sugar cane with them from Madeira and built up a flourishing sugar industry. And the Dutch captured Pernambuco, the new colony's biggest city, which was a stroke of luck for them. It meant freedom for the Jews; they came flocking in from Amsterdam. But the Portuguese returned to the attack. After a valiant defence in which the Jews fought side by side with the Dutch soldiers the city fell into Portuguese hands. Then the Jews knew that the hour had come. They fled on board sixteen ships, before the Inquisition could lay its hands on them. We do not know much about where the majority of these refugees went. Some of them went back to Holland, others found refuge in Dutch colonies in the West Indies.

But destiny's searchlight lingered on one of the ships, the *Santa Catarina*, with twenty or thirty Jews on board. After incredible adventures in gales and encounters with pirates in the Caribbean they made for North America and landed at New Amsterdam, the capital of the Dutch colony, which formed an enclave in the middle of New England. This was the beginning of Jewish settlement in America in the proper sense of the word. It is commemorated by the fact that tradition calls the *Santa Catarina* 'the Jewish Mayflower', after the famous ship which brought the English pilgrim fathers across the sea.

The Jews had expected an open door; after all they were coming to a piece of free Holland. But the governor, the elderly Peter Stuyvesant, an eccentric with a wooden leg, viewed them with a jaundiced eye and put every obstacle in their way that his fertile imagination could thing up. He got it into his head that they were merely the vanguard of a Jewish inundation of the colony. On top of that they were penniless; they had been forced to leave everything they possessed in Pernambuco. Stuyvesant sold what little they had at a public auction and put two of them in a debtors' prison.

But he had forgotten that the powerful West Indian Company in Amsterdam which controlled New Holland was largely financed by Jewish capital. So the board disowned their governor and gave him strict orders to change his policy about Jewish immigration. The only restriction was that 'poor Jews must not be a burden to the company, but must be looked after by their own people'.

However, in 1664 Dutch dominion in North America was brought to a full stop. King Charles of England decided to eliminate it and sent a fleet of warships. The Dutch colonists were sick and tired of Peter Stuyvesant's despotic régime and only fought half-heartedly. Although the governor defiantly declared that he would rather be carried out of the colony dead than give in, he swallowed the bitter pill and surrendered. New Amsterdam became New York.

It involved more than a change of name, a new era began for America. And also for the Jews. The English conquerors were more tolerant than the defeated governor and realized that the Jews were an asset to the new world. A favourable wind blew in their direction, and they enjoyed many privileges. They knew how to make use of them. Many became rich and a powerful Jewish community sprang up. The first synagogue on American soil was built in New York; it was called Shearit Israel, Israel's remnant. Its site was in Beaver Street between Broadway and Broad Street. A cemetery was laid down in the New Bowery, which was outside the city at the time. But Jews also went to Pennsylvania, Philadelphia, South Carolina and Georgia. It was in Georgia that John Wesley, the father of Methodism, said, 'there are Jews in this country who seem to me to own more of Christ than many who call him Lord'.

But Rhode Island offered the Jews the greatest freedom. It was not long before several thousands lived there. Thanks to their energy and industry Newport grew to be a dangerous rival to New York. Its splendour came to an abrupt end during the War of Independence when the English conquered the town and sacked it. The Jews left Newport and settled in New York, where they remained.

The American Jews rapidly began to play a role in trade and industry. Naturally they had not yet achieved complete equality of status. But they lived in very good circumstances compared with their European brothers. And equality was on the way for two reasons. All American colonists were refugees; they were seeking shelter from religious persecution. It was quite logical that sooner or later they had to grant others the freedom they craved for themselves. As a result the new world was fortunately free of the poisonous vapours which had infested the mental climate of Europe for centuries. Here humanity was given a new start, uninhibited by the hate and prejudice which the old world only managed to rid itself of much later.

The American War of Independence found the majority of Jews on the side of the patriots. Since childhood they had imbibed the prophet Samuel's famous warning against monarchy and it had left its mark. Israel did indeed acquire a king, because the Lord wanted to punish her. The uprising against the British king awoke deep instincts in them. Many Jews fought as volunteers under Washington's flag and not a few of them paid for the colony's freedom with their lives. Jewish financiers gave effective support to the cause of independence. The best known is a Polish Jew, Chaim Solomon, a New York merchant. He put his immense fortune freely at the provisional government's disposal. After Solomon's death a minister declared that without his help even Washington could not have saved the country.

But the Jewish contribution to America's freedom cannot be measured merely in men and money. Far more important was the heritage from their biblical fathers of three thousand years ago. The men in the War of Independence took their inspiration from the books of the Old Testament. The Puritan immigrants who had created the spiritual climate of New England were in reality more Jewish than Christian; they read the Old Testament more often than the New. Their God was Jehova, their law the Pentateuch, their models the prophets and kings of the Bible. The writers and orators who prepared people's minds for revolt made use of biblical ideas

THE CHAINS ARE BROKEN

and turns of phrase. Even the words engraved on the bell of independence are taken from Leviticus: 'Proclaim liberty throughout all the land unto all the inhabitants thereof.' In those days people took their guidance from the pulpit. And clergymen often chose their texts from parts of the Bible which could be crystallized in the slogan: 'Rebellion to a tyrant is obedience to God.' For so ran the motto which Franklin, Adams and Jefferson wanted inscribed on the seal of the United States, together with a picture of Israel crossing the Red Sea. But the Old Testament's influence did not only make itself felt in revolution and war. The institutions of ancient Israel were transferred to the newly-created republic. One of America's greatest jurists has said that 'in the creation of our new constitution, the Hebrew contribution is of overwhelming importance.' Yes, the small scattered groups of Jews along the coast of the Atlantic Ocean lent the new country the best thing they possessed, their heritage from the distant past. Perhaps they themselves did not fully realize its importance, for the living are too close to events to see them in perspective. But we do.

No one should be surprised that the American Jew gave their country everything they had—blood, money, ideas. For when the thirteen colonies proclaimed their independence on July 4, 1776, the tone sounded so new that the Jews thought they heard the bells of the age of the Messiah chiming. The proclamation said:

'that all men are created equal,
that they are endowed by their Creator with certain unalienable rights,
that among these are life, liberty and the pursuit of happiness.'

And the United States' first constitution of 1787 lays down that no religious test shall ever be required as a qualification for an office or post in the United States.

With such words young America unfurled the flag of freedom. Here began the belated long-winded process which was to stamp the modern age and which broke the Jewish people's chains.

THE CHAINS ARE BROKEN

The brave new world beyond the sea has the honour of being the first to understand that a country's Jews have the same natural rights as other citizens. But ideas also came to the fore in old Europe. Towards 1700 a change in the intellectual climate could be observed. From time immemorial theology had reigned in unchallenged majesty as the queen of knowledge. But now the church's eldest daughter, the school, was starting to come of age. The liberal disciplines became so independent that they drove the church and theology over to the defensive. Newton had shown that the universe is subject to unalterable laws. This weakened the idea of God's intervention in the world. Belief in witchcraft and demoniacal possession was a thing of the past. But even orthodoxy and veneration for time-honoured traditions disintegrated, for now the age of enlightenment proudly claimed that life should not be regulated by commandments reputed to come from God, but by the dictates of reason.

All these ideas were popularized and spread, first in France and soon afterwards in England and Germany. The result was often a fierce reaction against those thousand-year-old props of society, the power of the church and the monarchy. In his letters Voltaire used to write as a postscript: 'Ecrasez l'infâme!' (Crush the monster) and everyone knew that he meant the church. The French encyclopaedists were busily preparing the soil in which the revolution's ideas would soon appear and grow vigorously.

But for the Jews it was a dawn which slowly set the horizon alight before the sun rose. A new spirit awoke in people's minds, a hitherto unknown word was whispered in corners: tolerance. Why hate one another because the other person has a different religion? Have not all religions got the same goal of creating good people? Frederick the Great proclaimed that in his kingdom everyone was saved in his own way. In which case it cannot be sinful for the Jews to be different from Christians. Men are men, regardless of race and religion.

In 1781, towards the end of his life, Mendelssohn was visited by Jewish leaders from Alsace who asked him to write a petition to the French cabinet asking for them to be granted civil rights. Mendelssohn was clever enough to see that it would carry more weight if it was written by a Christian. He persuaded his friend, the Prussian official, Christian Wilhelm Dohm, to take up his pen. The result was a book, *Concerning the Improvement of the Jews' Civilian Status*.

In our eyes this heavy work in two volumes is a rather banal recital of truisms: the Jews' obvious faults have their root in Christian persecution; they will right themselves the moment the authorities give them freedom and the country will profit by Jewish industry. But in those days such words struck a new note and Dohm was bitterly attacked by the old-fashioned ecclesiastics.

But there was one man with whom Dohm's ideas found favour, the Emperor of the Holy Roman Empire. Joseph II favoured enlightened despotism. He reacted strongly against his mother Maria Theresa's ultra-Catholic régime and introduced reforms; it was he who abolished serfdom. As far as the Jews were concerned he had already done away with the yellow badge of Jewry and the capitation tax. But Dohm's book inspired him to go even further.

On January 2, 1781, the emperor issued his famous *Toleranz-Edikt* (Edict of Tolerance). In it he cancelled a series of the worst mediaeval restrictions imposed on the Jews in his country. They were entitled to earn their living as artisans, merchants and manufacturers, they could even lease land and cultivate it. However, if they wanted to *buy* land they had to be baptized first. In addition public schools were open to them and they were entitled to run their own schools.

The tendencies in the edict are obvious. They encouraged the Jews to let themselves be absorbed by their surroundings. Perhaps the emperor dreamed that the whole age-old Jewish problem would be solved by large-scale assimilation. Other ordinances pointed in that direction; they made the Jews liable to conscription, forbade them to use Hebrew and Yiddish in legal documents and required them to adopt current German surnames.

Naturally the Jews in the emperor's country scented that it was not his intention to give them facilities for nothing. Nevertheless they appreciated the *Toleranz-Edikt*. And we must not forget that Joseph II was the first European monach to use a battering-ram and work a few stones loose in the

THE CHAINS ARE BROKEN

wall surrounding the ghetto. The major breach was made by the men of the French Revolution.

But before we move on to that chapter, we ought to stop for a moment. For the emperor made the whole question of Jewish names a topical issue. And it is such an interesting and fascinating business that it is worth going into in some detail.

A name is only a word, a few letters and sounds. But behind it is the personality with whom it stays for life, from the cradle to the grave. And once he has gone, his name lives on in memory of him. He inherited it from his father and gives it to his children. There is a gleam of eternity, a touch of immortality, about ancient family names. Investigating them is like following a river back to its source; it becomes a journey through the centuries and their changing cultures.

To Israel's people their name was something permanent, it was part and parcel of the man who bore it. Only great men changed their names and even that was a very rare event, as when Jacob became Israel, unless there was some very serious reason for it. In the Middle Ages the Jews resorted to *Shinnuy Ha-Shem*, name changing, as a last resort. For death took place when *Malak Ha-Mavet*, the angel of death, pronounced the name and summoned the dying person. If the name was suddenly changed, there was a hope of fooling death's messenger. Dangerous illness could be allayed in the same way. But one had to be careful with the new name and be sure to choose a righteous one. For 'the name of the godless crumbles away'. Generally the new name was Chaim, which means life, or Raphael, God heals.

If a family lost a long line of children, in the end they did not dare give a name suited to a new-born child, but were content to call it *Alter*, old. When the angel of death came to fetch a baby and came on one who was called old, he was confused and forgot his errand. In a Yemenite family of my acquaintance one newly-born child after another died of smallpox. At last in their anxiety they gave a new little girl the name of Bath-Ja, which means God's daughter, and hoped that so lofty a name would protect her. She was attacked by the deadly disease, but survived it.

A name was something so personal that people took pains

to avoid two people with the same name living in the same town. In any case they could not join the family. No one could marry a girl who had the same name as the suitor's mother. If their love was so great, that the two *had* to have each other, the girl had to change her name before the marriage. Right up until modern times Russian Jews have considered it a bad omen if the son-in-law has the same name as the bride's father.

Naturally the Jews mainly used biblical names, and rightly so. Phonetically, they are certainly the most beautiful of all peoples' names, sonorous and rhythmical. But even in late biblical times when young Jews travelled in foreign parts, not to mention the dispersion, when Jews lived scattered aboard, it was the custom to have two names. One was Greek or Latin, which did not attract attention and was easily understood, the other Hebrew, *Shem-Hakodesh*, the holy name, which was used in the synagogus and Hebrew documents. John Mark and Simon Peter are two well-known examples from the New Testament.

In the dispersion the Jews gathered in colonies. Where they were numerous, they were rapidly forced to add an additional name to the one by which they were actually christened to distinguish between them. Hundreds of thousands of Jews lived in the Babylon of the Talmudic age and we find a rich inventiveness when it came to signifying a person's special character. There is a Simeon Ha-Zadik, the righteous, and other Simons, with the surnames He-Hasid, the pious, and Ha-Zanua, the modest. Or they have a title, Cohen, priest, Sofer, scribe; we hear of Johanan the sandalmaker, the baker Juda, the flax merchant Jacob and Zakkai the butcher. With others striking characteristics were emphasized; Abba was surnamed Ha-Arekha, the long. Samuel on the other hand was called Ha-Katan, the short. And even in those days it was the custom to call people after their home town, Levi from Jabne, Barhja from Basra, Joseph the Galilaean. Meir does not occur in the Bible, but great teachers in the Talmud period made the name famous; it means the bright one and still exists as Meyer.

Such names conceal the seeds of the genuine family names. These grew up naturally in Babylon and Spain, the first great

THE CHAINS ARE BROKEN

centres for Jewish settlement in exile. The development runs parallel with Christianity's, family names were a necessity in legal documents covering buying and selling. In the Jewish cemetery at Toledo we can still read seventy-five inscriptions which give us an insight into ancient surnames: Abudarham, father of drachmae, i.e. a mint-master or tax inspector, Abulafia, father of medicine, doctor, Dayan, judge, Alaskar, the red, Albo, the white, Bueno, the good—in other words both professions and characteristics were used. In France and Italy we find strange circumlocutions. The Parchi family came from Florence, the city of flowers, because Perka means flower, the Hararis from Montpellier, for *Har* means mountain, as does *mont* in French. In Rome the Portaleones got their name from the Lion Gate, the entrance to the ghetto.

In the Middle Ages the Jews had the odd custom of composing a title by fusing the first letters of a man's names together to form one. Famous examples are Rambam, from rabbi Moses ben Maimon, Rashi, from rabbi Solomon ben Isaac, while a later instance is Besht, from Ba'al Shem Tov, all of whom are mentioned in an earlier volume. There was great keenness among scholars to join the ranks of the men who achieved this honour. It meant that one's name was used so often that it was practical to abbreviate it.

After the persecutions of the crusading epoch only a few Jews lived in Germany. At the end of the thirteenth century they owned a mere fifty-four houses in Mainz; a hundred years later Frankfurt's Judengasse numbered 681 souls, while we have a register dated 1546 from Prague with 1,200 names. In such small communities everyone knew each other and it was superfluous to invent surnames. The very first Jew whose name we know was simply called Isaac. He formed part of Charles the Great's embassy to Haroun al Rashid's court in 795. The oldest gravestone in the cemetery at Worms is the one over Sagira, Samuel's daughter. But naturally the development among the Jews at this point in history had to follow the general tendency, even if Jewish naming usage lagged many decades behind the Christian one.

There is no lack of material at our disposal if we want to study this phenomenon. We know 5,934 gravestones in the old cemetery at Frankfurt am Main and no fewer than 22,000

THE CHAINS ARE BROKEN

in Prague, covering the period from 941 to 1787. We constantly find the obvious use of both characteristics and professions, Kelin, long, Jafa, beautiful, and Bechor, first-born. But German names begin to mingle with the Hebrew, Schwartz, Goldschmidt and Buchhändler. In Bohemia it became the general practice to add an 's' to one's father's name: Abeles, Perles, Selkes, son of Selig.

And now we have reached Emperor Joseph II's time. With him came a turning point in Jewish name giving. An ordinance dated July 5, 1787, ordered every Jew to bear a German family name in the future. Other countries followed suit; France in 1808, Baden in 1809. The authorities estimated that names in the national language would make things easier for the departments which administered taxes and the legal system. But the order is also one of the first signs of a certain rise in the Jews' status.

There were towns where the new regulations were introduced precipitately and brutally. The Jews were summoned before a commission which decided the case. The small bewildered frightened ghetto Jew trembled when the question what did he want to be called was roughly barked at him. If he did not have the answer pat, the official in question, usually a non-commissioned officer, decreed what the Jew and his family had to call themselves. These sergeants were not always noted for delicate feelings, if anything they were eager to show their power. So they often threw the Jew out through the door with a name like Eselkopf, Ochsenschwanz, Temperaturwechsel, Stinker, Bettelarm or Lumpe—Ass's head, Oxtail, Change of temperature, Stinker, Pauper or Scoundrel. Railing and Butterfly were two of the best names. At a trial in Vienna in 1878 some witnesses were heard whose names spoke of such treatment. What else can we make of them—Powder ingredient, Engine wire and Nutcracker? Many of these caricatures of names have clung to the families. But the families' achievements have wiped out the odious wound inflicted on them. The Heilbuth's were named after a fish, the halibut, but no one gives it a thought today.

However, most of the time the Jews knew very well what they wanted to be called. Aaron's descendants, the Kohanites,

THE CHAINS ARE BROKEN

proudly underlined their priestly dignity and were called Cohen, Cohn, Kahn or Kaplan. Katz does not mean cat; it is an abbreviation of Kohen Zedek. In the Slavic languages Cohen became Kagan, familiar to us as Kaganovitch. Levi's tribe is hidden behind many circumlocutions, Levy, Levinson, Halevy, but can also be made out in Lehman and Löve. The last named can equally well stem from Juda, a fact we shall return to later. It is less well known that Segal is an abbreviation of Segan Lewija, leaders of the Levites. On the other hand Levin has nothing to do with Levi. The name actually comes from Leib, which in turn stems from Löve. In other words one should not come to too abrupt conclusions when Jewish names are concerned. Schatz has as little connection with the identical German word for treasure as Katz has with cat. It is an abbreviation of Shaliah Zibur, the messenger of the congregation, and means cantor. Sachs does not mean the German word for scissors, nor does it come from Saxony; it is a contraction of Serah Kodesh, the martyrs' holy race.

Many people simply chose to translate their Hebrew names into German or Latin. Asher, happy, became Selig, Seligmann, or the Latin Felix. Baruch, the blessed, reappeared as Benedict or Benedix, Chaim was Germanized as Heimann and Heine. Heinrich, Heine's great-grandfather was called Chaim. Lazarus, from Eliezer, ended up as Gotthilf, Jacob had the emphasis placed on the last syllable and became Koppel. Marcus and Marx come from Mordecai, Slomann comes from Solomon.

The aged Jacob's blessing of his twelve sons at the end of the Book of Genesis set its mark on Jewish name giving. It says there that 'Judah is a lion's whelp'. So Juda became Löwe. Jacob also says that 'Naphtali is a hind let loose'. Consequently Naphtali became Hirsch or Hertz in German, in French Cerf, in the Slavic tongues Jelin or Jelinik. And Jacob says about Benjamin that 'he shall ravine as a wolf'. So Benjamin was turned into Wolf or Wulf.

Of course the Jews often followed the Christians and chose their father's name with son added to it. Abraham's son became Abrahamssohn, Abramowitz in Polish, Abramowsky in Russian to name one example. The Hebrew word for son,

THE CHAINS ARE BROKEN

ben, can be distinguished in Benario, from Ben Aryeh, in Benda, from Ben David, it can even be traced in names like Bech, from Ben Chaim, and Brann, from Ben rabbi Nathan.

The great majority of modern Jewish names can be split into two groups, taken either from their professions or their home town. A study of the former names is a whole course in the callings the Jews chose for preference: Fleischer (butcher), Weber (weaver), Goldschmidt (goldsmith), Silbermann (silversmith), Steinschneider (engraver), Krämer (shopkeeper), Wechsler (money changer) and Delbanco (banker). The Jews have always loved music. As a result Geiger (fiddler), Pfeiffer (whistler) and Spielmann (minstrel) are typical surnames. But I must warn the reader once more. Goldschmidt does not always mean goldsmith pure and simple. It can equally well indicate that the family is of the tribe of Levy. For one of the Levites' tasks was making gold objects for the temple. Obviously the Jews did not get their new names for nothing. Some of them were even dear. Names with 'gold' in them cost a surcharge, Gold, Goldstein, Diamond, Rubin, Rubinstein, Silvermann. It is pertinent to remark here that the Jews liked to call their children after men who had shown good will to their people, Lessing and Dohm to name two examples. Napoleon, too, had a great reputation among the Jews. In Germany Bonaparte was translated as Schönteil, a Jewish name.

But if we compile statistics of the etymology of Jewish names, it leaps to the eye how natural it was for them to call themselves after the town or country they lived in. In Baden 41 per cent of all Jewish names fell into this category. Countless place names became Jewish surnames: Worms, Speyer or Spiro, Bing from Bingen, Frank or Fränkel from Franken, Dehn from Denmark, Picard from Picardy, Hannover, Oppenheimer, Prager, Berliner, East European ones such as Kalisch, Lubliner and Willner, and so on ad infinitum. I may add here that Hamburg became Hambro, the family who founded the celebrated London banking house and produced a proud scion in the man who was president of the Norwegian parliament in 1940. In Denmark we find Fridericia, Glückstadt, Nyborg and Mariboe.

This preference for place names tells a moving story of

THE CHAINS ARE BROKEN

how the exiled people were attached to the places which gave them asylum, however uncertain and short it usually was. It was always a central part of the Jewish character to stick to the home, the little spot in a hostile world where even slaves could feel free. But in the same breath it should be added that there are obviously names which betoken homelessness and the inextinguishable longing for the old country: Ellend, far from the home country, and Gaster, foreign.

Here we stop. The long journey through Jewish names is merely intended to point out how their study can lead to peaks which give a broad prospect of Jewish life through the centuries. I return to pick up the thread of the story. We are going to hear about the French Revolution.

'What is your programme?'

The question was put to the Comte de Mirabeau on the February day in 1789 when he announced his candidature in Aix en Provence for election to the French diet, which later as the National Assembly was to make the revolution explode and sweep countless outmoded obsolete institutions out of France's house. The questioner was one of Mirabeau's Jewish friends. And the answer came quickly:

'I want to make a human being of you.'

Mirabeau kept his promise. It was the great revolution which tore down the centuries-old wall round the ghetto and, in Europe, broke the chains which had bound the Jewish people.

In fact it was strange that France should be the country to do so. From time immemorial she had never had a Jewish problem to cope with, for the simple reason that practically speaking no Jews lived in the French king's realm. In 1394 all Jews were banished from the country by a royal decree. It was to take three centuries before they returned. When Louis XIV wrested the rich province of Alsace from Austria, the 50,000 Jews who lived there went with it. To make the picture complete I should add that some rich Sephardic merchant families already lived in Bayonne and Bordeaux; they were descendants of refugee *marranos*. In addition the government shut their eyes to a few score Jews who lived illegally in Paris.

THE CHAINS ARE BROKEN

Anti-Semitism was rife in Alsace; the province's oppressed penniless farmers hated the rich Jewish money-lenders. As soon as news of the fall of the Bastile reached them, the farmers not only stormed the nobility's castles, but also burnt down the Jews' houses and behaved so violently that many Jews sought shelter over the frontier in Switzerland. But the Jews had powerful friends in France. Mirabeau, the National Assembly's influential spokesman, was one of them. The year before the revolution he had visited Berlin and met Mendelssohn and Dohm. Their fight for Jewish emancipation had made an impression on him. And like the dynamic personality he was, Mirabeau did not make any secret of his opinions when he went back to France. Yet he was not the first Frenchman to talk in those terms. One of Louis XVII's ministers once said: 'It is odd that people blame the Jews for being unprofitable, when the same people prevent them from being useful.'

The National Assembly had scarcely begun to meet before Mirabeau proposed that France's Jews be emancipated and given equal status with other citizens. Many of the Assembly's prominent men supported him, including the abbé Gregoire, Clermont-Tonnère and Robespierre. They did not stop until the ship was brought into harbour, but the voyage was a long one.

Theoretically there was nothing to fight about. In the declaration of the rights of man made in August, 1789, it says:

'Men are born equal and remain free and with equal rights. All citizens are equal before the law. No one may be molested for his opinions, not even his religious views.'

These immortal words are an echo of the American Declaration of Independence. But in Europe they sounded for the first time in the French National Assembly when its members took a whole week debating the declaration paragraph by paragraph and finally settled on its formulation. With it the door of fate swung on its hinges. Old prejudices, along with injustice and violence, were locked out in the cold and darkness for ever by these words. As often as evil powers sneaked in again, there were men with faith and

THE CHAINS ARE BROKEN

enthusiasm who were ready to drive it back where it belonged again.

But anti-Semitism is so stubborn that even in the National Assembly, in spite of the recent excitement of the newly-won human rights, a struggle lasting years was necessary before it decided to apply its own declaration of liberty, equality and fraternity to France's Jews. As late as September 28, 1791, only two days before the dissolution of the National Assembly, in other words at the eleventh hour, it passed a decree, after endless tugs-of-war and myriads of intrigues, stating that 'the Jews in France enjoy the same rights as the other citizens'.

That is the first great milestone in modern Jewish history. The next came a hundred years later when Theodor Herzl opened the way home to Zion. It was the French National Assembly which took the decisive step in 1791, opened the prison doors for the Jews and put them on an equal footing with all the other citizens of the country. And the Jews' gratitude knew no bounds. With true Gallic verve one of them gave expression to it in words like these:

'As recently as September 28th we were the only people who seemed doomed to perpetual degradation and slavery. And the very next day, the immortal September 28th, 60,000 unfortunates were transformed into human beings. God chose the French people to give us back our rights, as in ancient times he used Antiochus and Pompey to degrade and oppress us.'

It is easy to be wise after the event. Today we can see clearly the fatal confusion which was attached to their emancipation. The Jews did not win their civil rights for nothing. They had to take an oath to France in which they renounced their former rights, especially their self-government. This meant that they were regarded as individuals, not as a people, and that they were expected to be willing to become completely assimilated to the French people. Clermont-Tonnère hit the nail on the head when he said:

'One may deny the Jews everything as a nation, but grant them everything as individuals.'

But there were serious consequences behind it. If the Jews did not accept this demand, they were banished from France.

THE CHAINS ARE BROKEN

The French did not intend to tolerate a state within a state. Naturally the Jews could keep their faith. On this point the National Assembly agreed to complete freedom. But now the French Jews were a sect like so many others. Not a people. The French mind thinks keenly and clearly and the members of the National Assembly put forward the antithesis: Sect versus nation. They recognized the former, but condemned the latter. It was to take a whole century of intellectual crises before Jewry itself found its way out of the dilemma. But in 1791 these snags were hidden in the mist of the future. For the moment all was peace.

The French emancipation did not stagnate at home. The revolution's ideas proved themselves even more explosive than the primitive grenades the soldiers hurled at the republic's enemies. Ideas have never respected territorial frontiers; they are flying seeds which the wind bloweth where it listeth. The newly-created people's army marched out into Europe under the tricolour, with the motto *Liberté, Egalité et Fraternité* embroidered on it in golden letters. Clattering horses' hooves and the heavy tramp of marching feet were drowned by drumbeats and the fiery tones of the Marseillaise. The old aristocratic Europe was shaken to its foundations. In the Judengassen in the towns on the Rhine the Jews could hear the distant echo of gunfire from Valmy and Jemappes, the two battlefields where the revolutionary armies, singing *Ca ira*, won their first victories. It was about the retreat from Valmy that Goethe remarked:

'In this place and on this day a new era in history begins. You will be able to say, "I was there".'

The Jews were the first to profit by the new era. As soon as revolutionary soldiers captured a town, they put an end to religious inequality, they ordered the ghetto's walls to be knocked down and summoned the pale inhabitants of its narrow congested alleys out into the open air of the market place to listen to the proclamation which set them free. Now each one of them could call himself 'citizen' instead of the despised 'Jew'. They reported to the citizens' army, promenaded proudly in uniform and carried weapons; they sought election to the newly established town council. Yes, it was a new world.

THE CHAINS ARE BROKEN

Nowhere were these truly revolutionary events felt so much as in Italy. As early as 1792 the troops of the republic invaded Nizza and incorporated the town into France. An observer described the event in the words: 'the ghetto's walls began to dance!' The dramatic events acquired impetus when the young general Bonaparte swept the Austrians and their allies out of Italy in a victorious *blitzkrieg*. Venice fell in 1797; the last of the famous doges was deposed. We possess enthusiastic accounts of what the Jews experienced in this town which had once given the ghetto its name.

Monday, July 10, 1797, should have been a day of sorrow among Venice's Jews. It was the evening before 17 Tammus —the fast day when memory lamented the first breach in Jerusalem's wall when Titus stormed the holy city. With a feeling for dramatic effect, that was the very day chosen to bring freedom to Venice's ghetto at long last. The citizen's army paraded in the square in the Ghetto Nuova, a swarm of spectators filled it, they could see Catholic priests who wanted to show fraternal feeling for their new co-citizens. A tree of liberty was planted and the gate of the ghetto was pulled down; people chopped it to matchwood and threw the bits onto a bonfire. Christians and Jews joined in a gay *carmagnole*, while a flickering gleam from the flames fell on the hundreds of singing jubilant men and women.

The Jews in the Roman ghetto sang even louder. In the spring of 1798 the French army marched into Rome. The Pope was taken prisoner, but the Jews were free. They tore the yellow badge from their clothes, the brand of Cain, the symbol of their degradation. One of them was elected to the Roman senate. True enough that there was a severe repercussion. While Napoleon was occupied in distant Egypt, the Neapolitans succeeded in capturing Rome. The Jews were immediately driven back into the ghetto and the Inquisition re-established. The newly-elected Pope Pius VII again forced the Jews to listen to sermons about conversion. But it was only an episode. By and large the Italian Jews were free so long as Napoleon held the reins of power. As late as 1812 Italian Jews were soldiers in the great army's ill-starred campaign against Moscow. Rumour has it that they sang their Jewish psalms to the tune of the Marseillaise.

THE CHAINS ARE BROKEN

The first northern European country which came under French control was Holland, the new Batavian Republic. Strangely enough the Jews there could not agree. The traditionalists were afraid that new customs would undermine the faith and weaken their hereditary self-government. But the French ambassador made the decision out of hand; there was nothing to discuss. He ordered the Dutch National Assembly to pass the decree which gave Holland's 50,000 Jews civil rights. A few years later one of them was not only a member of the assembly, but also its president.

In Germany too events progressed, even if the tempo there was more like a sedate jog-trot. In the new kingdom of Westphalia, where the Emperor set up his brother Jerome as king, a decree of 1808 gave the Jews the same rights as their brothers in France. The old Hanseatic towns of Lübeck and Bremen had to go the same way. Even Frankfurt am Main, the capital of the confederation of the Rhine, followed suit belatedly, in spite of its century-old dislike of the Jews. But here the Jews had to pay a fantastic sum, twenty times the annual protection tax, for their freedom. After the catastrophe at Jena in 1806 the new age finally reached Prussia. With the annexation of extensive provinces of partitioned Poland the country had increased its Jewish population enormously. In 1812, in the middle of the febrile preparations for the War of Independence, the decree ordering Jewish emancipation came at long last. The only shadow was that Jews were still barred from government service. Only Saxony, 'the Protestant Spain', was inflexible; there the old state of affairs continued.

Shortlived as Napoleon's victory was, it changed the face of Germany. The Holy Roman Empire had only been a name. Now even that vanished. Even in countries where France was not the actual master, its spirit was active. A cleansing storm of freedom swept through the German countries and took a lot of stale mediaevalism with it. The only tragedy was that the Germans did not learn the lesson of their own free will, but at the point of French bayonets. This inevitably meant that there was a reaction simply sitting waiting for Napoleon's fall.

THE CHAINS ARE BROKEN

Napoleon first came into close contact with the Jews during his campaign in Egypt and Palestine. Until then he had only had a hazy conception of Jewry. He shared his countrymen's bigoted opinion that they were accursed and should be treated as such. But his powerful intelligence both as commander and statesman enabled him to overcome his prejudice when he realized that there were advantages to be had. In Palestine he saw the brilliant possibilities inherent in the Jewish people's age-old dream of their fathers' country. After the conquest of Gaza he issued a proclamation in the camp at Ramleh offering the Jews the chance of reconstructing David's throne in Jerusalem and urging them to enlist under the French flag. His words met with no response and the whole expedition ended in a fiasco which the emperor could never forget, even at the height of his subsequent triumphs.

In 1806 the emperor found himself in the midst of the Jewish problem again. His star was at its zenith; he made a halt in Strasbourg during his triumphal procession to Paris after the victory at Austerlitz. There was unrest in Alsace. Every day Napoleon was inundated with complaints about the Jews. They had subjugated the whole of the country's population, so the story went. Half the property in the province and often whole villages were in the hands of Jewish usurers. We have already heard of anti-Semitism in Alsace. From ancient times it was a privilege of Strasbourg that no Jews were allowed to live in the city or even spend the night there if they were passing through it. The Jews' enemies were ingenious; they whispered in Napoleon's ear how these homeless people did everything they could to dodge their military service. Undeniably a sore point to raise with the soldier-emperor. He himself remembered how often he had angrily watched the long train of Jewish canteen-keepers and provision-dealers who followed the army in the field. Napoleon resolved to take up the problem of France's Jews and provide a radical solution to it. The question was on the agenda at the first cabinet meeting after the emperor's return to Paris. Napoleon was in a bad humour; he inveighed against the Jews and threatened them with every kind of misfortune. But on more careful reflection he decided to tackle the matter more adroitly. An imperial decree was issued summoning a kind of Jewish parliament consisting of 112 Jews from every part of his extensive empire. The Jewish notables met in the Hôtel de Ville in Paris. They were immediately presented with a series of questions, twelve in all, for discussion and solution. Ostensibly they were concerned with rather banal matters—marriage, divorce, Jewish customs and opinions. But there was a purpose behind them. From the answers the government wanted to judge whether the Jews thought they owed their faith greater loyalty than the state. If that was the case Napoleon intended to put the clock back and put the Jews on the same footing as before the revolution. He, too, did not mean to tolerate a state within a state. However, the answers turned out quite satisfactorily. In one of them there was a reference to the ancient Sanhedrin. It was a spark which caught the emperor's imagination and set it afire.

When Napoleon acted, he liked to keep an eye on the muse of history. He was a true impresario with the whole world as his stage and mankind as his troop of actors. The emperor decided to do no less than add a new chapter to the Bible. He ordered the revival of the ancient Sanhedrin, the seventy-one great men who at the beginning of our era formed Israel's great council. Napoleon's Sanhedrin also had seventy-one members, forty-six rabbis and twenty-five laymen; its president bore the Hebrew title Nasi. In the winter of 1807 it met in Paris and was given the twelve questions for re-discussion. The emperor wanted the answers to have the same authority as the Talmud.

To tell the truth Napoleon had enough to attend to during these years when he was redrawing the map of Europe. But he managed to control the Sanhedrin as well; he never lost sight of it for a moment. He intended to make it his willing tool and use it to solve the Jewish problem, but only in the way he wanted it solved. This implied the total incorporation of the Jews with the French people. Imperial commissioners supervised the Sanhedrin's meetings and it proved submissive enough to answer the questions in the way expected of it. The high point was reached on the day when the seventy-one declared that all Frenchmen were their brothers. They were bound by French law and they would defend France *jusqu' à la mort* (until death). At the moment the ceremony reached this point, all the members of the Sanhedrin stood up and repeated in chorus: *'jusqu' à la mort!'* A truly Napoleonic gesture.

This has been called 'the sin of 1807'; the Sanhedrin sold the Jewish people to keep the emperor's favour. Is that true, I wonder? Or is there the second possibility that they saw through the emperor and made use of the proven age-old Jewish method of bowing before the storm? Who knows; perhaps these descendants of a people who have survived innumerable tyrants waited with a secret knowing smile for the wheel of history to turn once again and cast him who was now high down into the dust. The private correspondence which has come to light from those days shows that there were men of both types to be found among the Sanhedrin's members.

But Napoleon was satisfied; he thought he had achieved his goal. When the Sanhedrin was dissolved, he managed the empire's Jewish affairs with the same purposefulness as when he issued the *Code Napoleon*. A decree of 1808 set up a central consistory in Paris with local consistories under it throughout the empire to manage all Jewish affairs. Its main task was to encourage the enlistment of soldiers. Young Jews were not entitled to nominate a substitute. Simultaneously the decree imposed a series of disagreeable restrictions on the daily life of the Jews, forbade them to move, closed the frontiers to commerce and other callings. The French Jews were disappointed and indignant; the *décret infame* (the infamous decree), was the name they invented for it. As a matter of fact it did not have lasting results. The provisions were in force for a limited period of fifteen years. When the time ran out, Napoleon had fallen and died, and his successors did not renew the *décret infame*.

There is no doubt that Napoleon's policy vis à vis the Jews had momentous consequences by giving impetus to assimilation. But the Sanhedrin was a subtle diplomatic stroke, it caught people's eyes and fascinated the Jews far beyond the frontiers of the empire. When Napoleon conquered Poland, Jews wearing caftans and ear-locks flocked round the army and offered it all the help they could. Napoleon's name was loved among Europe's Jews; legends arose; Heine was deeply

THE CHAINS ARE BROKEN

stirred by the Napoleonic myth. Napoleon was of overwhelming importance for Jewish history because he broke up the old feudal Europe and spread the revolution's ideas throughout the continent, with Jewish emancipation as a natural consequence. Not that the Jews were in any sense close to his heart, or that he understood them. But history used him as its tool.

Yet spring had come too soon. The winter cold returned and froze to death many flowers which had ventured forth. The fall of the empire threw Europe into the grip of reaction. Once again the Jews were in the melting-pot.

III

REACTION

THE arched portal of the brilliant Congress of Vienna was the entrance to a period of black reaction in every country in Europe. Napoleon's conquerors, first and foremost the three great powers, Austria, Russia and Prussia, dictated what the new map of Europe should look like. It bore a striking resemblance to the old pre-revolutionary one. But they also revived people's political and social ideas. The detestable revolution was crushed, now the slogan was *restauration* (restoration). Things were to be restored to the good old order before the Twilight of the Gods came. For the next few decades the men of the Holy Alliance fought indefatigably for the Christian state as the surest bulwark against a new revolt.

The Jews were made to feel the significance of this. After happy dreams of freedom they awoke suddenly and saw the Middle Ages emerge into the light of day again. Naturally they worked with feverish zeal to keep what they had won. Between the negotiations Congress danced. In the homes of rich Viennese Jews as well. Here refined beautiful Jewesses entertained victors such as Talleyrand, Wellington and Hardenberg, while smiling coquettishly behind their fans they pressed their people's case. From every country in Europe Jewish communities sent their agents, known as *shdatlanim*, to Vienna to save what could be saved. For the first time in modern history an international congress put the Jewish question on the agenda. The Jews were on the verge of reaching their goal, but in an unguarded moment victory slipped from their hands.

Before the revolution Germany had been a broken interminable pattern of several hundred miniature states which supported countless princes. The newly-formed German federation had to be content with 'the thirty-six kings'. And the congress discussed a proposal that the newly-won civil rights should be kept 'in the German states which had granted them'. The proposal was both liberal and fair, but the Jews had many enemies in Vienna. And they were clever. One of them, the representative of the Hanseatic city of Bremen, recommended a minor amendment, the word 'in' should be replaced by 'by'. It was a hot day when apathy and inattention had spread in the hall. Without anyone knowing how it actually happened, the proposed amendment slipped through and was adopted. It meant that nearly everything was lost for the Jews. The German states where Jewish emancipation had been introduced 'by' the state itself could be counted on the fingers of one hand. Almost everywhere French power had forced the reform through 'in' the state. Jewish hopes collapsed like a house of cards. They felt that they had been shamefully cheated.

Once again the Jews fell upon evil days. But painful as the reaction felt, the new régime was not quite so harsh as the old one had been. Before the revolution oppression of the Jews had been the rule, the bright side the exception. Now there were light patches on the map of Europe, even if conditions there could not exactly be called favourable. But in spite of everything the Jew was no longer the same inferior being he had been as a matter of course before, marked by the yellow badge, an incomprehensible dialect and narrow horizons, shut in behind grey walls. He had breathed the air of freedom and seen the wonderful world outside. Injustice could no longer be restored.

In France Louis XVIII respected the signature of his unfortunate namesake and predecessor on the law of emancipation of 1791. The Jews kept liberty and equality, even if they might be a bit short on fraternity. Nor did Holland falter, and in Denmark the country's handful of Jews received extensive liberties as early as 1814, but did not acquire full citizenship until the June constitution of 1849. The other Scandinavian countries followed suit, even if the tempo was slower. Jews, like Jesuits, were simply forbidden to go to

REACTION

Norway. The poet Henrik Wergeland fought valiantly against this mediaeval decree. In 1851 his fight bore fruit and the country was opened to Jewish settlement.
But black shadows fell in Germany and Italy.

'We spilt our blood in vain at Leipzig and Waterloo.'
That was the complaint of the German patriots when the Holy Alliance oppressed the people and crushed the liberating movement which had freed the country with a firm hand. But if a people's elemental forces are subdued, they make new ways for themselves. A wave of xenophobia poured over Germany. It was directed at France and the Jews. France had infected the fatherland's holy soil, the Jews had profiteered during the war. But now the French were safely on their own side of the Rhine. So the wrath of the people was vented in all its force on the Jews. *Der Jud ist schuld!* (It's the Jew's fault!) was the cry in the streets.

Even the spirit of the age added fuel to the fire of anti-Semitism. It is enough to take a look at the country's three greatest minds to see how they disliked the Jews. On this point Goethe never outgrew his origins; he maintained the Frankfurt patrician's sneering contempt for the shabby inhabitants of the Judengasse. Already in the grip of his own philosophy of life, he took up a strong position against ethically minded Jewry which, so he claimed: 'denies the source of the highest (or Hellenic) culture.' Ludwig Börne once asked him angrily:

'Have you ever lifted so much as a finger to lighten the yoke of the oppressed?'

Sadly enough the same thing applies to the philosopher J. G. Fichte, the man who in the middle of the French occupation when French commands and drum beats were echoing outside in the streets, re-aroused German arrogance in the Academy in Unter den Linden with his inflammatory 'Talks to the German nation'. To him Jewry was 'a hostile state, widespread in every country, in a perpetual state of war with all the others', and he could think of no better remedy than conquering the Holy Land from the Turks and sending all the Jews back there.

Even a pioneer theologian like Schleiermacher, who—as

we shall hear later—was the lion of Jewish salons in Berlin and the spiritual adviser of beautiful Jewesses, opposed the 'naturalization' of the Jews and regarded it as an unrealisable demand, as long as they clung to their own laws and customs, and dreamed of a Messiah. He applied all his energies to leading his Jewish friends to the font.

No, none of the great men in the fields of German thought and literature lowered the barrier and barred the way to anti-Semitism's sudden fit of rage. The inevitable results followed. A stream of odious pamphlets flooded the country. In one of them the author advocated selling all Jewish children to the English. They would put them to work in the plantations of the West Indies instead of negroes. All Jewish men should be castrated and their wives and daughters sent to brothels.

In 1819 the agitators reaped their bloody harvest. Infuriated mobs stormed Jewish houses and shops. It happened in Würzburg, Karlsruhe, Hamburg, Frankfurt, Mannheim and Heidelberg; indeed the infection spread beyond Germany's borders. In Copenhagen and peaceful Danish provincial towns there were disturbances, the euphemistically named Jewish controversy. Precisely thirty years after the revolution Jewish dreams and hopes were drowned in the shouts and screams of the street. The stones which broke the windows in their houses also shattered the Jews' newly awakened faith in humanity and goodness.

Yesterday freedom. Today new chains. Both epochs left deep marks on the Jewish mentality and created complications which they took two or three generations to get over. Indeed many Jews have not got over them to this day. After the disturbances in 1819 it was the desperate ones who gave up. Some of them, in cold contempt, bought 'the ticket to European culture', as Heinrich Heine called Christian baptism. Others left Germany and fled. In their thousands, they made for America, freedom's promised land, to begin again from the beginning, as their people had so often done before.

But there were men who were strengthened by the defeat. They resumed the battle on the political front in the midst of the oppressive atmosphere of the Holy Alliance.

REACTION

They became revolutionaries and were largely responsible for instigating new popular uprisings, the revolutions of 1830 and 1848. There were 21 Jews among the 200 who fell in the street-fighting in Berlin in February, 1848. Christians and Jews were buried side by side in the victims' communal grave.

In this year of destiny the German Jews acquired a leader of unusual stature. Gabriel Riesser came from Hamburg where his grandfather had been the chief rabbi. The relationship between the two, grandfather and grandson, is an object lesson in the development German Jewry had undergone, in spite of all the setbacks. More than two generations, a whole world separated them. The old chief rabbi had fulminated Mendelssohn's German translation of the Bible in his synagogue as a profanation of the holy scriptures. His grandson was a doctor of law from Heidelberg University; he felt that he was a German and was on familiar terms with liberal politicians.

With his knowledge, intelligence and exceptional eloquence Riessler should have been the very man for an academic career. But he ran his head against a wall of prejudice. Only those who could produce a certificate of baptism could be appointed. Riesser flatly refused to become an apostate, as many others were lured into becoming. He was just as much a German as a Christian. 'There is only one baptism which initiates a man to belonging to his people,' he said, 'the baptism in blood spilt in the battle for freedom and fatherland.' His outlook was clear, the Jew did not belong to a national minority, he merely had a different faith from the majority of the people. Jewry was not a nation, but a religion.

Gabriel Riesser built his own rostrum. It was the periodical *Der Jude* (The Jew). Even the title shows his courage; nothing was to be concealed or wrapped up. 'Malice and hate made this word a term of abuse. Nevertheless we shall not disown it, but devote all our abilities to making it honoured,' he wrote in the first number. He was a distinguished writer; he lavished his brilliant wit in the camgaign against prejudice and restrictions. Here at last Germany saw a Jew who did not plead, but claimed his obvious right, unconditional emancipation.

THE CHAINS ARE BROKEN

Then came the *annus mirabilis*, the wonderful year, 1848, with the revolution which admittedly turned out a failure, but nevertheless cleared the way for freedom. Gabriel Riesser became one of the vice-presidents in the newly-elected German Diet in Frankfurt and a member of the deputation which offered the King of Prussia the imperial German crown. The King refused; he did not want to accept anything at the hands of the rebels.

The dramatic events, not only in Germany, but throughout most of Europe also brought the Jews freedom. But they were even more short-lived than under Napoleon. Reaction was in the saddle and everything went on as before. The Jews were disappointed once more. The stream of emigrants to America increased by leaps and bounds. But now they had not long to wait; the waves of progress were irresistible. Emancipation slowly worked its way to victory in the individual German states, one after the other. But first, the Empire, in its constitution of 1871, guaranteed full equality of civil rights as a general German law. The last fragment of the chain to fall to the ground was the Jewish oath. To swear *more Judaico*, in the Jewish manner, had branded the oath-taker. The Jew had to stand barelegged on a pigskin and with his hand on the Bible call down bloody curses on his head if his oath was false. In future the oath merely went: 'So help me God'.

Slowly and belatedly the German Jews progressed towards emancipation. They had to cut their way, step by step, through a primaeval forest of prejudice and hostility. Twice the way seemed to be completely barred. But it opened again and led to the goal at long last. The fourteen-year-old Moses Mendelssohn dared to take the first step on the road when he walked through Berlin's Rosenthaler gate in 1743. Not until 130 years later was the emancipation of the Jews written into the empire's constitution.

But the ink was hardly dry before their rights were encroached on and anti-Semitic propaganda reared its head again. It was true that the chains were broken, but they had not disappeared. The days were to come when they were forged around the German Jews again, more terribly than ever before. We can understand Einstein's outburst:

REACTION

'I never think about the future. It will come soon enough.'

By far the most Jews in Italy lived in Rome, Leghorn and Venice. All three towns relocked the gate in the ghetto wall as soon as the last French soldier was driven out in 1814. Grey and hopeless, the Middle Ages redescended on the Italian Jews. But even in Italy the Jews were not the same as before. There were some real men about, and more and more had the courage to fight for their rights. The nascent *risorgimento* had a disproportionately large number of Jews in its ranks and accepted Jewish emancipation as a matter of course. *Risorgimento* means revival; it was the name the patriots gave their movement when they fought for Italy's unity and freedom. Both Mazzini and Garibaldi received inestimable help from the Jews. Cavour's secretary was a Jew; he was called Isaac Artom and, behind the scenes, played a big role in the epoch-making events which in 1870 finally made Victor Emmanuel of Sardinia king of united Italy. It was a natural phenomenon for the Jews to acquire political equality within the House of Savoy's possessions as early as 1848, but in the other Italian countries the road was as long and difficult as in Germany.

1848, the year of the revolution, certainly inspired hope, even in papal Rome. Pius IX was driven out of the city. Once again Jews and Christians celebrated when they saw the dust rise in dense clouds as the Ghetto wall fell in ruins and its gates burnt on a blazing bonfire. In Rome's newly-elected senate Jews sat on equal terms with Christians. But the light was extinguished again; the Pope returned to the Vatican. The Jews had to assemble in church every sabbath and listen to sermons aimed at converting them.

But public feeling was about to swing in the Jews' favour. Eight years previously, in the Near East, a drama had unfolded which had made a sensation and done more than anything to create a hitherto unknown sympathy for the Jews. It was the ghastly Damascus affair. On February 5, 1840, Father Thomas, the prior of a Franciscan monastery in Syria's ancient capital of Damascus, disappeared. Father Thomas was a popular man in the city. He was good at healing the sick and had the entreé to many houses, including

THE CHAINS ARE BROKEN

Jewish ones. The monks were certain that some of these Jews had kidnapped the prior. For they had to use Christian blood, so the story went, in their unleavened Easter bread. A veritable affair of ritual murder developed, after old familiar patterns. The governor was alarmed, he had a number of Jews imprisoned and immediately put to the torture. Surprisingly enough this did not succeed in extracting a confession. But tempers were aroused. Attacks were made on synagogues and Jewish houses in various Turkish possessions, including Rhodes and Smyrna. The governor was a zealot. If torture would not work, he had other methods. Sixty Jewish children were imprisoned and locked in a cramped cell. There they would be left to starve to death slowly. That would certainly make their parents so submissive that they confessed.

But now something happened the world had never known before. The European press took up the affair; newspapers carried reports from Damascus describing the macabre events in full detail. Public opinion was aroused and turned in favour of the mistreated Jews. The case was debated in the House of Commons; London's Lord Mayor spoke at a big protest meeting; some governments instructed their ambassadors to make representations to the Sublime Porte at Constantinople. The Turks gave in to this outside pressure. The surviving prisoners in Damascus were set free; the governor was condemned and beheaded.

The affair had far-reaching consequences. Jews throughout the world suddenly felt united. In spite of all the differences between them they were tied to the same destiny. Not yet in freedom, but so much the more in suffering and danger. Christianity had shown that it too could show sympathy when injustice and cruelty became overpowering. Even the Pope had sympathized.

It is a long way from Damascus to Rome. But in 1858 the Pope's subjects heard of a new affair. This time events took place on their doorstep. On June 23rd a section of papal soldiers marched up to a Jewish house. On orders from the Inquisition they took away a six-year-old boy, Edgar Mortara, and handed him over to be brought up in a monastery as a Christian. The boy had been dangerously ill. A nun who had nursed him baptized him when she thought the boy was going to die. He recovered, but the sacrament had been administered. In other words the boy no longer belonged to his father and mother, but to the church. His despairing parents called for help, but no authority was able to act against the will of the Inquisition, and neither it nor the Pope would budge.

They had forgotten the lesson of Damascus, that the press has power in our age. The story of the abduction became a sensation which every newspaper covered at length. Once more world opinion was aroused and called for intervention in the affair. Napoleon III and Franz Joseph, the great Catholic monarchs, appealed to the Pope, but Pius IX did not deign to answer them.

'I snap my fingers at the whole world,' His Holiness is supposed to have said in a moment of irritation.

The Pope had to pay dearly for his stubbornness. The Mortara affair was such a challenge to general feelings of decency that it was largely responsible for clearing the way for the revolution of 1870.

In that year the troops of the new Italy entered Rome and made the world city the capital of the youthful kingdom. The Pope became 'the prisoner in the Vatican'. But the Jews acquired full citizenship. In 1555 Pope Paul I had erected the wall round the ghetto. After 315 years of degradation the Roman Jews had at last become free men.

One spring day in 1956 I was invited to a reception in the West End of London. It celebrated the three hundredth anniversary of Israel ben Manasse's achievement when, in Cromwell's days, he persuaded England to open her doors to Jewish immigration. In 1956 the country could look back on 300 years of Jewish activity, and both Jews and Christians were celebrating the event. At the meeting I am talking about the speaker was Cecil Roth, professor at Oxford, a great authority on Jewish history. In his speech he emphasized that during these three hundred memorable years England had practically speaking abstained from discrimination against her Jews.

'That is something unique in history,' said the professor. Suddenly he stopped speaking, was silent for a few seconds and looked at my chair. Then he cleared his throat and continued:

'With one exception. Denmark.'

The meeting rose and broke into spontaneous applause that lasted for over a minute.

Of course everyone knows that Cecil Roth's words must be taken with a grain of salt. Literally speaking they would not apply to anywhere on earth. Both east and west of the North Sea emancipation had to overcome obstacles before it was fully recognized. But as regards the Jews' social status, the professor's words are almost fully applicable. Such disadvantages as did affect the Jews in the two countries were the exceptions which prove the rule. It is of interest to note that they shared them with other groups of the population who deviated from the authorized church. In England they were called dissenters.

The Jews could live where they wanted in England, follow the calling they liked and move freely among their fellow citizens. The Jew only noticed that he was different in the City of London. There he could not obtain freedom, and only freemen had the right to open retail shops.

The first Jews in England were of Sephardic stock, refugees who came straight from Spain and Portugal, or made a detour via Amsterdam and Antwerp. Among them were merchants of great importance; they traded in the East and West Indies, importing silver ingots for example. For a long time trade in Jamaica was almost a Jewish monopoly. But when misfortune befell Poland's Jews and Polish refugees spread throughout Western Europe, the Ashkenazim also came to England in large numbers, mainly to London. Synagogues grew up inside the City—Great School in Duke's Place, Aldgate, the Hambro synagogue and New Synagogue. But the majority of the new immigrants were humble people, shopkeepers and artisans. They settled in the East End, in Whitechapel, with their centre in picturesque Petticoat Lane. A great many streets eventually looked like Polish Jewish towns. Here could be seen Hebrew shop signs, kosher butchers and countless small synagogues. Petticoat Lane was a market street with open-air stalls; it bulged with all kinds of goods from vegetables and eggs to stuffed monkeys and toys. The shops

REACTION

stayed open on Sundays and people from all over London flocked there to buy things. Poultry was sold in a side-street, called Goulston Street. On the Sabbath and holidays it was hard to make one's way through the countless piles of cages full of chickens, geese and ducks. They cackled, quacked and squawked, making the deafening spectacle echo far outside the East End. The customer bought his wares alive and carried the flapping screeching creature to the butcher, who stood ready with the handle of a sharp knife between his front teeth so that his hands were free. He twisted and turned the bird to make sure that it was ritually without blemish, put it under one arm with a practised grip, while he bent its head back with his fingers. With the other hand he seized the knife and cut its throat with a lightning stroke. The dead bird was thrown into a basket where the blood flowed out of it. Everywhere one could see people carrying the freshly killed birds home to the kitchen.

In our day the Jewish imprint on the East End is disappearing. The German blitz hit the East End severely and smashed these little streets with their alien East European character. Today many of London's Jews live in new airy parts of Hampstead. But a hundred years ago, as the prosperity of the East End's Jews increased, they began to leave its ghetto-like streets and move into better districts. We find their synagogues in Great Portland Street and Bayswater.

Sephardic and Ashkenazic Jews rapidly combined. The seal on their kinship was a famous marriage in 1812, when the Sephardic Moses Montefiore married Judith Cohen, who was of German origin. Her sister later married Nathan Meyer Rothschild, so that two prominent Jews, one Ashkenazic and one Sephardic, became related by marriage.

There was a less hostile attitude towards the English Jews. The numerous humble people among them came into close contact with their Christian neighbours. Shortly after 1800 the London Society for Promoting Christianity among the Jews was founded. The awkward title was usually abbreviated to The Jews' Society. Its work was carried on from both a school and a church, Jews' Chapel. The number of proselytes the society won was microscopic, but its indirect effect was important. It helped to establish respect and affection for the people to whom the Christian church owes both its Bible and its Saviour. But it was the Jewish sportsmen—and this is typically British—who really broke down the wall between Jews and Christians. Daniel Mendoza was the boxing champion of England and boxing is a sport which we think highly of. A series of Jewish boxers developed their branch of sport to such a extent that it finally came to call for skill and intelligence rather than brute force. The English aristocracy praised this form of 'the noble art of defence' and admired its champions and teachers.

On one point the English Jews met with a protracted struggle. It was of a political nature. Admittedly Jews had the vote, but, like Catholics, they could not be elected to the House of Commons. In 1829 the Catholics succeeded in winning equality on this point. The following year the Jews set out to achieve the same thing. The difficulty was that a newly elected member of the House of Commons had to take an oath on the Bible, i.e. on both the Old and the New Testaments, with the words: 'Upon the true faith of a Christian'. And a Jew cannot do that. An amendment to the law was required. England's famous historian, Thomas Babington Macaulay, introduced the necessary proposal in the House of Commons. His speech on this occasion, a magnificent specimen of great rhetoric, is often quoted:

'In the infancy of civilization, when our island was as savage as New Guinea, when letters and arts were still unknown to Athens, when scarcely a thatched hut stood on what was afterwards the site of Rome, this contemned people had their fenced cities and cedar palaces, their splendid Temple, their fleets of merchant ships, their schools of sacred learning, their great statesmen and soldiers, their natural philosophers, their historians and their poets.'

In burning words he asked the House of Commons to open the doors to Isaiah's countrymen and the descendants of the Maccabees.

The House of Commons followed Macaulay and passed the law, but the House of Lords threw it out. Year after year the same proposal came before the House of Lords and every time it was rejected. At last people decided on direct action. The Liberal majority in the City of London elected the future Baron Lionel de Rothschild as its representative in the House of Commons. On the day Rothschild appeared, the House was packed, the tension almost unbearable. What would happen?

Rothschild walked slowly and dignifiedly into the hall. The Speaker put the usual formula for the oath to him.

'I want to be sworn in on the Old Testament,' he replied.

'Mr Lionel de Rothschild, you must leave the House,' said the Speaker.

The House of Commons was in an uproar.

'Take your seat,' was the cry from one side.

'Leave the house,' the shout from the other.

Rothschild withdrew.

The attempt was made every time there was an election. The result was always the same. And the House of Lords clung steadfastly to its opposition to changing the oath.

It was not Rothschild, but another eminent English Jew, David Solomon, who became the hero in the drama which was soon to be enacted. Solomon was elected to the House of Commons as member for the constituency of Greenwich. He appeared in the House, quite simply refused to take the oath, but sat down in his seat and, indeed, even dared to speak and take part in divisions. His undeterred behaviour and the valiant words with which he justified it made a deep impression. But they also caused such a tumult in the room that the session was dissolved. Three times he took part in divisions. Each time he was fined the gigantic sum of £500. Solomon paid, but continued to hold his seat.

This was sport. The whole country followed Solomon's battle. He proved a good loser, and nothing makes a man more popular in England than that. The following year he was elected Lord Mayor of London. Finally the House of Lords had to give in. The new law gave a Jew the right to take his oath using the words: 'So help me God'. In 1885 Lionel de Rothschild was raised to the peerage and took his seat in the House of Lords. The last barrier had fallen.

During one of the heated debates on this question in the House of Commons the spokesman for the Opposition argued

THE CHAINS ARE BROKEN

strongly against giving the Jews seats in the House. In a celebrated answer, the member for Maidstone, Benjamin Disraeli, said that the Jews had outlived Assyrian Kings, Egyptian Pharaohs and Arabic Caliphs. In all probability they would also outlive the right honourable gentleman who had just sat down.

Disraeli himself was a Jew, of old Sephardic stock, born in 1804. In England in those days there were not a few members of proud Sephardic families who even grieved about the almost imperceptible discrimination they were the victims of. Religion meant nothing more to them, they were willing to do what lay in their power to prevent religious prejudice from hindering their sons' careers. So they had them baptized and let them be absorbed by the English aristocracy. Disraeli's father was one of them; he took his thirteen-year-old son to the baptismal font.

The young Disraeli rapidly developed as a sparkling mind, always restless and active, sharp in both thought and speech, with marked artistic talents. At the age of 22 he wrote the novel *Vivian Grey* which brought him sudden fame. Shortly afterwards he travelled to Jerusalem to find himself in the country which once had been his father's. The result was another novel, *Tancred*.

When he came home again Disraeli threw himself into politics. He topped the poll at Maidstone, but his behaviour in the dignified House of Commons was so strange that his maiden speech was a fiasco. The House hissed him. When he could not get a hearing, he stopped, but as he sat down a few members managed to hear his exit line:

'I sit down now. But the time will come when you will hear me.'

They were prophetic words. Disraeli ultimately became the leader of the powerful Conservative party, in which he was known as the Chief, was several times Prime Minister and raised to the peerage as Lord Beaconsfield. His popularity was enormous and among the common people he was nicknamed Dizzy. Gladstone and Disraeli were two born antagonists in English politics. Disraeli felt repelled by Gladstone in every way. He did not blame him so much for

REACTION

always having a trump up his sleeve, as for claiming that it was God who had put it there.

He said that Gladstone was a worthy man in the worst sense of the word.

The ageing Queen Victoria cherished an almost romantic friendship with Disraeli. When Gladstone tendered his resignation as Prime Minister, the Queen was so eager to accept it that it seemed rude. All she thought about was recalling Disraeli as his successor. Disraeli was the typical empire builder; we have only to recall that it was he who acquired the Suez Canal for England and the role he played at the Congress of Berlin in 1878.

Although he was baptized, Disraeli never made any secret of his Jewish origin, but gladly seized an opportunity to emphasize it proudly.

'Agree that one half of Christendom worships a Jewess, and the other half a Jew,' he said.

And in *Tancred* he asks caustically: 'Suppose the Jews had not prevailed upon the Romans to crucify Jesus, what would have become of the Atonement?'

In his speech in the House of Commons about Jewish emancipation he issued this challenge:

'Where is your Christianity if you do not believe in your Judaism? . . . over every altar . . . we find the tables of the Jewish law . . . All the early Christians were Jews . . . every man in the early ages of the Church was a Jew . . . If you had not forgotten what you owe to this people, if you were grateful for that literature which for thousands of years has brought so much instruction and so much consolation to the sons of men, you as Christians would be only too ready to seize the first opportunity of meeting the claims of those who profess this religion.'

England had many Jews with an international reputation, Ashkenazic families such as Rothschild, Solomon, Goldsmid and Hambro. The most conspicuous Sephardic family were the Montefiores, their most famous man Sir Moses Montefiore. His piety, long journeys and achievements on behalf of his suffering people in three continents cast the glow of legend over a life which lasted more than a century, for he lived from 1784 to 1885.

Montefiore was a banker in the City like his father; he amassed a large fortune and achieved high social recognition. The Queen knighted him and he filled important positions of trust in the Jewish congregation. Moses Montefiore was a devout, strictly orthodox man. Every morning at 7 o'clock he went to prayers in the synagogue, he dated his letters according to the Jewish calendar with Hebrew letters, observed the dietary laws rigorously, even when travelling, and refused to be present on the day he was instated in his office as Sheriff of Kent, because the day coincided with the Jewish New Year.

Montefiore was in Palestine seven times, accompanied by his wife, the Judith Cohen mentioned earlier. He undertook the last journey when he was 91. We must remember that a journey to the Holy Land in those days was a big undertaking, not always devoid of danger, for there were both bandits and illness to beware of. But Montefiore was a Zionist before Zionism existed. Jerusalem stood on his coat of arms in letters of gold. He believed firmly that the Jewish people would return to the ancient land and made practical preparations to that end. He bought land, started plantations and built houses and mills, some of which are still standing in Jerusalem. Montefiore was always active when he saw his people in need. He hastened to Damascus to aid his fellow countrymen during the affair and helped to arouse the world's conscience. He went to Russia and tried to improve conditions for the Jews under the Tsarist régime. The Mortara case took him to Rome. We find Moses Montefiore's name linked with almost all events in Jewish history during the century for which he lived.

IV

JUDENSCHMERZ

THE room was called a salon. The name was elegant, the prosaic facts more ordinary. The salon was a long room in the top storey of an old Berlin house, as 'narrow as a worm' people said with a smile. Some scattered tallow candles, did their best with their weak flickering gleam to disperse the darkness which stole in through the small windows when winter days drew to a close. The refreshments served were more than modest, a few cakes and a glass of wine. But every day of the week when Henriette Hertz held open house, the guests swarmed through the door, they crowded into the cramped salon, eagerly conversing or listening to lectures and discussions on literary or philosophical topics. Here one could see everyone who had a name in Berlin, writers, musicians, philosophers, doctors and diplomats—even the royal family allowed the young princes' tutors to take them there. As if by magic every talented young man who lived in Berlin or merely visited the city was drawn into the circle. In 1797 Schleiermacher wrote that the reason that it was so easy for young scholars and men about town to meet was that 'the man who wants to meet good society finds it here and anyone with talent is welcome.'

Henriette Hertz's salon was not the only one in Berlin. It became quite the fashion among well-to-do intellectual women to open their drawing-rooms to gifted witty people. Henriette Hertz's two friends, Dorothea Mendelssohn and Rachel Levin, also held highly popular salons. But they were only satellites revolving round the sun. For many years around the turn of the century Henriette Hertz's salon

THE CHAINS ARE BROKEN

was the intellectual focus of Berlin and the hostess its queen; she was called Berlin's Madame Récamier.

The strange thing was that Henriette Hertz, Dorothea Mendelssohn and Rachel Levin were all Jewesses. If one of them wanted to go on a journey, she could only leave Berlin through the Rosenthaler Gate and she had to pay *Leibzoll* at the same tariff as an ox. But in their salons Berlin's best society looked up to them and obeyed their slightest wish. How can we explain such a fantastic contrast? Well, the Jews' political emancipation only advanced at a snail's pace and, as we have seen, it was to prove short-lived on the first occasion. But a cultural emancipation had suddenly exploded inside a narrow circle of rich Jewish families. It did not come as a peaceful development, but as a violent revolution. And it had such extensive momentous results that we must go into it in more detail, especially if we are to understand these Jewish women and the joy and suffering they experienced.

When prisoners from dark prisons suddenly come out into the bright sunlight, they are blinded. They shade their eyes, but cannot make out the road they must take. Mendelssohn was the pioneer who had made the first breach in the ghetto wall and shown his people the road to freedom. But now the revolution and the age of Napoleon blew a gale over Europe. It was an age of fermentation and frantic development, a total reassessment of all values, political, social, scientific and religious. In the universal cry for liberty and equality the barriers which had long cut the Jews off from the world also fell. With insatiable voracity many of them threw themselves on the intellectual sustenance which had so long been denied them.

The rich were the first. And there were rich Jews in Germany around 1800. Rapid economic development had created a prosperous upper class. From the days of the Seven Years' War and more than half a century afterwards one war had followed on the heels of another. For alert business men this meant great opportunities. Here were contracts from the army, here one could speculate on the Stock Exchanges whose share quotations moved in seismic curves. This age did not see the sudden success of the House of Rothschild for nothing. But there were many small Rothschilds among

JUDENSCHMERZ

the German Jews. They earned money easily and amassed fortunes.

These newly-rich Jews naturally found it easier to enter Christian cultural circles than the ghetto's drab proletariat. And they went gladly. Modern liberalism and loose morals beckoned. It became indecent to talk Yiddish. The educated rich rapidly learnt German and fell upon the literature and thought of their fellow countrymen. Just at that time German culture reached its zenith; it was full of youthful vigour; it had all the elements which can influence and engross the human mind. It was the age of Goethe, Schiller, Kant and Herder.

The focus for this rapprochement between Jews and Germans was Berlin. The literature of the age of *Sturm und Drang* intoxicated Jewish readers as well and made them forget reality. A hot flood of romantic hysteria flowed into Jewish homes which had hitherto kept themselves tightly closed and isolated. This immoderate urge for knowledge and culture especially affected Jewish women. With their warm lively natures they learnt French to be able to talk the fashionable language; they read Lessing and seized Voltaire's books eagerly, intrepidly imbibing both his irony and his frivolities; they learnt English and soon discovered the books of the freethinkers. And naturally novels as well, which described love and romance, and offered young maidens sweet fare. 'We all dearly wanted to be the heroines of novels,' wrote Henriette Hertz later. The sorrows of young Werther created a furore in the minds of young Jewesses.

Jewesses. Yes, they led the way. We must not be surprised that it was mainly women who almost gave Jewry a fatal blow with their apostasy. It was connected with the whole status of the Jewish woman. Her life was indoors behind the walls of the home, in hidden seclusion. The man went out, he frequently visited the synagogue, the woman only seldom. Her religion was the ritual domestic round in the kitchen, wash-house, sewing-room and wardrobe. There her life was regulated by countless ancient regulations. And that *was* religion. Jewry did not distinguish between sacred and profane in the same way as many Christians. The Jew's faith embraced the whole of life; Jewish culture was a religious

THE CHAINS ARE BROKEN

unity. Since time immemorial this has been a source of unique strength and staying power.

But if the religious life of the home chilled and began to disintegrate, the woman had idle hands. She had nothing with which to fill the setting which was her life. So her faith was stunted. After all it only consisted of a few rituals which no one had taught her to understand. And when she went out into the beckoning bewildering world, she was a *tabula rasa*, a blank tablet. The first comer wrote his message on it. Unreflecting and ungrieving, countless Jewish women let themselves be absorbed by their surroundings and were lost to their people.

But there was a sequel with the best of them. In these years the word *Judenschmerz* (the suffering or pain involved in being a Jew) was coined. It was not only a word, it often became harsh reality. It attempts to express the feeling of loneliness which assails a man out in no-man's-land. He has left his own people, but discovers that he is not welcome among the foreigners he sought out. They reject him coldly, with merely a shrug of the shoulders, while the door shuts in front of him. Now he cannot go back, for he has burnt his boats. And treachery is not so easily forgotten.

This was the *Judenschmerz* many Jews felt the pangs of when they let themselves float with the current and become flotsam for the rest of their lives. There were no end of rootless destinies sitting around in Europe's great cities, brooding in solitude and melancholy apathy. They realized that their existence was superfluous; they were homeless.

Now we are back in the salons, in the midst of the mass of Berlin's intelligentsia. There is smiling and laughter, witticisms fly back and forth through the salon like tennis balls. And over all others the young sparklingly witty intelligent Jewesses shine like stars. But somewhere behind the eyes' happy light we can sense a black spot where lurked the *Judenschmerz* from which they never entirely freed themselves.

Henriette Hertz came from a Sephardic Hamburg family, the Lemos. Her father was a doctor. From him she inherited her intelligence, from her mother her energy, from both unusual beauty. From the time she was a little girl, everyone worshipped her charm. This gave her a self-confident manner, but also endowed her with something dominating and naturally she did not escape becoming self-centred and vain. When she danced at a ball, the spectators stood on chairs the better to see the strikingly beautiful girl dancing a minuet with her dancing-master. The precociously mature girl attracted so much attention in the street when she went to school that her father was alarmed. He promptly took her away from school and taught her himself at home.

Henriette felt deeply attached to her father and he achieved sensational results with his clear-headed girl. She must have been something of a linguistic genius, for in addition to German she had a perfect command of French, Spanish, Italian and Greek, as well as a knowledge of Portuguese, Latin and Danish. Later in life she took up the study of Turkish and Sanscrit. But she was particularly attracted to literature. She acquired a wide knowledge and developed so acute a literary sense that poets and critics quoted her judgments and accepted them as authoritative.

Henriette Hertz was only twelve and a half years old when the plates were broken on her engagement, in accordance with Jewish tradition. The suitor was Privy Councillor Dr Marcus Hertz, doctor and philosopher. He was weakly, small and ugly, twice as old as she was and called his beloved 'child'. On her side it was anything but a love match but she bowed obediently to her parents' wishes. Dr Hertz had to wait two years before the wedding, so that the 'child' was just over fifteen.

Naturally their married life was never supremely happy, but it was harmonious nevertheless. He lived for his knowledge, she tried to be an affectionate spouse to him, as well as a warm-blooded woman can be to a distracted unworldly man. When he died in 1803, she wept bitterly over him.

It was Dr Hertz who introduced her to his circle of scientists, writers and philosophers. And Henriette Hertz established her salon, the first place where Jews and Christians met on the same footing. Let us see for ourselves the woman as admirers have described her in letters and paintings. Her figure was tall and stately, she carried herself like a Spanish noblewoman of the highest lineage. Her features were delicately drawn, her complexion a graceful harmony of delicate tones; she never used make-up. The pale face formed an almost shocking contrast to the jet-black hair. Her beauty was in blossom until late in life and attracted men's admiring looks. But there was sadness in her smile; her friends called her 'the tragic muse'.

Among the many people who frequented the salon, an inner circle rapidly grew up; it was called the League of Virtue, in the fashion of the time. For some of them the name was the only virtuous thing about it. The members were on intimate terms with each other; they corresponded in code, using Hebrew letters. Here were Dorothea Mendelssohn, the philosopher's daughter, Friedrich von Schlegel, and the Protestant theologian Friedrich Schleiermacher, at the time chaplain to the Charity Hospital in Berlin. It was no coincidence that these two men belonged to the salon. They were the most radical spokesmen of romanticism and turned Henriette Hertz's salon into a nursery for the new school of thought. Schlegel became Dorothea Mendelssohn's destiny, Schleiermacher Henriette Hertz's, although in a less momentous way.

Schleiermacher had come to Berlin in 1794, where he made his 'Speeches on Religion to the Educated among its Despisers', as the pompous title read. In Berlin Schleiermacher made his decisive breakthrough to romanticism. His romantic theology gave full rein to the sensitive emotional side of his being, with its strong aesthetic leanings. His whole being longed for love and he found that there was something in his nature which women understood better than men. As a cleric he had an unparalleled reputation and soon won a large enthusiastic public.

Schlegel introduced Schleiermacher to Henriette Hertz's salon. The two young scholars were intimate friends, sharing the same room for a time. Schleiermacher at once found his spiritual home in the salon. A curious relationship developed between the clergyman and the beautiful Jewess which was precariously balanced on the razor-sharp edge between friendship and eroticism. Schleiermacher spent every afternoon

JUDENSCHMERZ

with her. When Mr and Mrs Hertz spent the summer in the country near Unter den Linden, he used to visit them weekly and spend a whole day from morning until night. She used to call him *mon bijou*, my jewel.

The friendship between Schleiermacher and Henriette Hertz naturally became a favourite subject for gossip in Berlin. It was even the target of caricaturists. They showed her tall well-built figure walking with Schleiermacher. But he was so little and thin that she had put him in her décolleté. He stuck out of it and held her under the arm. They themselves claimed that the relationship was platonic. And if we take their characters into consideration, it was probably true. The tittle-tattle made no impression on Dr Hertz. If anyone whispered malicious gossip to him, he answered with a philosophic smile and frustrated the gossip's friendly intentions by not saying a word.

Dr Hertz's death meant the death of the salon. He left no money and Henriette Hertz was in straitened circumstances. On top of which she had to support her old blind mother and an unmarried daughter. The old story repeated itself. When she was poor and lonely, most of her friendships died. Henriette Hertz had tasted the sweetness of fame. Now she slid into oblivion and was on the verge of destitution. But she did not give in. This strong woman resumed the struggle. She cut down on her requirements, started to give language lessons and made herself a scanty living.

Of course she received attractive proposals of marriage, she could even have been governess to a princess. But the condition every time was that she be baptized. And as long as her mother lived, she could not bring herself to take that step. The old lady was one of those women who, with every fibre of her being, clung to a Jewry she knew little about and understood even less of, but which she cherished in the cockles of her heart, for without it life would have been quite inconceivable. Her daughter knew that she would break her mother's heart by renouncing Jewry, so she refused the tempting offers.

But no sooner had her mother closed her eyes than Henriette Hertz bowed to Schleiermacher's ideas and was baptized into the Protestant Church. The thin threads which had bound her to her father's faith were broken at long last. For her Jewry had long been a mummy—as Schleiermacher put it. The reward for being baptized soon followed in the form of a small annual pension, which the king granted her.

Henriette Hertz lived a long time, to the age of 83. She is one of the destinies whose life lies between two fronts and never really belongs to either of them.

A few decades before the salons blossomed forth, Moses Mendelssohn's house was a centre of enlightenment in Berlin. Many of the age's great minds went in and out of it. And Mendelssohn's second eldest highly-gifted daughter Dorothea sat modestly in a corner, listening to the conversation. She understood more of them than her father knew, she imbibed knowledge and impressions and was fascinated by the new books and ideas. Dorothea was a leader among her contemporaries and wanted them to share her literary interests. She organized a reading group for her female friends. Every day they gathered in her room to read aloud and perform amateur dramatics. But even if it had taken until late at night to learn the parts, early next morning Dorothea sat in her father's study, together with the rest of the household, an attentive listener to his *Morgenstunden*.

Moses Mendelssohn was a progressive, but on one point he did not deviate from the old traditions. Home life was patriarchal; he chose the husbands for his daughters. He was an old-fashioned Jewish father with supreme authority; the girl was not asked if she liked the man. When Dorothea was sixteen, her father married her off to a Berlin banker, Simon Veit. He was an honest tender-hearted man, but a philistine, with no cultural interests. He had an insignificant figure and an ugly face. Dorothea did not love him and never learnt to do so. The unhappy marriage was the first link in a chain of misfortunes which time was to hang round Dorothea Mendelssohn's neck.

Immediately after the marriage she naturally sought her interests outside the home. She was a friend of Henriette Hertz and rapidly became a star in her salon. There she met Friedrich von Schlegel. It was an epoch-making event in both their lives. She was thirty-two, he was twenty-five.

Young as Schlegel was, he had already won a reputation as

JUDENSCHMERZ

the man who opened up new paths for German poetry; he had dared to criticize Schiller himself. His whole being was poetic and idealistic; wherever he was, the air sparkled with wit. Dorothea Mendelssohn, Madame Veit, to give her her married name, was no beauty. Quite the opposite one might almost say. The friendly eye finds something that can be called pretty, even in the case of an ugly woman—two shapely hands, something noble in a facial feature, supple lines in body. Dorothea had no redeeming features. But a fire burnt in her mind, a shining flame which flashed in two soulful eyes. It made people forget everything else.

Schlegel was fascinated by her brain alone. He loved everything that was big and strong; he wrote his books in capital letters. In the same way people had to have big strong features before he could like them. Mere gentleness and beauty never captivated him. In keeping with his nature he found it far too weak. It did not flare and burn. He fell hopelessly for Dorothea's charm and loved her at first sight.

And she returned his love just as hotly and ardently. In Schlegel she saw the ideal figure of her most secret dreams, the romantic hero, who had floated vaguely before her from her childhood and whom she had so often pictured to herself during miserable nights in Simon Veit's arms.

Dorothea Veit and Friedrich von Schlegel were both lofty strong personalities, as if made for each other. They met at Schleiermacher's, who in fact shared rooms with Schlegel. The inevitable happened. The champion of German romanticism and the daughter of the Jewish philosopher were irresistibly drawn to each other. Within a few days he reached the goal of his irrestrainable passion. She became his mistress. And they dared to trample respect for the age's strong sexual conventions underfoot. She left her home and moved in openly with her lover.

The whole Mendelssohn family shuddered at the scandal and repudiated their lost daughter; most of the couple's friends gave them up. Schleiermacher intervened and persuaded Simon Veit to give his unfaithful wife a divorce so that she could legalize her relationship with Schlegel. This magnanimous man, who never understood why such a disaster should befall his home, went so far that he let her have the custody of their two small sons; indeed as long as Veit lived he continued to send her much-needed financial aid anonymously.

Dorothea stayed with Schlegel until his death. She faithfully shared his many vicissitudes and hardships, and put up with his constantly changing moods. It was difficult for the restless romantic to find regular work and an income. The pair wandered from place to place; Berlin, Jena, Dresden, Leipzig and Paris were stations on the way. In Paris Dorothea became a Christian and was baptized by a Protestant clergyman. Like so many romantics, Schlegel was enthusiastic about the Catholic Church. Shortly after her baptism the two were converted to Catholicism.

The year after Dorothea's break with her husband Schlegel aroused embarrassing attention by publishing a *roman à clef*. In a guise which was easily seen through he put his most intimate experiences with Dorothea at the mercy of a curious public. As the book's artistic merit was also dubious, it was harshly criticized. Only Schleiermacher defended it. He called it 'a good sermon with a bad text'.

Dorothea had to pay dearly for her love-affair. For the rest of her days she was given the cold shoulder in so-called good society; poverty and want were her daily fare. For many years she tried to contribute to their livelihood by writing. But when she was old she changed the pen for the needle.

'Enough books have been written,' she said. 'But I have never heard that there are too many shirts in the world.'

Schlegel died in 1829. She survived him by ten years. There was calm after her troubled life. She travelled a long way from Mendelssohn's quiet devout home to the restless world outside, which finally left her alone. All she had was her two sons, who both became distinguished painters.

Rachel Levin was the third of these unusual Jewesses who were torn loose from their fathers' people by German culture. And she was by far the most important, in fact the most eminent woman who ever queened it over a salon with her brilliant mind. She made an unforgettable impression on everyone who met her and it is not long since the age which

JUDENSCHMERZ

has been described so often, so that she still seems to be living to us even today.

Rachel Levin was quite small with a thin frail body, always ill and suffering; her life was a chain of infirmity and sickness which she bore with admirable heroism. For this delicate hopelessly ugly woman had a glowing mind; 'A very red heart' as a friend put it. With her powerful intellect she defied all indignities and was, as one of her circle said, 'an independent girl, of unusual intelligence, clever as the sun, tender-hearted to boot, original through and through. She understands and feels everything, her words are so striking and profound in their biting paradoxical form that one goes on thinking about them afterwards and is astonished by them'.

Rachel Levin was a few years younger than the two friends. She grew up in the home of a prosperous jeweller. Her father was a man with a will of iron; he ran the house with despotic obstinacy, but loved and idolized his clever weakly daughter. The last remnants of Jewish tradition had leaked out of the house long ago, Rachel grew up in 'a wood without religion'. When she met Jewish life she felt repelled, its character was not aesthetic enough for her. From birth she was a stranger to her people and their faith. Yet no one can escape his own shadow. The days were to come when the hidden longings began to stir.

But for the time-being German culture was her life. She opened the famous 'daytime salon' in her father's house and gathered artists, officers and diplomats around her. Jean Paul was a frequent visitor, the close friend with whom she could both laugh and cry; she was on familiar terms with Wilhelm von Humboldt and Heinrich Heine liked to frequent her salon. It would be necessary to name practically all the great names of the day if we wanted a complete list. Schlegel, Schleiermacher, Ludwig Tieck, Schelling, Steffens and Hegel were all to be met there.

But Goethe towered over everyone else. For Rachel Levin Goethe and life were one, his mind had charmed her in a way no other could. Her affection and respect for the great poet turned the salon into a real cult. And Goethe himself was not always insusceptible to hero-worship. He visited her

THE CHAINS ARE BROKEN

once and she felt that it was a patent of nobility. 'Goethe has given me the accolade of knighthood,' she wrote in breathless excitement.

Rachel Levin did not write anything herself. But in her letters, and she wrote a lot, even more than Voltaire, the springs of her mind and spirit flow in the original way which was her own. She also had a remarkable talent for inspiring contemporary poets to creative work. Rachel Levin was behind a large number of German poetic works.

But the years went by and Rachel Levin was in her forties. In those days that meant old age and the end of life for a woman. Her heart had been exposed to several storms, but she was still single. Then she suddenly married a Prussian diplomat, Varnhagen van Ense, but first she was baptized.

When it was over she noticed that the bond which tied her to her fathers was not broken, even though she had tried to cut it. In one letter she relates how she had had a dream about her own birth. An angel promised her great things. She would experience the world, something not given to many, her life would be rich and powerful. But then came an unexpected stab in the back:

'Be a Jewess.'

And the letter goes on:

'Now the whole of my life is a long haemorrhage.'

This painful feeling of schizophrenia was expressed on her deathbed in these ecstatic words:

'With enraptured pride I think of the flight from Egypt, of my origin and the long sequence of destiny with which mankind's greatest memories are bound up. What for so much of my life was the greatest disgrace, the bitter misery and misfortune of being a Jewess, I would not lose at any price.'

On the day of her funeral van Ense sent a large gift of money to Berlin's poor Jews.

We have followed the three women in their apostasy and seen the price they had to pay. They were only three. But their common destiny became a symptom. Thousands followed in their footsteps. Accepting baptism spread like an epidemic among the Jews in Berlin. And the fashion spread

JUDENSCHMERZ

throughout the whole of Germany, to Königsberg and Breslau, to Frankfurt and Hamburg. Jews were baptized in order to merge with the German people, to be able to marry a Christian, to ensure a career or escape the lack of rights which affected them. It is estimated that in the first eighteen years of the century more Jews were baptized than in all the previous eighteen centuries put together. In Berlin alone between a third and a half of all the Jews were baptized. And we should take note of the educated section of Jewry which was drained off.

All Moses Mendelssohn's sons, with the exception of the eldest, Joseph, floated with the current and finally accepted baptism. One of the sons, Abraham, married the daughter of an assimilated Jew. A Christian brother-in-law persuaded him to take the German surname of Bartholdy. This quiet modest man was the father of the famous composer Felix Mendelssohn Bartholdy, who was christened as a baby and grew up a convinced Christian. He became one of the great composers of church music. His father used to say with an ironic smile:

'Once I was my father's son. Now I am my son's father.'

The rush to the baptismal font increased to such an extent that the Prussian government was alarmed. These facile proselytes could never be an asset to the church. In 1810 Jewish conversion to the national religion was controlled. No clergyman was allowed to baptize a Jew, unless the Jew produced a certificate from the police stating that his intentions were sincere.

Obviously there were men whose apostasy caused serious reflection and searing pangs of conscience. Others took it more lightly. The wealthy David Friedländer, who wanted to see the door to Germany's highest posts opened to him, admitted cynically that he was willing to be baptized, on one condition, that the church exempted him from believing in the divinity of Jesus. All Berlin was diverted by the tragicomic episode and called it 'a dry baptism'. But there were also many who did not shrink from a wet baptism.

When we enter into the spirit of Jewry in the years when the ghetto's walls fell, we see freedom's golden rays melting the ice of the Middle Ages' frost and cold. It was a stormy

THE CHAINS ARE BROKEN

spring with natural catastrophes in its train. The melting ice made the flood overflow the banks. Jewry was to go through many bitter experiences before summer ripeness and peace let the river return to its normal level. Only then could the cool fertile stream flow down to the sea.

We have not reached that stage in this book. For the moment we are in the midst of the conflict, with its shrill dissonance which shared the heart's tragedy, on the borders between the ancient Jewish heritage and a new beckoning world. *Judenschmerz* could stand as the title for this split which cost generations their peace and happiness. The word was coined by Heinrich Heine. He knew it from personal experience. The poet's mind was a battle-field for forces which drove him in different directions and eventually killed him.

Heinrich Heine is even more typical of the modern Jew who broke out and never found peace abroad any more than the queens of the three salons. We shall follow his career and turn the searchlight on Dusseldorf where he was born.

V

HEINRICH HEINE

D USSELDORF was the capital of the duchy of Jülich-Cleve-Berg, one of the countless minor German states. As early as 1795 the French revolutionary army under General Kléber occupied the country and it was under French government until the fall of Napoleon. Not until 1815 was it incorporated with Prussia, when the little kingdom's special charm disappeared into Moloch's maw. French dominion put a stop to the old feudal system and governed the country on purely French lines. That meant that serfdom, feudalism and villeinage were abolished; the legal system was governed by the *Code Napoleon* and religious freedom was introduced. No wonder that the Jews of the Rhineland hailed Napoleon as a liberator from age-old oppression. Heine could rightly say that he had 'inhaled the air of France' from childhood.

In young Heine's eyes Napoleon was a mystic revelation, the symbol of the revolution's ideals of liberty; like Hegel he saw the universal spirit revealed in the figure of the French Emperor. He expressed this burning worship of Napoleon in unforgettable words in *Die Grenadiere*, one of his earliest poems. Elsewhere he describes the French soldiers marching into the streets of Düsseldorf, 'honour's happy men, who have marched round the world and conquered it, singing to the music of the band'.

As a fourteen-year-old boy he stood and watched the emperor's triumphal procession through Düsseldorf's Hofgarten. The lad's heart beat a tatoo and he rejoiced that the great ruler dared to defy police regulations and ride down the avenue. Normally it meant a fine of five rix-dollars. And lo 'the admiring trees bowed, the sun's rays filtered curiously

THE CHAINS ARE BROKEN

and shyly through the leaves and high up in the blue sky swam the only visible star'. He was envious of the horse the emperor rode on and stared at the white hand which gave the animal a friendly pat on the neck, the hand which had subdued anarchy's hydra-headed monster. The emperor's face had the colour of Greek and Roman marble busts; his features were nobly regular, like classical faces, and on them was written: 'Thou shalt have no other god but me'. Such was Heine's version of the universal genius, 'the man of ideas, man become idea'.

With his feeling for the theatrical Heine claimed that he was born on New Year's eve in 1800, 'I am one of the century's first men'. In reality he was born on December 13, 1797. His home was in Bolkerstrasse. Both his parents came from Jewish families which had lived in the Rhineland for centuries. His mother was by far the most important of the two. Her family, van Geldern, which was counted among the Jewish elite, had produced a long line of doctors. She called herself Betty, but her real name was Peira, from the Hebrew Zippora. She had not changed her biblical name for a German one for nothing. There were only faint traces of her Jewish heritage in her strictly rational mind. Almost the only thing was that she preserved her childhood habit of writing in Hebrew characters even when she wrote German. Betty Heine's faith was a cool deism, through her the son experienced French reason in its primitive form: thou shalt learn, know, be efficient. She was a great admirer of Rousseau, whose *Emile* was always on her table. The children's upbringing was her hobby-horse; she nursed them herself and gave them their first lessons.

So Heine did not inherit his sense of the fantastic from his mother. On the contrary if she found out that he had a novel, she took it away from him; she forbade him to go to the theatre and chastised the servants severely if they filled him with ghost stories. She was a realist. Her ideal was Rothschild; he had the sense to become somebody and earn money. Heine's mother lived to a ripe old age and survived her son. His love for her remained engraved on his mind. During the years when he lay on his sick-bed in Paris, 'the mattress grave', he concealed the true state of affairs from her. His letters to his mother are full of white lies, they tell of health, riches, friends, instead of pain, poverty and loneliness.

His father Samson Heine was the very opposite of her. As a young man he had been *Proviantmeister* (Supply Officer) of the Duke of Cumberland's army and taken part in campaigns in Flanders and Brabant. He never forgot his military past, but loved parading in the civic guards' dashing blue uniform and gallantly saluting his wife up at the window when the company came marching down Borkerstrasse. Samson Heine was a business man, but an unsuccessful one. His passions were actresses, horses and dogs. Unfortunately his income was not large enough for him to satisfy his loose inclinations. His son writes of him that 'a boundless appetite for life was the basic feature of my father's character, he was self-indulgent and cheerful, and saw everything through rose-coloured spectacles'. But for all his childishness, he remained faithful to Jewry, unlike his wife, in any case as regards external appearances. He it was who saw to it that the children had a scanty Jewish schooling. In Hamburg lived Solomon Heine, Samson's brother, a rich banker. The family's rich uncle later played a part in his nephew's life.

Actually Heine was not really called Heinrich, but Harry. He only Germanized the name after his baptism. His family heritage was made up of bewildering antitheses; his mother's rationalism was sharply opposed to his father's romanticism. He did not take any firm centre for life away from home. Nor was there any authority to be found outside the family's narrow circle. Harry Heine's childhood coincided with a period of ferment. Europe was a witch's cauldron of fallen thrones and rulers, who came and went like shooting stars. This unrest left deep imprints on a naked over-sensitive mind like the young Heine's and exploded in violent reactions. He was an unbalanced child, in both love and hate. The first of his words we know were spoken when he was a four-year-old in Frau Hindermann's kindergarten. He had put sand in her snuff-box and when she asked how he could think of anything so naughty, the boy answered:

'Because I hate you.'

After kindergarten his father sent him to Rintelsohn's private school, a typical Talmud-cum-Torah school after the

THE CHAINS ARE BROKEN

Polish model, where the commandments and biblical maxims were hammered into him. We find many reminiscences of this time in his poems. But the boy did not take it very seriously. One Sabbath two of his friends saw Harry biting grapes off a vine on his neighbour's sun-drenched side wall.

'The law only forbids me to *pick* grapes on the sabbath. It does not say that it is forbidden to bite them off,' he shouted.

Harry was fourteen when he went to the French school, the Lyceum, with Jesuit fathers as masters. The jump from traditional Jewry to Catholic Christianity was enormous. And the skinny boy with the chestnut hair, the sparkling eyes and ironic twist to his mouth did not have a good time of it among his new school-fellows. Nor was it so simple to learn Latin.

'If the ancient Romans had had to learn Latin first, they would never have managed to conquer the world,' he said. And a teacher saw him kneeling before a crucifix one day in one of the school's corridors. The boy looked up at the roughly-carved image of Christ and prayed:

'Oh you poor god, once so persecuted, if you can, please help me to learn the irregular verbs.'

On his very first day in the new school Harry found out that he was 'different'. He had his first experience of *Judenschmerz* and realized that he belonged to *das Urübelvolk*, another word he coined himself. (It means something like 'the people who have been evil from time immemorial'.) Harry hit back and learnt to defend himself with his ready wit, but new wounds were inflicted on his mind.

Harry was sixteen when he first fell in love. His beloved was Seffchen; she was sixteen, too, had finely chiselled features, big eyes, a very pale complexion and blood-red hair. She was also the executioner's daughter. Her father was naturally a pariah, shunned by everybody; eeriness and horror surrounded him and his family, a curse hung over the man who dared to approach his house. But eeriness always had a special attraction for Heine.

'I kissed her, not only because I loved the girl, but also to defy the old community and all its gloomy prejudices.'

'The course of my whole life was plotted in my cradle,' Heine once wrote. He was born the son of three fatherlands,

HEINRICH HEINE

Germany, France and Judaea, and never lived to see his fractured heart made whole. Jewry gave him, who nevertheless became one of its greatest poets, a miserable heritage. It was little more than a Jewish *instinct*. In spite of everything it was the strongest influence in Heine's life. It comes out in some of his finest poems, *Prinzessin Sabbat* and *Jehuda Halevy*, and finally helped to balance his mind so much that he became 'the hero in the mattress grave'.

But at first Harry Heine was neither famous nor a poet. The family discussed the boy's future. What was there to be done with him? There have always been two Jewish types: the practical realists, who go far and become somebody, and the dreamers, the impractical enthusiasts. Harry Heine was one of the latter. His attitude to money shows this. He was the opposite of a capitalist, liked to spend money, but never learnt to make, let alone save it. Uncle Solomon in Hamburg was one of the former, a self-made man who had risen the hard way, a classical representative of the dawning capitalistic era. Solomon Heine promised to look after his nephew and make a business man of him. So Harry travelled to Hamburg and lived in his wealthy uncle's home.

It was not a success. From the very first day he felt that he was locked in a golden cage. When he sat on the tall office stool with the heavy ledgers in front of him, his gaze turned to the window and green trees and golden sunshine of the Jungfernstieg outside. Down there he was at home. His uncle knew that two and two make four. To a poet they just as often make five. There were clashes between the two. In the uncle's eyes his talented nephew never became anything more than *der dumme Junge* (the stupid young man). 'If he had learnt something sensible, he would not have needed to write books.' Once he gave Harry a long warning lecture. When the old man had finished, Harry got up and walked out of the office with his head held high. At the door he turned round and discharged his exit line:

'You ought to know that the best thing about you is that you bear my name.'

But it was not the fault of the business that Hamburg became *die schöne Wiege meiner Leiden* (the beautiful cradle of my sorrows). Uncle Solomon's blonde daughter Amalia

THE CHAINS ARE BROKEN

was a bright coquettish girl. Heine fell in love with her and courted her. She was on the point of giving her heart to her poet cousin, but no, her father forbade the match. The daughter yielded obediently and did as her father asked. Harry felt betrayed and said bitterly:

'She was lovable and he loved her. He was not lovable and she did not love him.'

The wound never healed; for many years he sang of his anguish. One section of the *Buch der Lieder* is not called *Junge Leiden* for nothing. Heine was finished with Hamburg, an unsuccessful business man who had also had his heart broken.

He became cynical in his dispair. He sought solace among the loose women of the Jungfernstieg. He bought consolation for his *Weltschmersz* from more than one generous magdalen. He himself relates that he was never an experienced seducer, but often had to be content with bought love. This eventually cost him his health. A venereal disease, for which contemporary medical science knew no cure, took away first the use of his limbs and later, at far too early an age, his life.

Heine had touched bottom—financially as well. His father had not weathered the economic crisis which followed in the war's wake. He went bankrupt and so was unable to help his eldest son to make a career. Then uncle Solomon lent a hand. Perhaps he felt a duty to his nephew after the break between the two young people. At any rate he offered to pay for Harry's studies. Incidentally he did not escape with that. His wasteful nephew was quite satisfied to continue relying on his uncle's generosity for the rest of his life. Without a substantial annual subsidy from Hamburg he would have died of hunger. Gradually it became embarrassing for both of them.

Heine studied first at Bonn and later at the famous Georgia Augusta University at Göttingen. He chose law, but never became a friend of Corpus Juris, 'Egoism's Bible', as he called it. He was much more attracted by the lectures on German language, history and literature. He was critical of student life itself. He called the beer-swilling, cliché-ridden, duelling students 'patent pomade-stallions'.

They were the days of the Holy Alliance. Reaction brooded

over the German countries. The slogan was no longer liberty, equality and brotherhood, but feudalism, police power and censorship, all of them personified in Metternich, the man who once burst out:

'Ten times a day I say to myself: Good God, how right I am and how wrong the others are.'

Germany's liberal youth, first and foremost students, had believed that a united free Germany would arise from the blood spilt in the war of independence. They were deeply disappointed and found themselves spied out by the police as 'demagogues', liable to imprisonment and censorship. The stagnant *Biedermeier* age (1820-1848) was full of hidden tensions. They were only relaxed in the revolutions of 1830 and 1848.

As a good German patriot—for such Heine felt himself to be—he was a revolutionary and therefore under suspicion. Once in a way he was closely examined. In the students' beer cellar he displayed his keen wit for the first time in biting satires and gay persiflage. Perhaps Heine was revealing here something of the Diaspora Jew's exaggerated belief in airy theories and talking big; 'deadly words', 'singing flames', as Heine himself called them. There is something almost moving and awkward about the wordy perpetually arguing drifting Jew, who never had the reins of power in his hands, but had to be content to practise his 'word fetish'. Only today in the state of Israel can he begin to learn the ABC of politics.

Heine's student days came to a sudden end. After a duel he was given *Concilium abeundi,* i.e. he was sent down from the university. That gave the impetus to a decisive turning point in his life. Heine went to Berlin.

He went at a happy hour. The salons flourished and the young poet at once became familiar with Rachel Levin and her husband, Varnhagen van Ense. It was the very place for him, a centre of German culture. Rachel Levin was the first person of importance who showed sympathy for his art. She openly took up 'our little Heine', as she called him. And both she and van Ense kept anxious eyes open for the weaknesses in his character which could be disastrous for his development.

THE CHAINS ARE BROKEN

Heine began to display his talents in Berlin. He lived a fertile artistic life; he wrote and the first books appeared. They were a success and Heine's fame rose; second-rate poets began to plagiarize him even then. He made a journey to Poland to study the life of the Jews there; he was appalled at their misery and wrote a short book about them. For a brief period he worked for Jewish emancipation, was friends with Eduard Gans and Moses Moser, whom we shall hear of later, and took an active part in the *Verein für Kultur und Wissenchaft der Juden* (the Association for Jewish Culture and Knowledge). He also attended Hegel's lectures. He never became dogmatic. He liked to toy with the idea that he never really understood the Hegelian system. But the great ideas threw sparks into the poet's impressionable mind and made him an out and out radical, both politically and socially. For there is a revolutionary core hidden in the Hegelian dialetic.

Suddenly Heine broke off. He realized that it was time to take his studies seriously and pass an examination, get a job and free himself of his perpetual dependence on his uncle Solomon. So that he could study in peace he left Berlin and locked himself in a room in Göttingen. In July, 1825, he qualified as Doctor of Law, but only with very poor marks.

A few weeks previously—to be exact it was June 28, 1825 —Heine had sold his soul, to use his own words. In the Lutheran vicarage in the town of Heiligenstadt near Göttingen he let himself be examined in Christian knowledge for a stiff hour by the vicar, G. Christian Grimm. The vicar praised him for his knowledge and together with a colleague, the Rev. Bonitz, he led Heine into the church, where he baptized him. He received the baptismal names of Christian Johann Heinrich. After the ceremony the three men ate breakfast in the vicarage. The conversation languished, Heine barely contributed the odd word which politeness demanded. As soon as they had risen from the table he said goodbye and went.

The remarkable thing is that Heine's consciousness of being Jewish reached high tide at that very time. And seldom has any convert brought so little conviction with him to the font. He only let himself be baptized in order to earn his daily bread. Unless he was baptized all the callings in the country were barred to him. It was reason pure and simple which drove him to take the step he bitterly regretted later. Baptism was the ticket to European culture.

'If the law had allowed me to steal silver spoons, I would never have been baptized,' he wrote to his friend Moser.

Heine's calculations went wrong. From that day on his own people looked on him as an infamous traitor. And worse still, he suffered from self-reproach; he had the same bitter experience as thousands of his people, that a Jew does not sell his birth-right without simultaneously committing a kind of spiritual suicide. Nor did Paris let itself be bought for a mass—not by a Jew at any rate. No doors opened to Heine, however much he made his knuckles bleed by hammering on them.

In a letter to Moser a year after his baptism he writes:

'I often get up in the night, look at myself in the mirror and curse myself. Now I am shunned by both Jews and Christians. I bitterly regret that I let myself be baptized. Nothing has changed for the better; I have only had bad luck since.'

Restlessness drove Heine to travel constantly. He lived in Heligoland, visited England and made a long journey in Italy. Everywhere he made efforts to find a job, so that he could ensure his future and become independent of his uncle. He cut down his demands to such a bare minimum that he declared himself satisfied with a minor post under the Hamburg council. But no, wherever he looked, he saw a notice with the inscription: 'Entrance forbidden to you'. He seemed to hear a unanimous no from fate.

In the widst of his unrest he wrote book after book with feverish haste; he almost strewed them around him. The *Buch der Lieder* was a tremendous success. But the impractical poet did not know how to make money out of his works. His published, Julius Campe, swept up the profits. The *Buch der Lieder*, which finally sold a million copies, was bought outright by Campe for 50 louis d'or.

Things did not improve when the censor began to take an interest in his books and blue-pencil them. A few years later the Federal Council banned them altogether in Germany. It was not the only time that such a fate was to befall Heine.

THE CHAINS ARE BROKEN

During the Nazi epoch in Germany his books were also banned. But there are some of Heine's poems which every German loves so much that they cannot be suppressed—*Lorelei* and *Du bist wie eine Blume* to name examples. Even during the Hitler régime they appeared in the song books, but with the annotation: Author unknown. A classical example of the stupidity a dictatorship brings in its train.

In the summer of 1830 Heine was on holiday in Heligoland. He dreamed on the beach, listened to the scream of the sea-gulls and the eternal roar of the surf. As usual he was involved in crises.

'Women are my curse,' he wrote to a friend, 'I think that if I went to Novaya Zemlya I would be pestered by singers and dancers. As soon as I get rid of one, the next one bobs up.'

But he was especially despondent about the development of the political situation and grieved about his own fiasco in the guerilla war he waged for German freedom and unity. The cause he believed in and loved was at its lowest ebb. Even France, the revolution's promised land, was in the firm grip of the Jesuits, Italy was enslaved by Austria, and Germany . . . No, everything looked hopeless.

Heine was a rebel, a revolutionary, and we must not underestimate his influence in this connection. It is shown in his almost brilliant talent for coining slogans. The phrase world revolution was his work. Long before Marx he said that religion was the opium of the people, before Nietzsche, God is dead. But Heine's sympathy with communism was mixed with fear. He looked forward with anxious forebodings to the day when it would conquer and the 'the most odious of all tyrants, the mob, exercised its brutal dominion over a herd of sheep where everyone is sheared alike and bleats in the same way'.

He sought solace in books; the Old Testament, Greek poets and a great work about the revolution. He had presentiments that something great was afoot, 'like birds which feel that a storm or an earthquake is approaching.' It was the romantic side of the revolution which fascinated Heine, its leaders'

HEINRICH HEINE

self-sacrifices and naturally the wiping out of unjust privileges.

And the day came. The postman delivered a heavy parcel of newspapers. He opened and read them. The glowing news of the July revolution in Paris leapt from the headlines. The king had fled; the people had conquered. Once again the rebels at the blood-stained barricades had crushed tyranny. The cry in Paris was: 'Peace for cottages, war against palaces', the notes of the Marseillaise rang in the streets, the tri-color waved again in the citizens' city. For Heine this was 'sunbeams in printer's ink, they inflamed my soul to a raging conflagration. I feel as if I could set the whole ocean as far as the North Pole alight with the flames which burn in me.'

From that day Heine had finished with Germany. It had been his first fatherland. But now he felt that he 'had inhaled too much tobacco smoke, malodorous sauerkraut and coarseness' there. No, Paris was the 'New Jerusalem', the Rhine 'the river Jordan which separates liberty's holy land from the Philistines'. The following year he left Germany and went to Paris. He had only planned to visit the city, but he stayed there until he died—for twenty-five years, from 1831 to 1856.

Now Heine was in Paris, reduced to living by his pen and an annual allowance of 4,000 francs from uncle Solomon. He found everything wonderful, society life, the museums, the libraries, the restaurants and the colourful life of the boulevards. Especially the women. Heine never made any secret of his amorous adventures. On one of his first days in Paris he wrote to a friend in Germany:

'If anyone asks how I am, then say: like a fish in water. Or more accurately: tell everybody that if a fish in the sea asks another how he is, the latter answers: like Heine in Paris.'

The first years in Paris were a flourishing period for Heine, he was full of activity and restless energy. New books appeared, he acted as correspondent for German newspapers and used his influence on the liberal party in his homeland. From the very beginning his style had been his and his alone. Every line from his hand, whether erotic or political—his two main themes—sparkles with malice and sarcasm, but always concealed behind irony's cloak of elegance and charm. He draws a veil over his tragedy, hides his pain behind the light, the dreaming, the boastful or coquettish. Because he plays with muted strings, his voice sounds in a minor key and acquires the deep double tone which makes Heine Heine. Now Saint Simonism became a new gospel for him; in it he saw the way to liberty; liberty, always liberty, that was the exile's eternal longing.

Emancipation, not only for the Irish, the Greeks, the Frankfurt Jews and the West Indian negroes, no, the whole world shall be freed. First and last Europe, the continent which is now on the point of coming of age and tearing itself away from privilege and aristocracy.

It was also under Saint Simon's influence that Heine developed his famous antithesis: Nazarene contra Hellene. He purposely uses the word Nazarene so as not to say Jew or Christian. For the two are in the same boat. Their faiths are indeed different, but naturally one. For the Jew the body is merely the clay which houses *Ruah-Hakodesh*, the Holy Spirit. Christianity goes still further and stamps the flesh as the root of evil. They are both Nazarenes. And the Nazarenes are ascetics, iconoclasts, morbid spiritualists:

'Christ has conquered Olympus's gods, the Middle Ages are the age of asceticism, whose holy vampires sucked our blood.'

But the Hellene is the life enhancer, proud in his development, he sticks to reality. Heine wanted to be a Hellene and overcome the religion of pain which had turned Olympus into a hospital. With this Dionysian feeling for life he sought to get rid of the conflict inside him and achieve the harmony he constantly strove for. It was the solution of despair, and it was in vain.

Inner conflicts create irritability and lack of balance. They predispose to quarrels and bickering, and bring external conflicts in their wake. Heine did not escape from them, but was the centre of several bitter controversies. His long feud with Ludwig Börne saddled him with a duel and only brought him scant honour. But Ludwig Börne forms part of the picture of Heine and he played such a role in Jewish life at the beginning of the nineteenth century that we must pause and reproduce some features of his portrait.

Ludwig Böorne was some ten years older than Heine. Originally he was called Löb Baruch and he is one of the many important personalities produced by Frankfurt's cramped Judengasse. As a sixteen-year-old student he lived in Berlin in the celebrated home of Marcus and Henriette Hertz. She was thirty-eight at the time and in the summer of her beauty. The youth fell passionately in love with the mature woman and she had to use considerable skill to keep his passions in check. His letters to Henriette Hertz form a literary memorial to the little love story and are an important source of knowledge about her.

Ludwig Börne is one of many contemporary examples of a Jew who did his utmost to become German. He let himself be baptized and changed his name on baptism. He won little happiness from this step; he too had to experience how hard it is for a Jew to coalesce with a people which is not his. The reaction under the Holy Alliance lit revolution's flame in his hot-headed brain. Börne became one of the standard bearers of *Das Junge Deutschland* (Young Germany). The pen was his sharp sword; he had no mercy on the Philistines, nor on the anti-Semites. He directed this bitter outburst at them:

'Because you yourselves are slaves, you cannot suffer slaves.'

Nor is his great confession forgotten:

'Because I myself was born a slave, I love freedom, because I was born without a fatherland, I want a fatherland more than you, because my fatherland was as narrow as the Judengasse and the outside world began at its gate, the city does not suffice for me, nor the province, but only the great fatherland, as far as the language reaches.'

Like Heine Börne sought refuge in Paris after the July revolution. They were both fighting for freedom, but had different views on how it should be won. Börne disagreed strongly with Heine, because he found him too passive and vacillating. Heine only answered two years after Börne's death, with a book about him which was full of bitterness. It caused a great stir and cost Heine many friends. No one could reconcile themselves to the fact that he had attacked his friend after his death, when he could not defend himself.

But as the horizon darkened for Heine, he found peace at home; he married Mathilde. That was not her real name, it was Heine's pet name for her. She was a gay village girl from Normandy who had come to the great Babylon on the banks of the Seine. An aunt who had a boot and shoe shop lived there. Mathilde became an assistant in the shop and Heine bought shoes there. In this way they found each other.

One of Heine's bitter remarks about woman is that 'she unfortunately only has one way of making her husband happy but thirty thousand ways of making him miserable'. But he met completely unselfish love in Mathilde. She had no intellectual interests and never learnt to understand German.

'People say that Henri is a great poet. But I don't understand a word of what he writes,' she once said.

Perhaps it was this that bound Heine to her. He knew that she loved him for his own sake, not for his talent or fame. And in addition she had the temperament he wanted, gave him the same happiness as Tannhaüser found with Venus. She was woman through and through, with spontaneous charm, changed from fits of rage to smiles and laughter, and wept as bitterly over a dead parrot as when she lost her mother. Their marriage was rather like a seesaw. There is a story about their relationship which is probably untrue, but amusing and typical of Jewish satire.

When Heine lay on his deathbed he summoned a friend who was a lawyer so that he could dictate his will. The friend wrote from Heine's dictation:

'Mathilde shall inherit everything I leave.'

But when the continuation came, the friend stopped and looked at the poet in surprise. For it read:

'The condition on which Mathilde inherits from me is that she has remarried at the latest one year after my death.'

'Why?' he asked in astonishment.

Came a weak flash of the satire which had so often sparkled in Heine's eyes, as the dying man whispered in a weak voice:

'Can't you understand that I want to make sure that there is at least one man who is really sorry that I am dead?'

Heine had only been in Paris two years when one day in

HEINRICH HEINE

1833 he discovered that he could not move two of the fingers of his left hand. It was the first warning of the terrible illness which was approaching. He had never had a strong constitution. He suffered from violent headaches in his student days; he was hypersensitive to noise. An irregular life did not help matters. It was not alcohol which broke down his nervous system—'I can be satisfied with smelling the cork of a bottle of wine', he said—but sexual debauchery. The disease developed slowly but relentlessly. His eyes began to fail, in time his left hand, indeed his whole left side was lamed. The doctors tried to help him by prescribing ice-cold baths. It helped for a while, but no longer. In February, 1848, the disease entered its fatal phase.

The February revolution swept through the boulevards of Paris. For a long time Heine had not been out of doors. Now he dragged himself down into the street with his lame leg to take part in the great events. During a street fight he sought shelter in the Louvre. The great womanizer collapsed in front of the Venus de Milo, sobbing:

'She has no arms.'

The rest of his days he lay in what he called his *Matratzengruft* (mattress grave). The curtain went up on the tragedy's fifth act, genius's brave hopeless battle against the forces of destruction. The house was in a quiet side-street near the Champs Elysées. Over there swarmed busy living people, heavy carriages rumbled along, there was singing and music in the pavement restaurants. But here was calm, only occasionally did a gust of wind carry the gay sounds so far. One had to go up three storeys, 150 steps, then the way led down a long dark corridor before one reached the room, a light friendly room with a balcony. Half a dozen mattresses were piled on top of each other. On this bed one could see the poet's bloodless pale shrunken body, in a grotesquely distorted position with the legs bowed together. The white hands always kept their elegant lines. When he was aware of guests, he raised his damaged eyelid with his healthy hand, the same movement as when someone holds a lorgnette and turned his head back so that he could see the visitor. He could not turn his diseased eyes. If he wanted to read, the book had to be moved from right to left so that he could follow the text. Such is the description of a visit to Heine. This state of affairs lasted for eight terrible years.

'A Greek god would never treat a poet like this,' he sighed, 'but crush him with a thunderbolt.'

He was no longer the Hellene, 'the freest German since Goethe', who had smiled condescendingly at the depressing Nazarene. Now alas he was only a poor Jew, fatally ill, an enervated image of misery.

'Sic transit gloria mundi.' He often greeted his visitor with these words and called himself 'an unburied corpse'.

But while his body disintegrated and withered, his mind remained alive. Remarkably enough his brain was not attacked by the disease. And in the mattress grave he gave a fascinating example of the spirit's victory over death.

Heine found his fatherland. It was not Germany, nor France, where the goddess of beauty had no arms, but Judaea. He turned to the god of his fathers. Not in the orthodox sense, for Heine never entered a synagogue again. Nor did he bow to any authorized version of the faith—dogma was always a plague to him. Heine was the independent, free man, the outsider to the end. He knew that when he died neither priest nor rabbi would officiate at his funeral.

Keine Messe wird man singen,
keinen Kaddisch wird man sagen.

No one will sing a mass,
No one will say a Kaddisch.

But in his innermost thoughts the martyred Jew returned to Jehovah. He remained Heinrich Heine, in whom hope and despair, torment and blasphemous mockery blended. 'The great animal tormentor's hand' had laid heavily on him. God had been more than a match for him.

'I have returned to God after having herded swine with the Hegelians,' as he put it. And it was 'mankind's home chemist', the ancient Bible, to which he clung in doubt and temptation.

'My eyes opened simply by reading the Bible, the temple

treasure, which, God be praised, was not destroyed in the wicked Titus's flames.'

The new acknowledgment, the fruit of reflection on sleepless nights finds expression in his confession, written in one of the last years of his life, in these classic words:

'My predilection for Hellas has fallen off. I see that the Greeks were only handsome youths. The Jews on the other hand were always men, powerful, inflexible, not only in vanished ages, but right down to today, in spite of eighteen centuries of persecution and misery. If it was not a ridiculous self-contradiction for a champion of the revolution to boast of his birth, I would be proud that my ancestors belonged to the noble house of Israel, that I am a descendant of those martyrs who gave the world a God and a moral system, and fought and led on all the battle-fields of ideas.'

And he goes on to say of Moses:

'Unlike the Egyptians he did not fashion his works of art in brick and granite. No, Moses built human pyramids, he chiselled men into obelisks. He took a poor nomadic tribe and out of it created a people who would be a model for all other peoples, indeed it serves the whole of mankind as a pattern. He created Israel. What a gigantic figure Moses is. How little Mount Sinai seems when Moses stands on it.'

The sands of life ran out for Heinrich Heine on Sunday, February 17, 1856. At the end he whispered, once more with the trace of an ironic smile on his stiffening face:

'*Dieu me pardonnera, c'est son métier.* God will forgive me, it's his job.'

He himself expressed the tragedy of his life in words which apply to thousands of his generation's Jews:

'Jewry is not a nation, nor is it a religion. It is—a misfortune.'

VI

REFORM

M ASS apostasy is the first landmark in the history of the Jewish character and destiny in the century which saw the chains broken. A natural catastrophe of the spirit began and—to use a metaphor—the downpour came and the floods, and the winds beat against the houses which were built on sand. They fell and their fall was great. But the nucleus of this people which seems to possess immortality survived. It consisted of those who had built on a rock which lay so secure and so high that the water could not reach it. But harsh times awaited the Jews who remained in their father's house. At the close of the Napoleonic epoch Jewry's youngest generation were faced with a forest of bewildering questions and tangled problems. How to unite inherited tradition with the new times? Or to express the matter in the language of Hegelianism, the fashionable contemporary philosophy: 'Where is the synthesis between ancient Jewry and modern European culture?' It was not an academic discussion. It was a matter of life and death. The issue was a burning one and called for an immediate answer. We shall follow the generation which stumbled forward towards an answer and found a way through a dark and dangerous future.

Emancipation and assimilation, those are the two keywords which open the door for us. It is easy to say them and not even difficult to imagine what they stand for. It is far more difficult to penetrate the chaos of conflict and schism among the whole of the Jewish people which followed in their wake and split Jewry into countless factions which fought each other bitterly.

REFORM

Emancipation obviously signifies the battle for political and civil equality. Assimilation is more indefinite. It means the process by which the Jews let themselves be absorbed by their fellow-citizens. But there are many degrees of assimilation going from the Jews' use of the country's language and clothes to mixed marriages, where a Jew marries one of the aliens, and on to baptism and total absorption. As regards language and clothing assimilation was the general rule for the Jew wherever he was in dispersion. He spoke Greek in Alexandria, Spanish in Toledo, Arabic in Cordoba and German in the Rhineland. And where there was no specific law against it, he mainly dressed like the majority of the people among whom he lived. But when the wall around the ghetto crumbled, far bigger matters were on the agenda. Suddenly Jewry stood face to face with complete assimilation, with obliteration.

As a result the word assimilation became a battle-field for the Jews. The fight warmed up, not only with those who clung to complete obedient submission to every letter of the law, but also between many groups who were agreed that it was necessary to accommodate themselves to modern life but not on how much and which parts of their heritage they could offer on the altar of the *Zeitgeist*. The battle was a fierce one; it degenerated into unparalleled strife and discord.

Now Jewish discord is not only a modern phenomenon, but as old as Jewry itself, indeed it seems to form an inevitable part of this many-faceted people's life. 'When three Jews meet, four political parties are represented,' goes the saying and there is certainly an element of truth in it. Even in the olden days the shadow of political discord brooded over Jewish life. When the Romans under Titus laid the Jewish state waste, it was not the legions which decided the war. Long before they reached the holy city, sentence was passed on it. It was internal dissension, a regular civil war behind Jerusalem's walls which undermined their powers of resistance and prevented the Jews from meeting the crisis at full strength. Here we are confronted with the unfortunate tendency the Jews have for everyone to stick to their guns. And it is not only politics which splits Jewry. The spiritual division goes far deeper. It is an old experience that discus-

THE CHAINS ARE BROKEN

sion of life's highest problems arouses a veritable *rabies teologorum* (theologians' rage). Among the Jews it was even more savage than with the rest of us. And in the nineteenth century these bitter disputes often make the picture complicated to the point of confusion.

The problem was as follows: how to unite tradition and reason? Mendelssohn had set the ball rolling. He taught that Jewry is not a revealed religion, but legislation. A Jew can believe what he likes, so long as he lives according to the law. But this rationalistic view was already out of date and could never satisfy modern youth. For these young people did not want to subject themselves unconditionally to a discipline which had kept Jewry alive for thousands of years. The unfortunate thing was that the older generation did not have a philosophy which was capable of keeping the children when the discipline had disintegrated. And Christianity confronted both old and young, inviting them to seek shelter in its church. Where did the road lead in this dilemma?

In 1819 a small circle of intellectual youth collected in Berlin, especially learned university men. Between them they wanted to clarify the problems. This much they knew: the road to liberty led through knowledge. Not knowledge of the Christian cultural world. That was not an urgent concern; Mendelssohn had long ago shown the way there. No, they strove for enlightenment about their own world and past. They reckoned that if only they became familiar with Jewish history and literature, they would be equipped to create a respect which could preserve essential values in Jewry.

When they had gone so far, they organized the *Verein für Kultur und Wissenschaft der Juden* (Society for Jewish Culture and Knowledge). They set lofty goals for the new society. It was to establish institutions for Jewish research, both scientific and popular, open schools and seminaries, in fact encourage handicrafts and agriculture, and first and foremost try to dam the stream to the font.

This was the circle Heine joined when he went to Berlin. The moving spirit of the society was Leopold Zunz, who was already deeply engaged in Jewish studies. Moses Moser became Heine's intimate friend. The young poet admired

REFORM

Moser's wisdom and warm-heartedness, and called him 'Nathan the Wise's postscript'. Eduard Gans was more of a problem, a brilliant talent and an enthusiastic disciple of Hegel. He was only forty-one, but managed to create a furore as professor of history at Berlin University. His eloquence drew so many students that even the largest lecture rooms were too small, especially when he was teaching modern history. Here he spoke so frankly that at times the government denied him access to the university. The common denominator of the circle of friends was that they were all young, uncertain and fumbling. But also enthusiastic, thrilled by the idea of finding the way forward for themselves and the people.

Things went badly for the society. The ship sank almost before it had left harbour. Perhaps we can understand its tragic fate better when we read Eduard Gan's desperate attempt to use Hegelian historical philosophy on Jewry in words which sound dated to our ears, but contained the highest wisdom for the intellectuals of the age. He claims that the general development is 'the many's, whose unity is only in wholeness'. But Jewish life differs from it as a unity which did not become multifarious, because 'the Jews can never go under, nor can Jewry be dissolved. But in the entirety's great movement it would ostensibly go under and yet live, as the current continues out into the sea'. This had to suffice. We are not surprised that such airy talk left the great Jewish public cold and that the general run of people met the society's activity with complete indifference.

Gans was in despair and burst out:

'The only thing that holds the Jews together is fear. And the only interest they are willing to sacrifice from their earthly goods is poor relief.'

He gave up, applied for a professor's chair and was awarded it, but only on condition that he was baptized. His apostasy made a painful impression on his friends. Heine, who nevertheless went the same way himself later, burst out indignantly:

'The captain should be the last to leave the sinking ship, but Gans was the first to save himself.'

Shortly afterwards the society collapsed and was dissolved.

THE CHAINS ARE BROKEN

Leopold Zunz saw his hopes dashed. In a letter from him we find these bitter words:

'The Jewry we sought to reconstruct is a house divided against itself, a prey to barbarians, moneylenders, fools and simpletons. Long years will roll by and we shall constantly see this people as it is today, pushed into a corner, merely vegetating, while with dried eyes they look for the Messiah or sort the papers in junior posts in government offices, by turns rich or bankrupt, persecuted or tolerated.'

But in the midst of his hopeless dejection Zunz stuck to his post. Heine said admiringly of him that he 'is a man of responsibility and energy, he works and achieves great things while others are content to dream or have fainted by the roadside'.

Zunz was originally called Lipmann. The name we know him by was taken from the little Rhineland village of Zons from which the family came. He was born in Detmold in 1794, grew up in a poor home and lost both his parents when he was still quite young. He himself was delicate and sickly, but nevertheless lived to the ripe old age of ninety-two. Almost all his life he had to cope with financial difficulties, held a few scattered jobs in schools or as a journalist, advertised for pupils but only had a few. But he was never venal. Many times in his life he left a position because it required things of him which he could not give with a clear conscience. He dauntlessly said goodbye to a steady salary and stood in the street without knowing where he would find the money for his daily bread. Not until he was in his late forties did he find some kind of security as rector of a college.

In the midst of the *Mabbul*, the Hebrew word for the flood, in which the Jewish people whirled, he saw one firm point, what he called *Wissenschaft des Judentums* (knowledge of Jewry). He nailed the word like a flag to a flagpole over his head where it waved throughout his life. For him Jewry's inner conflict was solved by delving deep into its history and studying it according to modern principles. And suddenly he emerged before the public as Jewry's great historian.

Before his time Jewish history had been chaotic and neglected. The only thing people asked about old books and documents was whether the authors were also pious men, but

REFORM

lucid knowledge about time and place were hidden in the mist. Jewish history lacked two eyes, it had neither method nor system. It only became a science with Zunz. His achievement was to bring knowledge of Jewry into line with every other branch of historical research, so that today it can claim to be a faculty in every university of importance.

He never became a dusty historian. His books were always inspired by a topical practical need. In one of its despotic caprices the Prussian government forbade rabbis to preach in German. The answer was Zunz's great book on the Jewish religious service. In it he dealt with the prohibition and showed that throughout the ages, in Palestine as in Germany, preaching in the synagogue had always been in the language of the country in which the Jews lived. But that is only a detail in the book. The main thing is that the world saw here for the first time a strictly systematic examination of Jewish preaching and ritual during 1,800 years. And as these two subjects embrace everything in the life of the Jews, from philosophy to folklore, the book became a vast panorama of the Jewish nature during the long exile. Zunz shows that he is a great historian; he has a sense of context, is coolly reserved in his conclusions and classically clear in his formulation. Undoubtedly the popular conception of Jewry in his time was that it was a fossilized relic. On the contrary, Zunz points out, Jewry has always been a living growing plant.

But Zunz had not finished. Among countless treatises about almost every conceivable subject in Jewish history, he issued one epoch-making book after another. On Jewish names and the poetry used in the services, to name only two of the most important. He was not called the father of Jewish knowledge for nothing. He continued his vigorous activity right into his eighties. Then a great affliction struck him. His wife, who had stayed faithfully by his side during all their financial difficulties, died. He could not produce anything without *die Zunzin*, as their friends called her. Suddenly he was an old man; his zest for life and energy withered. He lived on until 1886, a mere shadow of himself.

Since his day the study of Jewish history has flowered steadily. The most important names are Heinrich Grätz and Simon Dubnow—the latter murdered by the Nazis. In other

THE CHAINS ARE BROKEN

words Jewish historical research is not much more than a hundred years old. Perhaps that is where we should seek the explanation of Christianity's curious ignorance of it.

The reader may ask why I have gone so deeply into a man like Leopold Zunz. Admittedly his life was devoid of drama; it was spent in a quiet book-lined study. Bent over books and documents he sat lost in his research. Of course he wrote a few books, but who reads them today? Yet the truth is that in such studies the bullets are made and the ammunition prepared which is fired in the great battle and is understood by everyone. And Zunz was by no means an unworldly pedantic theoretician. He took part in the February revolution, he was elected to parliament and it was his ideas which inspired the great movement which we call Reformed Jewry.

Leopold Zunz and his pupils marked an epoch in the view of the Jewish past. Before their time the Bible and the Talmud had stood as fixed unchangeable starting-points. In them God's revelation was found and that could not be altered or abolished. The smallest word, indeed every single letter and sign has a deep spiritual meaning and must be carefully thought about. Until God cancels the old revelation by a new one, every single ceremony keeps its validity. As long as people could remember, Jewry had built on these ideas.

But Zunz put himself in line with the modern Biblical research which emerged inside the church during the same period. He taught that the reality looked entirely different from what people had imagined. God's revelation simply is not definitive and final. The Bible and the Talmud point the way; they are certainly very significant, but they are only stations on the path of a long development which has always been going on. The ancient holy books are the crystallization of God's revelation in vanished ages. But God reveals himself anew in every epoch through the spirit of the age. Changing ages can very well alter ancient commandments and replace them by new ones. Such were the radical ideas of modern historical research which Reformed Jewry took over.

The reformed Jews were progressives. They found a great many things in the tradition antiquated and they realized clearly that Jewry no longer appealed to the people with the

REFORM

same fervour as before. They were deeply engaged in thinking about where the renewal could be found. They seized on the historians' criticisms of the hitherto sacrosanct tradition with enthusiasm. For it was an established fact that it no longer had the right to constrict them in its bonds and tie them so that they could not move. They were free as regards it. Some of them felt as if God had given them a new revelation. Here at last they found the instrument they had lacked for bridging the gap between past and future. Jewry should be modernized, reformed, so that Jews of the time could feel at home in it again. So they put themselves in line with the reigning religion and did everything possible to make Jewry resemble the church. There was plenty to tidy up. Reformed Jewry swept like a new storm over every field of traditional Jewish life.

Like all great movements it began in a small way. The prelude looked comparatively innocent. A rich influential banker, Israel Jacobson, lived in Westphalia. He had worked his way up from the bottom with industry and skill. In everyone's eyes he was a noble distinguished personality, deeply rooted in his fathers' faith. It pained him to see the indifference with which many Jews approached their religious life. The more Jacobson thought about it, the more convinced he was that the reason was that Jewry had petrified into formalism; the service had become unintelligible to modern men. But he was also a man with an aesthetic sense and found that life in the synagogue and the ceremonies at the service were not beautiful enough. The whole lacked decorum. This word came to play a prominent role in the controversy which was now knocking on the door.

The synagogue had been the place where people met from time immemorial. The word synagogue simply means a bringing together. In it the congregation was accustomed to gather for the service. Not only on the sabbath, but three times every day, for morning, noon and evening prayer, *Shaharit, Minhah* and *Ma'ariv*, and devout men sat in the synagogue all day studying ancient sacred books. But the synagogue was not only the religious centre, it was the assembly place where everyone met and shared sorrow and happiness with each other. Even during the service. Between the prayers people

THE CHAINS ARE BROKEN

sat and chatted comfortably with each other, there was whispering as they exchanged the latest gossip. Indeed men could equally well hear rates of exchange and prices, and conclude a rapid business deal. It was not devotion and quiet as in a Christian church, but loud chatter and confusion. This offended against decorum in the opinion of Jacobson and many others.

But there was more in the way, much more serious things. The service itself was incomprehensible and its form was offensive. Perhaps it had been good enough for the ghetto. Then the Jews only knew the life behind the wall. To them the traditional form of the service was perfectly natural. It was as it was and it could not be otherwise. However, it was not like that for men of the new generation who had been out in the world and known life there. When they came to the synagogue, it naturally offended them to be amongst all this bustle. But they could not follow the service either. They hardly understood the old Hebrew prayers. In their daily life they tried to be modern westerners, but in the synagogue everything was old, alien and eastern. Here stood men with striped shawls over head and shoulders, looking like wanderers in the desert; the women, like slaves in a harem, were shut in behind thick curtains in a side room or on a remote balcony. Youth put the synagogue's service on one side of the scales, the church's on the other. The scales turned decisively in favour of the latter.

Jacobson decided to reform the service. He had the opportunity to do so. High up in the Harz mountains, in the village of Seesen he had once built a school where the children were taught both Jewish and general subjects on modern principles. The school had acquired such a reputation that many Christian parents also sent their children there. Here Jacobson owned a synagogue and in it he began to experiment gradually with the reform of the ritual. He proceeded slowly and cautiously. The first change was translating the Psalms into German; it was the prayers' turn later. Many people went to Jacobson's synagogue, both the school's children and their parents, when they were visiting. They spread the report of Jacobson's reformed service to all parts of Germany.

REFORM

In 1815 Jacobson moved to Berlin. He at once found someone who shared his views, another banker, Jacob Beer, father of the famous composer Giacomo Meyerbeer. Like Jacobson, Beer was a cultured man with refined taste. The two wealthy men decided to put their ideas into practise and began to hold services in their homes according to the new principles. Jacobson's eldest son was to be *bar mitzwah* on the very day the new services began in Berlin. The language was German, men and women sat together, unintelligible prayers were suppressed and Jacobson altered the traditional form of the boy's festival so radically that by mistake it resembled confirmation in a Christian church. But the most conspicuous change was that the psalm singing was accompanied by organ music.

That was a challenge. From ancient times the Jews have hated organ music. It reminds them of a church and, far worse, of the *autos-da-fé* in Spain. It was the custom of the cruel Dominican monks to put an organ alongside the stake. When the flames were burning the victims to death, the organ music rang out and drowned the dying Jews' last cry to God: *Shmah Israel*, Hear Israel, the Lord our God, the Lord is one. Orthodox Jews listened with horror to the rumour of the presumptuous man who dared to make use of the accursed instrument. But to the reformers the organ was a symbol. When they used it, the service in the synagogue gradually resembled the church's. The gap between the two religions had shrunk.

Jacobson and Beer were not permitted to experiment for long. The orthodox Jews in Berlin complained to the government, which forbade any other kind of Jewish service but the traditional one. But the fire had already caught in many minds; the movement could no longer be stopped. In the free Hanseatic city of Hamburg other reformers built a synagogue. Later they acquired an annex in Leipzig, the city with the big markets, where Jews from all over Europe used to arrange to meet. Naturally they attended the new services, with the result that many of them were impressed and took the idea home. Reformed Jewry spread in many countries; it reached Austria, Holland, England, Denmark and Sweden (especially in the synagogue at Gothenburg).

THE CHAINS ARE BROKEN

Alterations in the service were only a beginning. The reformers who received Jacobson's heritage went much further. Jacobson had acted from religious and aesthetic motives. His successors set themselves political goals. They found that the reformation of Jewry could be used as a crowbar to force open the door to emancipation. They made the movement march in step with propaganda for civil equality. But these radical reformers cut so deep into the traditional faith they they came close to cutting Jewry's vital nerve.

For millennia the Jewish people had felt that they were in *galuth*, in the exile which is God's punishment for the sins of their fathers. But the punishment does not last for ever. One day the Messiah will come and free Israel. In a wonderful way he crushes its enemies and leads the exiles home in triumph to the ancient land and makes Jerusalem queen of the earth. On mediaeval maps the Holy City is drawn as its centre. It was to be so again. The temple would arise in new brilliance and the temple service, which had had to stop during exile, be renewed.

That was the dream. During persecution and in exile the Jew has watched out for him who is to come. He has longed, he has hoped and prayed. Every year at Easter the dream was put into words in the greeting: next year in Jerusalem. No Jew doubted this blazing hope which gave life a meaning. In the midst of his debasement, he knew that he was a king's son in spite of everything.

The reformers took the dream away from him, at first as the result of learned studies. The theologians stripped the Messiah dream bare. Layer after layer came off it. And at the very core they found that the noblest, original element in the belief in the Messiah is not the king of David's house who will reconstruct Israel's power. They provided a different conception of the Messiah from the nameless prophet exiled in Babylon who wrote the last part of the Book of Isaiah and saw visions of the suffering Lord's servants and dreamt of justice and peace. He was not to be an individual; the Jewish people themselves are the real Messiah in his view. So that it was not just God's wrath which drove Israel into exile but his foresight. The Jews were scattered among the heathens to proclaim to them God's will and stand as an example of

REFORM

righteousness and truth. Every Jew is a priest, anointed to serve at the altar of mankind. And the culminating idea follows that Jewry is not nationalist, but universal. The ultimate salvation is not Israel's alone; it belongs to the whole world.

It is easy to find a political purpose in this sensational break with tradition. In any case the new outlook was used for political ends. Now anyone could see that the Jew had no national aspirations. And once again we are faced with the stubborn assertion that Jewry is not a nation, but a religion. The Jews belong to a particular sect, just the same as the Catholics or Protestants, and are as German as they are. The reformers stopped calling themselves Jews; they were 'Germans of the Mosaic faith'. They also changed the name of the synagogue. Now it was called the temple. This favourite word had hitherto been reserved for the fallen sanctuary in Jerusalem. But now everyone could see that Berlin or Hamburg or any other town which erected its 'temple' was just as good as Jerusalem. 'Stuttgart is my Jerusalem,' a Jew of that city exclaimed. In their synagogues the reformed Jews abolished the old prayers about the revival of the Jewish state and cut out of the ritual the word *Am*, people, when Israel was named. In fact there were reformers who were willing to give up the old calendar, by which the year was reckoned from the creation of the world, and make zero the date of the national battle at Leipzig in 1813.

Once belief in the Messiah had gone, the ideas of the reformist movement went through Jewry like a landslide. It was a trifle in comparison when the service was moved from the Sabbath to Sunday. It was a question of coming into line with the church as far as possible. Inevitably there was a modification of the strict dietary rules. *Minyan* was no longer valid. The word means number, ten in fact. That was the quorum required before a Jewish service could begin. People stopped using the prayer shawl and phylacteries, *tallit* and *tefilin*. *Shulhan Aruk* disappeared; large sections of the Talmud were scrapped, indeed in some places the inviolable Torah was amended and the rules governing marriage and divorce revised. All this continues to this very day. As late as December, 1957, I found an advertisement in a Jewish New

THE CHAINS ARE BROKEN

York paper inviting people to *Chrishnukka*. I.e. Christmas has been merged with the Jewish *Hanukka*, the feast of cleansing the temple. Both holidays are celebrated in December, but there the similarity ends. So it was naturally convenient if Jews and Christians could celebrate together with a turkey, Christmas tree, presents and everything else that goes with the occasion.

These hasty pencil strokes must suffice to sketch the portrait of the reform movement. They show quite clearly that the name reformation is a misrepresentation. For reformation means a return to the source. The Lutheran Reformation cut through the church's thousand-year-old tradition and went back to the church's origin, its Biblical foundation. But the Jewish reformers did exactly the opposite. They quite openly cut off a heel here and a toe there, and adapted Jewry to the taste of the age. Their reformation was not a reformation, but a form of assimilation.

It goes without saying that the reformers called down a storm on their heads. They aroused sorrow and anger among all strictly orthodox believers. Some congregations split; they formed two factions, each with its own rabbi, one reformist and one orthodox. Passions ran high in the countries where the new ideas took root, with Germany in the forefront; polemics and excommunications were interchanged. It would take us too far to follow this lengthy conflict in all its details. But if we consider some of its protagonists, we catch a glimpse of the struggle as seen from both sides.

The reform movement had highly gifted and learned spokesmen. The foremost among them was Abraham Geiger. Like Ludwig Börne and the Rothschilds he came from Frankfurt's Judengasse. He was born there in 1810 in a learned rabbinical home. At the age of three he read both German and Hebrew and had gone so deeply into his Hebrew Bible that his father did not hesitate to let him start on the Talmud. At School Geiger was so far ahead of his school fellows that he complained at home of having no work to do. So his father took him away from school and read with him at home. The boy had barely become *bar mitzwah* when his father died. At the funeral he not only gave the traditional *Hesped*, memorial speech, in Hebrew, but also recited a translation into German, to the devout family's displeasure.

It was characteristic of him. Even at this tender age he was already moving away from strict orthodoxy. For a time he even thought of not following in his father's footsteps. Instead of theology he plunged into historical and linguistic studies, especially Arabic and Syrian. The result was a highly-praised dissertation on Jewish influence on the Koran. Bonn University rewarded the seventeen-year-old student with its top prize. Nevertheless theology prevailed in the long run. Geiger completed his studies and became the rabbi of Wiesbaden. Some years later the far more important post at Breslau became vacant. Geiger was a candidate for it and as a result entered the stormy period of his career.

In Breslau the congregation had an orthodox rabbi who was called S. A. Titkin. Under the influence of the reformist ideas it had been decided to appoint another rabbi in addition to Titkin and the new incumbent was to be one of the modern theologians. The choice fell on Geiger. His arrival in Breslau took the form of a great drama. All the German Jews followed the development of events in suspense. For it was clear that Titkin and the orthodox branch of the congregation intended to use every conceivable means to get rid of Geiger. There is no doubt that they did their best. Before his final appointment Geiger had to deliver a trial sermon in Breslau's great synagogue. In the meantime Titkin succeeded in obtaining a ministerial ban on it. The intrigue misfired; Titkin had forgotten to take the city's chief constable into account. The latter was a liberal man who was already impressed by Geiger's personality. The big blue envelope containing the government's letter lay on his desk on the morning when Geiger was to preach. He did not open the letter until after the service, but by then it was too late.

However, Titkin did not give up. He devoted his energies to preventing Geiger from acquiring Prussian citizenship. If he did not get it, it was impossible to hold a post inside the frontiers of the kingdom. Titkin fired off a whole arsenal of accusations against his dangerous opponent. Geiger was forced to stay in Berlin for fifteen long months in order to plead his case personally in the government offices. At long last he won through and had his appointment confirmed.

Geiger was a man who made an impression. His stature was short and skinny, but those who met him only saw his face. It was clear-cut, almost leonine. In the fashion of the day he wore his hair long; it fell down over his shoulders in soft folds. He was very shortsighted and wore strong double glasses. Behind them his eyes shone with a strange unforgettable brilliance. Geiger lived in the sermon's golden age. He was an exceptional master in the pulpit. His language was classically pure and beautiful, backed by sonorous diction, its content was original and profound.

Throughout his life Geiger remained the eternal student, always reading, discussing and hungry for new impressions. He created his own forum in the *Wissenschaftliche Zeitschrift für jüdische Teologie* (Scientific Journal for Jewish Theology), which today is a gold mine for the study of the reformers' battle in one of Jewry's most disturbed storm centres at the time. Geiger was never tired of emphasizing that Jewry is not something definitive and finished, but a steadily growing process. What we call tradition was itself once the result of a growth or a revival. He demands inexorably that both the Bible and the Talmud should be studied historically. They are stages on the way and new development is constantly going on. Geiger had a much discussed clash with Zunz. He attacked Zunz because, in spite of his critical attitude, the master never went all the way, but stuck to the old customs—for example he always used *tefilin* and observed the dietary laws strictly. But Zunz answered:

'It is religion that should change us, not we who should change religion.'

Zunz also asserted that one-sided negative criticism is the way to apostasy.

The conservative orthodox Jews had their important spokesmen. The most prominent was Samson Raphael Hirsch, for many years rabbi of Frankfurt am Main. He was just as learned as Geiger and possessed a dialectical ability which made him a dangerous opponent. Hirsch transformed Frankfurt into the stronghold of orthodoxy in Germany, but became important far beyond his narrow field of activity there. In his famous book *Nineteen Letters from Ben Uriel* he pro-

REFORM

duced in classical German language a fearless defence of Jewry in its traditional form.

The essential result of the long-drawn-out conflict was a New Conservative Jewry. It agreed to minor changes in the service, cut the most incomprehensible obsolete prayers out of the liturgy, permitted preaching in German, used a male choir and in time it even accepted organ music in the synagogue. But it clung unswervingly to the dietary laws, the Sabbath and prayers in Hebrew. The historian Zacharias Frankel, for many years rabbi of Dresden, was the talented spokesman of the New Conservatism. At a rabbinical meeting in Frankfurt he had a clash with the reformers which created an uproar.

About 1848 the battle subsided. The result was a decisive defeat for the reformers. They did keep one or two bridgeheads in Germany, but they never won support among the masses. Their message had been too one-sided and intellectual for that. On top of that the reform movement lost much of its best blood in the great emigration from Germany to England and especially America. But the emigrants took the reformist ideas with them and started the movement in America. It took root there and to this day has its strongholds in many American congregations. It has made an indelible mark on American Jewry.

But the reform movement also managed to make deep inroads into Europe's Jewry, primarily in Germany, of course. It forced its opponents to arm themselves with knowledge and clear ideas, and many antiquated and in modern eyes laughable traditions were relegated to the attic. For tens of thousands of Jews it was a bridge which helped them over the gap between the Middle Ages and the modern era and so preserved them for their people.

Their weaknesses are obvious to us who can see the events in the perspective of a hundred years. The reforming Jews were caught in the false illusion that Jewry is only a religion and has nothing to do with nationality. No one should blame them for failing. In their day national feeling out in the Christian world was still in embryo. It did not break through until the popular risings against Napoleon and as yet had simply not penetrated the Jewish consciousness. It was fifty years later before Jews began to wake up and see that concepts such as nation, religion and tradition are so closely interwoven in Jewry that no one can separate them if Jewry is to remain Jewish.

But perhaps it was the reformers' optimism which made the movement fatally lopsided. Admittedly they were born in a generation which believed in progress. The Jew had left the ghetto, now he had to become a world citizen all of a sudden. Tolerance and liberty were on the way, the enemy in full retreat. So Jewry no longer needed its old defences. For peace would cover the earth as the waters cover the sea. The sun rose and the mist was dispersed, while hate, stupidity and hypocrisy vanished never to return.

The reality was quite different. One fine day the optimistic dreams and bright visions burst like soap bubbles. The future which lay in wait for the Jewish people was to prove both harsh and bitter.

VII

THE FRUITS OF PEACE

THE old Judengasse in Frankfurt am Main no longer exists. It was so narrow that the sunlight never reached the paving of the street and it was in urgent need of clearance. The old rickety houses were torn down long ago and replaced by more permanent dwellings. But they too have gone. Air raids during World War II wiped out whole districts of Frankfurt and the old Judengasse went with them. Here not even the stones can speak, for there are none left. Yet memory whispers about is former appearance. The families who had their origin there and are scattered all over the world treasure faithful traditions which go from father to son, from mother to daughter, about their forefathers' wretched lives and the injustice they suffered. But there is pride in their voices when the talk turns to the Judengasse. For it was a nursery for young shoots which later rose and grew into the forest's most celebrated trees. The homes in the narrow street fostered children with ability and the will to succeed. I have already mentioned some names: Ludwig Börne and Abraham Geiger are two of them. Now we come to the history of the family from the house with the red shield, who without exaggeration helped to shape Europe's destiny for almost a century.

From olden times Frankfurt had been one of Germany's most important towns. As early as the Middle Ages it was given privileges as an 'unmittelbar Reichstadt'. The town lay so near the Rhine's broad waterway that it became the transit port for Germany's trade with the west. About the time of the French Revolution Frankfurt had 35,000 inhabitants, of whom a tenth were Jews. And it was as business men that

THE CHAINS ARE BROKEN

the Frankfurt Jews found their chance and seized it.

In the old days the houses in the Judengasse were not numbered. People knew them by the sign or picture on the house signboard, an animal, a tree, a ship. The inevitable result was that the house's inhabitants were also known by the signboard and got their name from it. As far back as 1585 we know the owners of the house which later was numbered 148 but previously had a red sign. From that year they added *zum rothen Schild* to their name. Later the name Rothschild was to fly round the world. We know very little about the actual founder of the family, Amschel Moses Rothschild. He was probably an itinerant provision dealer and lived with his family in an attic room at the top of the crowded house. He died in 1754, when his eldest son, Meyer Amschel Rothschild, was only eleven years old. But the young boy carried a field marshal's baton in his knapsack.

Old Rothschild had had great plans for his intelligent alert son. He was to go further than his father and become at least a rabbi. The boy was registered in a famous *yeshiva* in Fürth, but had hardly begun his studies when his father died. He did not leave enough money for the boy to be able to take his examination, so the young Rothschild was forced to give up his studies. Instead he went to Hanover where he obtained a position in the Oppenheim's banking house. He could easily have stayed there for the rest of his days and lived in modest but decent conditions and perhaps some day been promoted to book-keeper. But the young man had higher aspirations. When he felt that he had learnt what the Oppenheims could teach him, he resigned and returned to Frankfurt. Rothschild bought the parental home, settled there and became his own master. His honesty, punctuality and discretion soon aroused attention among older colleagues and they gradually began to use him as a confidential middleman in difficult and important transactions.

When he was only a boy his father had instructed him in his hobby, numismatics. Now it was more than a spare-time occupation. In those days every business man was forced to have a sound knowledge of the various coins. Germany was divided into several hundred small states and each of them set great store by having their own monetary system. So

THE FRUITS OF PEACE

money-changing had a prominent place in business life. In it lay the germ of Rothschild's adventurous career.

Many high-born people were interested in numismatics. They found their way to Rothschild's shop and he took care always to have rare coins in stock. General von Estorff was one of these collectors. Later the same Estorff happened to become a courtier at the court of the young Prince Wilhelm of Essen. Wilhelm was the grandson of the old Elector of Hessen-Kassel. Moreover he was of the highest birth; his mother was daughter of the King of England, he himself was married to a daughter of King Frederick V of Denmark. For the time being his own status looked modest; he was only landgrave of the Lilliputian state of Hanau, in other words a star which was a long way from reaching its zenith. But it was on the way up. Rothschild saw that there were possibilities and began to back Prince Wilhelm. He was lucky. The Prince was a passionate numismatist. Rothschild offered him rarities at favourable prices through General Estorff. The Prince began to take note of the little Jew from Frankfurt.

The Elector and his grandson were very rich. They had made their fortunes by trading in men. Before the age of universal national service princes used to hire out their soldiers wherever there was war. It was excellent business; high wages were paid for well-trained troops and good compensation for dead and wounded. During the American War of Independence, England especially hired Hessian soldiers and sent them overseas. The soldiers fought and died; the two princes raked in millions. When the Elector died, Prince Wilhelm inherited not only his title, but also his fortune. Suddenly he was the richest man in Europe.

He needed plenty of money. Wilhelm was what was called a free-thinker, extremely tolerant in religious matters. But he also claimed tolerance for himself. To the indignation of the whole country he kept a harem of mistresses and had, so it is said, seventy-four children by them. But the new Elector also knew about money and made his fortune multiply. He had an unusual talent for choosing the right collaborators. Rothschild finally became his most distinguished agent. It took many years before the suspicious monarch learnt that

THE CHAINS ARE BROKEN

here was someone in whom he could have unlimited confidence. That only came when he really had need of Rothschild.

They were stormy times. First came the French Revolution with wars in its wake, which was most dangerous for Wilhelm when Napoleon extended his sceptre over Europe. The Elector was a fanatical opponent of the French emperor and had to flee his own country. Napoleon declared that the House of Hesse-Kassel had ceased to reign. While Wilhelm was in exile, Rothschild managed his financial affairs. Clear-sightedness and boldness enabled him to steer his way between countless dangerous reefs. When the Elector finally came home, Rothschild was able, like the good and faithful servant, to return the talents with interest. Obviously Wilhelm had hoped to see some of his fortune salvaged. But now Rothschild's servants started coming into the castle. They placed heavy chests and barrels full of gold on the floor in front of the Elector. Bowing low Rothschild handed over to his sovereign the numerous portfolios full of securities. Then he counted up the interest. It was more than the Elector had thought possible. From that day he believed unswervingly in Rothschild's genius and honesty, and opened the way for him to Europe's other princely houses. It should be added that Rothschild had charged a good percentage as commission and used Wilhelm's fortune for speculations on his own account. The war made him a very rich man.

Amschel Meyer Rothschild was tall and stately, with pronounced Jewish features and a simultaneously good-natured and clever, almost sly expression. He wore a small Vandyke beard, *bar paryk*, but as a Jew could not powder it. His clothes were modest. When he went out, he wore a three-cornered hat. He was very charitable. If anyone saw a line of happy-looking beggars in the Judengasse, he could be sure that Rothschild had walked past and given them alms. Apart from his success in business he remained a ghetto Jew; he never learnt to speak correct German, but struggled along with his Yiddish, to the amusement of his distinguished clients, and his letters were crude and awkwardly expressed.

At the age of twenty-five he married the young daughter of another Frankfurt Jew. She was called Gudula and was seventeen at the time. They settled in the old house and lived happily together. Ten children, five sons and five daughters, grew up in the rich secure home. Amschel Meyer died at the age of seventy, but did not live to see Napoleon's final fall. Gudula survived him for many years; she lived to be almost a hundred. Although she was as rich as Croesus and could have had every conceivable comfort, she refused categorically to leave the dark old house in the Judengasse. Her elegant carriage could not drive up to the door, the alley was too small for it to pass. It had to leave her at the corner and both she and her guests walk over the rough paving-stones. Like many of the women in the Judengasse Gudula Rothschild was rather superstitious and feared that her sons' luck would fail if she did not keep watch where their cradles had stood. Her vitality was unimpaired to the end. Not until she was past ninety did she begin to ail and complain to the doctor of being tired. He answered respectfully that unfortunately it was not in his power to make her younger. She snapped at him:

'I do not wish to grow younger, by God. But he has to make me older.'

The parents took great care over their children's upbringing. The daughters were married to capable merchants and the sons followed in their father's footsteps as a matter of course and carried on the business. They never forgot the day when their father showed them five sticks. He tied them into a bundle and tried to break them. He could not do it; the bundle was too strong. Then he undid the bundle and it was a simple task to break the sticks one by one. He told them to remember this lesson and always stick together. If they only consulted each other and carried out everything jointly, no power could break them. Alone they would be defenceless.

On his deathbed he repeated the admonition. He enjoined them to remain faithful to Jewry and see to it that the young people of the family married each other. He said that in that way money was saved on dowries and the heritage remained in the family. It was like moving money from one trouser pocket to another. His descendants faithfully observed the old man's command about marriage. The family is one of the most inter-married in Europe. 'Only a Rothschild is worthy of marrying a Rothschild,' they say in the family. According to all eugenic principles it should have proved fatal. But every rule has its exception and it is a fact that the Rothschilds preserved their high intellectual qualities right up to the fourth generation and have done so to this day to a large extent. Obviously the chromosomes have produced special sports now and then, like drawing a blank in a lottery. The Rothschilds have included eccentrics and idlers who let others do the business on the stock exchange and while they concentrated on racehorses and other expensive amusements. But they had the money to do so. On the other hand there were others, and surprisingly many, who developed into hothouse specimens of bankers.

The old father was a man with foresight. He realized that the snug Judengasse would prove too cramped for birds with a wing-span like his five sons'. So he sent the four youngest away from home at an early age. With his sure strategical business instinct he chose key positions for them. He let the eldest, Amschel, stay at home to manage the old firm. Amschel was the head of the family from his father's death until he himself died in 1855. Karl founded his bank in Naples and became financial adviser to the Vatican. Solomon settled in the imperial city of Vienna, James in Paris. But the first to leave home and shoot rapidly across Europe's economic heaven like a gleaming meteor was Nathan, who settled in London. The father's prediction proved right. They stuck together and in fellowship the five brothers developed such strength that for a long time they were able to dominate extensive areas of Europe's economic life. Indeed there were occasions when they literally had control over war or peace. The Rothschilds always threw their weight on the side of peace. Twice they prevented the incipient outbreak of war by refusing to finance governments which were ready to embark on military adventures.

There is something of the brilliance of legend over the saga of these five brothers and their successors. We must limit ourselves to following Nathan Rothschild in London. He was the most important of them all and concentrated in himself the family's genius and moral standards.

THE FRUITS OF PEACE

Pure coincidence drove the twenty-one-year-old genius to London. A traveller in English drapery showed his collection of samples in the house of Rothschild. Nathan dealt with him, but the agent behaved boastfully and made the young Rothschild feel that it was he, the Englishman, who knew all about business, whereas he was only a continental European. Nathan persuaded his father to send him away; he would show that he was capable too. Without being able to speak a word of English he travelled to Manchester. But he did have his exceptional abilities and also a letter of credit for £20,000, in our days worth a good million.

As soon as Nathan came to England he noticed that goods in Manchester were cheaper there than on the continent. And the cheapest of all was to buy them from the actual factories in Manchester. In other words it was worth while sitting here, buying the goods and sending them home. But not only that. With his sharp eyes he discovered many opportunities. He arranged with the factories to deliver the raw materials himself, both wool and dyes, for them to manufacture. In this way his profits trebled. Nathan went further and incorporated new fields. Now he also dealt in colonial produce, spices, wine, sugar and coffee. In a few years the £20,000 became £60,000. He learnt to believe in himself and his lucky star. Later he described it as follows:

'My luck depended on one axiom. I said to myself: what another can do, I can do too. Therefore I became the man with the proof that I was superior to everyone else.' Then he added with a smile:

'It is not enough to like money. It must also like you.'

Manchester soon became too small for Nathan Rothschild. In 1804 he settled in London and soon after acquired British citizenship. No sooner had he set up his office in the City than he attracted attention by daring operations. His first great coup was the financing of Wellington's expeditionary corps in Spain. The English were in financial difficulties there and it was both troublesome and dangerous for the War Ministry to send large sums of cash all that way. Rothschild undertook the task. In the very middle of the blockade he succeeded in getting the money through by secret channels. With the help of the fine-meshed net of business houses the

THE CHAINS ARE BROKEN

Rothschild brothers had already spun across every country, the money was forwarded through enemy territory and came into Wellington's hands. When the general was marching towards Paris in 1813, Rothschild repeated the achievement. The British government appreciated his important services and from then on made use of his banking house without a second thought.

One of the secrets of the house of Rothschild's success was its highly developed intelligence system. It was before the days of the telegraph and a properly organized postal service. The transmission of news was slow and uncertain. But the Rothschild brothers kept in daily contact with each other by pigeon post and their agents and sea captains had orders to send in rapid comprehensive reports of everything they observed. If they gleaned important news, they were royally rewarded. The Rothschilds were nearly always a neck ahead of their competitors, and often of governments, in their knowledge of the latest developments on every political or economic front. Nathan Rothschild seized his greatest and most celebrated chance after the Battle of Waterloo.

It was natural that such a thrilling and fantastic story was on everybody's lips. And it was no less interesting to retell it from generation to generation. With the passage of time, too, the story has swollen and acquired quite improbable proportions. We hear that during the crisis of Napoleon's hundred days Nathan Rothschild went hurriedly to Belgium. While the Battle of Waterloo was being fought, he watched it on horseback from a hilltop. As soon as he was sure that victory belonged to the English, he gave the horse free rein and galloped to Brussels. Without wasting a moment he hired a carriage at a sky-high price and ruthlessly forced the coachman to hasten to Ostend. But once there it was impossible to cross the Channel. A veritable hurricane was driving the waves in over the harbour; all crossings were suspended. Rothschild had to cross. He found a skipper and offered him 500 francs to take him to Dover. The man shook his head. He did not want to risk his life, even for such absurdly high pay. Rothschild would not be deterred. He kept on raising his offer: 800, 1,000, 1,500 francs. Still the answer was no. Not until he reached the fantastic figure of 2,000 francs did the

THE FRUITS OF PEACE

skipper give in. Luck was with them; they did get across. Half-dead with sea-sickness Rothschild climbed into his carriage and set off for London.

Two hours later he stood in his place in the Stock Exchange, by the first pillar on the right when one comes in from Cornhill. He was completely exhausted, as pale as a corpse and his knees were knocking. He looked as if he had grown ten years older overnight. The room was atremble with nervousness. In hushed voices everyone discussed the English defeat at Waterloo. It was certain that the battle was lost. Just look at Rothschild. He is like a ruined man. The Stock Exchange lost its head; prices plummeted. Fear spread like a cyclone. It ended in panic. Valuable securities were put on sale at ludicrous prices. No one noticed that Rothschild nodded to his agents or gave whispered orders that now was the time to buy. Whole mountains of securities came into his hands at rock-bottom prices. The following day the news of the victory at Waterloo reached London and all share prices soared. Rothschild had made a fortune of a million.

So runs the legend. The reality was hardly as dramatic. But there is a grain of truth in the story which is powerful enough on its own. In fact Rothschild stayed at home in London during the battle, but he was the very first to receive news of the victory through his information service. He hastened to the Chancellor of the Exchequer and told him the news. Of course he also made use of his knowledge on the Stock Exchange, even if his profits were a good deal more modest than the story says. But the fact is that the story of the House of Rothschild itself is so unbelievable and tangled that romantic tales about it grew luxuriantly. It is tempting to recount a random selection of the countless anecdotes which circulate. But we must take care not to lose ourselves in them. However, one story which is correct in every detail may be told, because it throws light on the House's methods of work.

Before Rothschild's time merchants paid for their goods in gold or notes. Rothschild simplified the problem by introducing the now universal bill of exchange. Immediately after the reform was launched, Nathan Rothschild presented the

THE CHAINS ARE BROKEN

Bank of England with the first bill of exchange for a large sum, made out to him by James in Paris. However, the bank refused to honour it on the grounds that it was against the rule to honour bills of exchange from private individuals. Nathan took his revenge.

When the bank opened next morning Nathan appeared in person and took up a position by the head cashier's counter. Simultaneously eight of his collaborators stationed themselves in front of the other cashiers' counters and blocked every one of the bank's places for doing business. Rothschild took a five-pound note out of his bursting wallet and asked for it to be changed into gold. Surprised to see the great man himself fetching money the cashier handed over five gold sovereigns with the utmost politeness. Rothschild examined them carefully and slipped them into a leather bag. Then he took out another note and asked to have it changed too. And so he went on. Not only he, but also the eight other members of the firm. It lasted until the bank closed. Naturally the manoeuvre attracted attention, but the surprise became a panic when Rothschild announced that he intended to do the same thing every day for two months in the first instance. On the first day alone he had drained £210,000 pounds from the bank's gold reserves and all other business had been at a standstill. The world's mightiest bank was defenceless against a single man who knew what he wanted and was in a position to accomplish it.

'They have no confidence in my bills of exchange. I have the same right as regards their bank notes,' he said.

The Stock Exchange was highly amused; this was sport. But the bank summoned an emergency meeting of the board and it decided to offer Nathan Rothschild an apology and a statement that in the future the Bank of England would be ready to honour every bill of exchange from the House of Rothschild.

The head office of the firm of N. M. Rothschild is at 2, New Court, St Swithin's Lane, one of the smaller alleys behind the Bank of England in the City of London. Events of worldwide importance have taken place in this modest house. Government loans have been granted and mighty enterprises begun. The men who came to confer with the head of the

firm were treated curtly and firmly. A somewhat conceited statesman from abroad was shown into the holy of holies, the principal's office. Nathan Rothschild sat bowed over his papers. He did not look up and merely said:
'Take a chair.'
'Excuse me,' said the visitor who was not used to being treated so unceremoniously, 'You obviously didn't catch my name. I am —— ——'
'Then take two chairs,' snarled Rothschild.

But if the tone was brusque, great things were happening there, both in Nathan Rothschild's time and when his son Lionel took over the reins. To name examples, it was there that a substantial section of Cecil Rhode's empire building in South Africa started. Its connections reached as far as Spain from which country the Jews had once been driven out. Lionel Rothschild concluded the negotiations with the Spanish government for financing the quicksilver mines at Almadèn and in return was nominated Knight of the Order of Isabella the Catholic. Undoubtedly a gesture to make to a Jew.

The most famous episode in the House's history was the gigantic loan of four million pounds to Disraeli when in 1885 he suddenly saw a chance of acquiring almost half the shares in the Suez Canal and thereby guaranteeing this main artery of the empire for England for a long time to come. Lionel Rothschild heard the request while he was eating dessert after lunch. By the time he had sucked the juice from a grape he had made up his mind. He said yes.

But once the firm set up rigid barriers. When the Russian government wanted a government loan in London, the House of Rothschild clung uncompromisingly to one irrevocable condition—that the pogroms in Russia must be stopped before negotiations began. When that did not take place, they broke off all relations with St Petersburg and virtually cut off the chances of a Russian loan in the City. Perhaps it is not known that Rothschild's refusal had consequences. The Russian government turned to Paris instead of England and obtained the loan they wanted. The result was a strengthening of the friendly relations between Russia and France, which later led to the entente between the two countries.

THE CHAINS ARE BROKEN

But there is one more consequence to be noted. When the Tsarist régime collapsed in 1917 and the Russian government loan stock was quoted at zero, England was spared a loss.

The House of Rothschild continues to flourish to this very day. Obviously the German and Italian branches have long been sawn off, and the Nazi invasion of Austria in 1938 meant that descendants of the House of Rothschild were arrested. Hitler made use of his chance and obtained a loan of a milliard as ransom. But in St Swithin's Lane business went on steadily. As late as 1952, 210 years after the birth of Amschel Meyer Rothschild, the firm set up a subsidiary, the British Newfoundland Corporation with a monopoly of the exploitation of enormous tracts in Labrador and Newfoundland with boundless quantities of uranium and many other materials.

In the general consciousness the House of Rothschild stands as the type of Jewish capitalism. Jews and money belong together, and have done so since the Middle Ages. To be rich as a Jew is a popular saying. The state of Israel will easily make ends meet. World Jewry's excess of wealth is at its disposition. So say both friends and foes of this new country. But when talking about this question it is important, here as always, not only to see things in black and white, as one's sympathies lie, but also to have a sense for nuances and apportion light and shade correctly. How much is there in the chatter?

If we look at the matter historically, we must begin by stating that in Jewry's classical age, in biblical times, the Jew was a farmer, not a merchant. He did not become one until the dispersion. He was forced to it, because Christianity barred all other doors to him. The Jew could not own land or cultivate it, in the towns the guilds and corporations locked him out. Business and dealing in money was his only way out. So the Jew went into trade and in the course of time developed outstanding aptitude as a merchant. But in reality the great majority of Jews were financiers in miniature. True enough in the Middle Ages as in later times there were Rothschilds before the Rothschilds, merchant princes and financial giants who kept the belief that Jews are rich alive.

THE FRUITS OF PEACE

But it is nevertheless a fact that a third of the ghetto's population lived on charity. And as a general rule the rich men's wealth only lasted a short time. Their fortunes were seldom handed down to their sons. Long before that it had either been stolen or confiscated.

But there are two periods in history when Jews played a decisive role in economic development. I have described the first in *The Three Rings* when barter was succeeded by payment in jingling coins, when the Jews began to lend money and take interest on the loans. The other turning point came in the Rothschild's day and coincided with the opening of the epoch of modern industrialism, the nineteenth century (after the Napoleonic wars) when national economy gave way to a world economy. The world had been a small enclosed one. All at once it became big. Modern means of communication and political expansion moved the wings of the world theatre far out to the sides and pushed the backdrop so far away that it could scarcely be seen. It was necessary to find new methods of payment. The old-fashioned transport of gold and silver bullion for cash payment proved impractical and prohibitive. This was where the private banker intervened and arranged payment in bills of exchange and cheques, as we saw in the case of Nathan Rothschild. These private banking firms gave Europe's economic life its special imprint during the first half of the century. In this field the House of Rothschild was only one of many, but it was the one people noticed. Of course we ought to name some of the other Jewish banking houses. There was Solomon in London, a series of Mendelssohns in Germany, descendants of the philosopher, and Jacob H. Schiff in America. It is ironical to think that the descendants of the boy who was banished from Berlin in the 1740's because he had read a German book ended up as prominent bankers and industrial magnates. The family's name is Bleichröder.

The fact that the Jews played the main part is not really remarkable. From time immemorial the ghetto Jew had been forced to occupy himself exclusively with money matters. Usually in a shabby petty degree, second-hand dealer, pedlar and usurer in the same person. But the jump from that to a large-scale financier was only a question of degree. When the wall fell and the Jew went out into the world, he had not only generations of training in financial affairs in his blood, he had also inherited his fathers' enforced talent for adaptation. Now he was free. He looked at conditions with fresh eyes and was ready to find new ways to solve old problems. But the Jew had even more innate qualifications. He was used to being mobile, often on long journeys which had given him international connections. He found his own people in every country. It was easy for him to choose agents to represent him abroad.

The private bankers' achievement was not so much that they themselves provided the necessary capital, as that they made other people's capital mobile. They created a sensitive machinery with the help of which the capital required was procured and made available to industry and trade. In addition the banks were in a position to transfer it from one country to another if the need arose.

But their day was a short one. On the whole they began to flag after 1848 when the big joint-stock banks began to come to the fore. Once again it was Jews who discovered this new form of banking activity, the brothers Isaac and Emile Pereire with their Crédit Mobilier at Paris in 1852.

But money is only a servant. It must work, create values and distribute them. In the gigantic nineteenth-century development of industry, traffic and trade there are many fields where we find Jewish influence quite incommensurate with their numerical representation in the general population. As regards the latter, statistics show that Germany in 1871 had 420,278 Jews, which was 1.2 per cent of the population. In 1925 the figure was 564,379 and the percentage down to 0.9. In other words assimilation had made considerable progress. Spiteful voices whisper that Hitler had only to wait and see. In the course of a generation or two there would not have been many Jews left to plague the German people.

Obviously we must limit ourselves to suggestions when it comes to Jewish contributions to Europe's technical, industrial and commercial progress. But here are some characteristic examples. Sir Isaac Lyon Goldsmid took a prominent part in organizing London's docks, Major Samuel Isaac carried the Mersey Tunnel project through, Sir Ernest Cassel

THE FRUITS OF PEACE

financed the Assuan dam, something Nasser seems to have forgotten, and was the man who started the construction of the London underground. In Germany Emil Rathenau founded the Allgemeine Elektrizäts-Gesellschaft, the world-famous AEG, which gave the country its electricity system. He was the father of Walther Rathenau, the Foreign Secretary who tried to convert Germany to reason after World War I, but fell a victim to pre-Nazi terrorists. We find Jewish influence behind branches of the chemical industry, coal and steel production in Upper Silesia created by Moritz Friedländer, Simon Levy and David Löwenfield. Jews were also connected with the building of railways and shipping. It is enough to name Albert Ballin and his Hamburg-Amerika line.

From ancient times Jewish merchants were interested in the importation of those four staple articles, sugar, tobacco, coffee and tea. In Egypt coffee was simply called the Jews' drink. The cigarette industry in England was founded by Jews. Other Jewish specialities have always been candle-making, diamond-cutting and jewellery.

In the ghetto the Jew played a part as a second-hand dealer. His importance in this field can scarcely be over-estimated. He bought up old clothes, cleaned and repaired them, and sold them to people who could not afford to buy new garments. That meant the majority. So the clothing of the poorer people was in his hands. There are few spheres where the results of industrialization spring to the eye as much as they do with clothing. Today we see the average man, and even more so his sons and daughters, dressed like the rich. Of course the quality of cut and material is poorer, but there is not so much difference. In this social revolution, and it is nothing less, the Jewish tailor has had the same influence as his great-grandfather, the second-hand-dealer in the Ghetto. The countless refugees from Russia meant cheap manpower. Many of them became managers and factory owners. Looms and sewing machines reduced the prices of clothes to a fraction of what they had been. The same injection of Jewish industriousness and initiative can be shown in the boot and shoe, and furniture industries.

Selling the goods was just as important as producing them.

THE CHAINS ARE BROKEN

That modern phenomenon of sales technique the big store was the brain-child of Jewish business men. We only have to think of Lewis and Marks and Spencers' in London, Tietz and Wertheim in Berlin and the Nordiska Kompaniet in Stockholm. The modern popular large restaurant works on the same mass-distribution principle. The cheap and popular Lyons in London was founded by a Jew.

While the February revolution's storm swept through Paris in 1848 and carried all before it, the Comédie Française was re-christened the Théâtre de la République. Every night it was filled to overflowing, not so much for the play which was on as to be there at the finale. When the curtain fell, a young proud actress stepped forward, dressed as the genius of France and sang the Marseillaise. When she came to the third verse about the holy love of the fatherland, she suddenly unfolded her gown. Lo and behold it was the tricolor. She had wrapped herself in the three-coloured flag of liberty. Amidst tumultuous enthusiasm the audience joined in the singing of the revolution's immortal hymn.

The actress was Elisa Rachel Levin, known simply as Rachel by everybody. It was quite natural in Paris in 1848 for the people to see themselves symbolized in the figure of a Jewess. And today, a hundred years after her death—she died in 1858—Rachel still ranks as one of the great, perhaps the greatest of all tragediennes on the world stage.

This lovely flower grew in a muddy ditch. Her cradle stood in the inn le Soleil d'Or (the Golden Sun) in a village in Switzerland. Her father was a pedlar and trudged from village to village with his chest on his back. He had permanent stalls in market places in both Switzerland and Germany. Later he took the family to France where they lived for a time in Lyons, but later settled in Paris. The mother helped to earn their daily bread; she sold needles and silk ribbons from door to door. The amount the parents could scrape together was not enough, so their two daughters, the elder Sara and the little skinny Rachel slipped into coffee houses and inns where they played the guitar and sang. After each number they gathered up the small change the clients threw to them.

On one of the occasions we call coincidences the director

of the Royal Conservatoire in Paris heard the nine-year-old Rachel. He was what we call a talent-spotter today and realized at once that he had discovered something out of the ordinary. There was talent in this little frozen emaciated girl. He tested her, found that her talent lay in the direction of recitation and put her in the hands of an eminent teacher, Saint Aulaire. It was a thorny path for the weakly girl with the perpetual cough. She was hungry and ragged, but full of energy. She got a modest job with the Théâtre Français. New obstacles cropped up. Her patron died unexpectedly. And when she at long last made her debut in vaudeville at the Gymnase, it was not a success. The director of the Théâtre Français, Provost, was in the audience. After the performance he advised the girl that she had better sell flowers.

In her despair she went to a well-known Jewish actor, Samson. He was the first to see in which direction her wonderful talent lay; she was a born tragedienne. Samson studied the great tragic roles with her; he was her indefatigable spokesman at the Comédie Française and finally persuaded the theatre to let her make her real début as Camille in Corneille's *Les Horaces*. It was an unheard-of sensation, a success so brilliant that Paris lay at her feet from that evening. France's leading critic wrote: 'There is no surprise and no triumph to be compared with this evening.' When Rachel came out into the wings after the final curtain with her arms full of flowers, she met Provost. She curtsied coquettishly and said:

'Look, I followed your advice. Now I'm selling flowers.'

France had got its great tragedienne. She brought the forgotten classical dramatists, Corneille and Racine, into fashion again and acted them with a genius which packed the theatre; people stood in long queues to buy tickets. With her sculptural carriage, the tremendous pathos she put into her recitations and her severe marble face Rachel gave the classical tragedy new life. The annals of the drama know no triumph like her *Phèdre*. A hundred times she played the part which is described as 'a revelation of human suffering which is never forgotten by the man who has seen it'.

She made money, fabulous sums, both in Paris and on tours in Europe. In St Petersburg in the middle of a severe winter admirers covered the stairs to her dressing-room with flowers. What a change from the freezing girl in shabby inns! Of course Rachel was envied by some; intrigues and ambushes lay in wait for her. She had her vulnerable points, she who loved glory and wealth. Her father managed her financial affairs and was hard and demanding. The daughter got the blame for her father's actions.

As with all children of the stage people loved to pry into her private life. And Rachel made no secret of the fact that she had numerous love affairs. Her lovers were men of high rank. Napoleon's natural son, Count Colonna-Walewski, gave her a son whom she loved dearly. Rachel always refused to marry. 'I only want tenants, not owners,' she said.

But in one thing she was above all criticism. Rachel never disowned her Jewish origin and remained a Jewess until her death. The distinguished circles she moved in hoped that they could convert the great actress to Christianity. First and foremost Louis Philippe's Queen, Maria Amalie. When Rachel once asked the Queen for a Favour, the answer was:

'Yes, if Rachel is converted first.'

The Archbishop of Paris dearly longed to bring her into the fold, but she stood firm in the face of all attempts at persuasion. Once she had to recite a scene in Madame Récamier's salon with the words: 'I see, I know, I believe.' When she spotted the archbishop among the guests, she cut the line out. She did not want to arouse false hopes in him. Even the Tsar of Russia tried his hand with the same result.

Rachel's career was as short as it was brilliant. From her childhood she battled against tuberculosis. No doctor could heal her. During a tour in America the disease got the upper hand. She sought a cure in Egypt but came home even sicker. For three years she was bed-ridden; it was such a long-drawn-out fight against death that her friends could hardly bear to see her. Rachel was not thirty-eight when death finally released her. As with every Jew, her last words were: 'Shmah Israel.' (Hear Israel, the Lord our God, the Lord is one.) The mourners included everyone of importance in France, actors, poets, journalists and politicians; they all followed the Jewish actress to her grave in the cemetery of Père Lachaise. Even

THE FRUITS OF PEACE

today one still finds fresh flowers on her grave.

It is a concomitant of homelessness and a perpetually vagabond existence that the Jew is often forced to re-orientate himself in new curroundings. In almost every generation for two thousand years many Jews have moved into an alien world of unknown ideas and customs, and met men who worked from quite different premises from their own. We have seen how this innate ability for adaptation produced results in trade. But it also turned a strikingly large number of Jews into actors and actresses. Mainly the latter. No one can say why for certain. Rachel was one of them. Her destiny runs strangely parallel to that of Johanne Luise Heiberg, the Danish stage's greatest artist. She too was born a Jewess and grew up in a dirty poor home, but ended as the queen of Danish intellectual life. In subsequent generations names like Sarah Bernhardt and Elisabeth Bergner shine.

Music is close to the art of the stage. Moreover it has always been the Jew's favourite art form. It lives among the common people and is as necessary as bread. So it is not surprising that there are almost swarms of Jews among practising musicians. Among creative artists we can point to Mendelssohn-Bartholdy, Giacomo Meyerbeer and Jacques Offenbach.

Obviously we cannot keep statistics of intellectual life. The wind bloweth where it listeth. We hear its sough, but we do not know where it comes from or where it is going. But nevertheless it is quite surprising to discover that of the forty-four Germans who won the Nobel Prize before the fatal year 1933, eleven were of Jewish stock. Even the briefest survey of European cultural life during the period after the chains were broken shows to what extent the emancipation bore fruit for everyone's benefit. We think of writers such as Jacob Wasserman, Lionel Feuchtwanger, Emil Ludwig, Arnold and Stefan Zweig, Franz Werfel, Ernst Toller, Arthur Schnitzler, Marcel Proust, Henri Bernstein and André Maurois. And above the exact sciences shines a name like Albert Einstein, the man who said in an ironical moment that if his theory of relativity proved correct, Germany would claim that he was German, France that he was a world

THE CHAINS ARE BROKEN

citizen. But if it proved wrong, France would say that he was German and Germany that he was a Jew.

In previous volumes of this history of the Jews I have often mentioned that the Jews worked as doctors. Medicine and the art of healing were often an almost exclusively Jewish occupation. We catch a glimpse of modern Jewish medicine if we read an amusing ironical article by a Christian doctor in Riga:

'A Nazi who has caught syphilis cannot let himself be treated with salvarsan, because salvarsan was discovered by the Jew Ehrlich. Indeed, even its diagnosis is unjustifiable, because the Wassermann test is also a Jew's work. If the patient is suspected of having gonorrhoea he must not investigate the bacilli causing the disease, because the doctors, Neisser and others, who discovered gonococci, were Jews. If he suffers from a weak heart, he must avoid using the classical remedy, digitalis. For that was found by Ludwig Traube. If he has toothache he must not have a cocaine injection, for that was the discovery of Karl Koller. Typhus could not be treated, for that meant using the methods of the Jews Vidal and Weil. If he suffers from diabetis, he must do without insulin which was the direct result of the researches of the Jew Minkowski. If he has a headache, he must not use pyramidon or antipyrin, because Spiro and Filehne were Jews. If he suffers from fits, he is incurable, because the only effective cure, chloral hydrate, was discovered by the Jew Oscar Leibreich. The same sort of thing applies in the field of psychiatry. Psychoanalysis is the work of the Jew Freud.'

The article went on at even greater length, but we have surely heard enough. If the author had written it today, he could have added the anti-polio vaccine which the American Jew, Dr Salk, produced.

Karl Marx was a Jew, but only by birth. He was born in 1818 in a totally assimilated home. His father, a typical Rhineland lawyer, had been baptized two years before the birth of his famous son and took care that he too was baptized at the age of six. So the boy grew up in surroundings

THE FRUITS OF PEACE

which were quite alien to Jewry. Under the influence of Hegel the most radical political and social ideas soon conquered the young highly-talented Marx. It cost him many a stay in prison. In 1848 he was an enthusiastic participant in the revolution. In the same year he collaborated with Engels in writing the Communist Manifesto with the opening words: 'Workers of the world, unite!' When reaction followed the revolution, Marx had to leave Germany. He sought refuge in Paris, but as he took part in revolutionary activities there as well, the French government expelled him. Finally he found asylum in England where he found the peace necessary for a productive literary life which lasted for years. One of the fruits was his great work, *Das Kapital*.

But he was ignorant about Jewry. Just as ignorant as many Christians are about his Communism. To them he is a Jew and his ideas Jewish. But Marx was not only alien to his fathers' people; unlike Disraeli, who was also baptized as a child, he actually hated them. He identified Jews with the Rothschilds. One of the few remarks about them to be found in his works was made when he was about twenty-five and reads:

'The Hebrew faith repels me. What is the basis of Jewry? Self-interest. What do the Jews live by? They are dealers. What God do they worship? Money.'

Although born a Jew, Ferdinand Lassalle was just as un-Jewish as Marx. Even he was not really sure whether he had been baptized as a child. Lassalle was a few years younger than Marx, but although he became one of the revolution's zealous standard bearers, also under Hegel's influence, the two were bitterly opposed to each other. Lassalle's life was a restless one; he was the eternal agitator—'the terrible Jew' people called him, afraid of his ideas. But German Social Democracy honours him as its father. In 1863 he founded the German Workers' Union which gave birth to the party.

A bloody full stop marked the sudden end of his passionate and romantically fascinating life. He loved a girl and she loved him, but her father forced her to marry another. Lassalle challenged his successful rival to a duel. He was fatally wounded by the first shot. He was only thirty-eight.

It was the Liberal Party which supported the Jews in their

THE CHAINS ARE BROKEN

fight for emancipation. So it was quite natural for the majority of Jews to join their champions once they had got the vote. But not all of them. Quite a few Jews were members of the Conservative Party, both in England and Germany. It was a Jew, Friedrich Julius Stahl, who developed the Conservative Party's doctrines in Prussia. Ironically enough it can be said that two Jews were the spiritual fathers of the proletarians and the Junkers respectively, Marx and Stahl.

The politicians' most distinguished weapon is the press and the Jewish contribution to modern newspapers is a not unimportant chapter in their history. Many lively young Jews, newly escaped from the ghetto, found an outlet for their powers in the press. We often know our own influence by the reaction of our opponents. Hitler and his cronies angrily labelled the liberal press 'Jewish newspapers'. They were not entirely wrong; there were liberal newspapers owned by Jewish capital and a long line of distinguished journalists were of Jewish stock.

It was J. M. Levy who started the *Daily Telegraph* and so laid the foundations of a more popular paper. The modern news service, transmitted via news agencies, was created by Jewish journalistic pioneers such as Reuter, Wolff and Havas. In Germany the Ullstein firm owned the *Berliner Tageblatt* and the *Vossische Zeitung*, while important papers such as the *Frankfurter Zeitung* and the Viennese *Neue Freie Presse* were also in Jewish hands.

The tree is known by its fruit. And a hasty tour through many spheres of European life, like the one we have just made, merely confirms that the fruits emancipation bore were both seminal and nourishing.

VIII

HEP ! HEP !

HEP! HEP! is anti-Semitism's signature tune. That was the cry a little less than a thousand years ago when the Crusaders stormed the Jewish districts in the German towns on the banks of the Rhine. Before they risked their lives in the bloody war against the heathen Saracens in the East, they wanted to settle with Christ's oldest enemies in the West. In my book *The Three Rings*, you can read what the sombre consequences were for Europe's Jewry. But the cry of hep-hep did not die with the Middle Ages. The ominous words rang out again in many towns in Germany and neighbouring countries during the sudden anti-Jewish hysteria in 1819. And it is still heard today wherever public feeling boils over with agitation and hate.

Strangely enough no one knows exactly what the cry means. One theory is that it is made up of the initial letters of *Hierosolyma est perdita* (Jerusalem is lost). Others are convinced that it comes from the Old German cry *Hab, hab!* (Give, give!), the rest of the sentence, 'tax to the Emperor', being left unsaid. As a curiosity I mention that a celebrated etymologist interprets it as the call used to summon goats in France. It was applicable to the Jews because their beards were like goats' beards! The Jews did not always listen to the challenge in silence. Sometimes they shouted back: 'Jep, jep!', another contraction, this time of *Jesus est perditus* (Jesus is lost).

The cry Hep, hep! is old and its meaning uncertain. The word anti-Semitism on the other hand is new and no one can doubt what it implies. In fact it only dates from 1879. In that year a slim volume, little more than a pamphlet, lay on

THE CHAINS ARE BROKEN

the counters of German booksellers. The title was: *Der Sieg des Judentums über das Germanentum* (The Victory of Jewry over Teutonism) and it was a libel, a spiteful attack on the German Jews.

The author was William Marr and he himself had been one of them. I am almost tempted to say 'naturally'. For the phenomenon of its bitterest and most dangerous enemies being former Jews has followed Jewry like a shadow for two thousand years. Bitter, because their apostasy rankled with them, and they tried to drown the voice of conscience, dangerous, because they knew Jewry from inside and where to hit hardest. Wilhelm Marr was the son of a Jewish actor; he had accepted baptism and moved in a circle of radical journalists. Not for long, because the others ejected him, to be quite frank on grounds of dishonest conduct. But his book was a success; it became the year's best seller and went into many editions.

Its epigraph is *Vae victis!* (Woe to the conquered!). And the conquered are the Teutons, the conquerors the Jews. We read how a Jewish group of peoples, who had made themselves hated everywhere in the East, were torn from the soil of Palestine by a Roman Emperor's fiat and transplanted in Europe. There the Semites set to work to put everyone else under their yoke. They succeeded. Like the born materialists they are, they quickly usurped power over trade and industry, and won wealth and might. First and foremost they had made Germany their target and the country was now well on the way to becoming *verjudet* (Jewishized). They not only dominated capital, but also the press and through it public opinion. The Liberal Party obeyed them, the legislative assembly was their servant, soon they would also hold the reins of government. Just as the Mongols once subjugated China, the Jews would conquer Germany. With one difference, that whereas the Mongols ended up by becoming Chinese, the intention was to make the Germans Jews. Semitism had already conquered Teutonism. It was the last moment for the Germans to arise and ward off the disaster, otherwise they were faced with *Finis Germaniae* (the end of Germany). The stir the book caused was crystallized by the formation of a League of Anti-Semites which was to save the German fatherland from the threatening danger. The society's periodical was entitled *Zwanglose antisemitische Hefte* (roughly, numbers of an anti-Semitic magazine appearing at irregular intervals).

Wilhelm Marr has the honour of being the man who let the word anti-Semitism out of the stable. We meet it here for the first time. Later it was taken into the language as a name for hatred of the Jews. In reality it is misused, for there are other Semites besides the Jews. But the vital thing about the word is that this time people were not against the Jews for their unbelief, i.e. on religious grounds, as the Catholic church was for many centuries, but hated them as a race which was an alien ethnical element in Germany. This was something entirely new in Jewish history.

When Wilhelm Marr's book came out in 1879, it was not new. The first edition actually appeared as early as 1873. But then the book attracted no attention and it took six whole years to sell out the edition. Only with the second impression in 1879 did it come to the fore. For events had happened which had made the situation ripe for the great breakthrough of modern anti-Semitism. Germany was its motherland; from there it spread through other European countries and flew across the sea to distant continents.

When the newly created German Empire—'the second Reich'—dictated its harsh conditions to France in 1871, it started an epoch in Europe whose consequences the present-day world still has not managed to escape. *Blut und eisen, die gepanzerte Faust* (Blood and iron, the armoured fist) had conquered. Prussia's official historian, Heinrich von Treitschke, taught that the country which has shown itself strongest in history is in the right for that very reason. In Germany the concept of the state had become a new fetish and the various countries of Europe entered the epoch of the armaments race. An armed peace was the only one anyone believed in. And into this complex of lethally dangerous possibilities filtered industrialization with all the sweeping changes which followed in its wake and the increasingly bitter clash between capital and labour. The world entered on the age of the class struggle. Obviously all this had consequences for the Jews, primarily the German Jews.

THE CHAINS ARE BROKEN

As the reader will remember their emancipation coincided with the establishment of the German Empire. And they saw it as their natural duty to put themselves immediately at the service of the new Germany. Their assimilation was already so far advanced that they felt as one with *das grosse Vaterland* (the great fatherland), in fact they did everything to prove themselves more German than the Germans. Jewish arrogance was effaced. The conflict between the orthodox and the reformers had already split solidly built religious unity and the chill spiritual breeze, which put out the light of so many religions and swept over the whole of Europe during these decades, had a disastrous effect on the German Jews who wanted to share in the latest developments. If they had been farmers with their national centre of gravity in the country, they would have kept their balance better. For it is a time-honoured experience that the currents of fashion are weakened once they come out into the open country. But from ancient times the Jews had been huddled together in narrow alleys in the towns which had let them in. And now the stream of new arrivals went to the big cities, especially the new capital of the empire. In 1871 Berlin had 36,000 Jewish inhabitants. By 1880 the number had jumped to 54,000 and it was to go on rising steeply for many decades. And wherever there are large numbers of Jews, there is always danger in store for them.

The first squall to give warning of the storm which was on the way hit the country in 1873. It appeared on the economic front. The victory over France and the incredibly high compensation which the conquered had to pay—and actually did pay at a far quicker rate than anyone had thought possible—naturally created a boom in Germany. It did not bring much prosperity in its train. A fever spread; everyone wanted to earn easy money; new companies were formed; they shot up like mushrooms. They were built on a scale hitherto unknown, yet everything petered out in gambles, imaginary projects and swindles. The word *Gründer* (founder) acquired a tinge of humbug about it which has remained. The inevitable crash came in 1873 and whirled countless spectators into the abyss. As always on such occasions the middle classes were hit the hardest.

HEP! HEP!

The Jews were singled out as the guilty ones. *Der Jud ist schuld*. Naturally there had been many, many Jews among the speculators on the Stock Exchange who danced in the rout around the golden calf. Undoubtedly a disproportionately large proportion of the German Jews were business men. But they were still few in comparison with the others, often people with prominent names, including many noble ones with great reputations. But no one gave that a thought in the heat of the moment. It must have been the 'golden International' which provided the secret backers of the catastrophe, the Jewish capitalists' international society, just as Catholics and socialists had their black and red Internationals.

Obviously such an explosion never comes unheralded. The explosive is matured during a long incubation period. In Germany dislike and envy of the Jews had accumulated. People whispered that wherever you pointed in the community, your finger picked out a Jew, and most strikingly in the press. Influential papers with large circulations such as the *Berliner Tageblatt* and the *Frankfurter Zeitung* were published and written by Jews. In reality these young journalists had broken away from their origins long ago. But no one gave that a thought; they *were* Jews.

'The Jews have seized the press!' was the cry and even reactionary papers like the *Kreuzzeitung*, the feudal landowners' sheet, and the Catholic Centre's *Germania* were labelled Jewish, i.e. non-German, regardless of the fact that their articles were mostly ultra-national. But it was not only the press. The Jews were infiltrating everywhere. Just look how the Jewish moneyed aristocracy was rising. There were Jews in many fields, even in government offices. In the street no one could help seeing signs with Jewish names which intimated that here lived a doctor, a dentist or a lawyer. So even the liberal professions were threatened.

Painful as all this was, it was only a pinprick in comparison with what happened when the Jews got into trouble on the political front. The liberal parties had helped them to win political freedom and the Jews rallied behind them. They turned out to be a good horse to back, because a favourable wind was blowing for the Liberals in Germany. As from 1867 Bismarck had had to make an alliance with them in order to

THE CHAINS ARE BROKEN

ensure the parliamentary majority needed to achieve German unity under the Empire. But in the 70's the wind began to blow from a new direction.

Bismarck himself, the gigantic figure in German politics for almost the last half of the century, cast a by no means unfriendly eye on the Jews. After all it was he who had given them emancipation, not only out of political necessity, but also because he sympathized with them. On several occasions during his career he solemnly condemned anti-Semitic agitation. In 1878, when the Congress of Berlin made the terms after the Russo-Turkish War, the Iron Chancellor was at the height of his career, he was 'the arbiter of Europe'. Bismarck forced through a clause in the peace treaty signed by the great European powers ordering Rumania, Serbia and Bulgaria to repeal all laws discriminating against the Jews. Indeed in one of his none too frequent cheerful moments he remarked that 'the offspring of a German stallion and a Jewish mare' could easily turn out well. He might well have been thinking of recommending the combination to his sons. Bismarck believed that when the Jews interbred with the German race they would act as an effervescent element which have to be paid considerable attention. He himself was on terms of personal friendship with many Jews. But internal political intrigues drove Bismarck into the arms of anti-Semitic parties. And this had bitter consequences for the German Jews.

They had already made enemies in the Reichstag. We need only mention that the reactionary and chauvinist parties recruited rom the landowning and officer classes looked on the Jews as a class of the community which was critical of their feudal ideas. The triumphantly advancing middle class, which supported liberalism and numbered many Jews among it, was viewed by them with deep aversion. But the Jews had also quarrelled with the Catholic church and with it the powerful Centre Party. When Bismarck conducted his celebrated *Kulturkampf* (Cultural battle) and reduced Catholic influence by the May and Falk Laws passed in 1872 and 1875, he had collaborated with the Liberals and also with the Jews. In return this made the church's traditional hate felt, this time on the political front.

HEP! HEP!

In 1878 Bismarck broke with the Liberals. The Conservatives had a great success at an election and the Iron Chancellor found it opportune to ally himself with the reactionaries in order to put a brake on the dangerously growing Social Democrats. We have come to the turning point. We can say that this is when anti-Semitism was born, even if the word first came into the world the following year through Wilhelm Marr's activities as an author.

Deep down inside Bismarck was a dyed-in-the-wool reactionary from his youth. His Liberal period had only been a parenthesis, a waltz he danced out of political necessity. When it was over, he had to rely on his Junkers from the East Elbe, an attitude the old Emperor approved of with all his heart. In return the Chancellor had the whole weight of the Liberal opposition against him—the Liberals whom every honest reactionary regarded as the discovery of the Jews. In fact two of their spokesmen, Eduard Lasker and Ludwig Bamberger, actually were Jews! Was further proof needed? It became all too tempting to use anti-Semitism as a batteringram in the political battle against the opposition. In an atmosphere which was heavy with reaction, militarism and chauvinism, things rapidly so arranged themselves that the soil was ready for the growth of anti-Semitism.

Now we can understand why Wilhelm Marr's scurrilous anti-Jewish pamphlet had a greater success in 1879 than it had in 1873. It appeared at an opportune moment and they were strong men who had a use for it.

Deutschland erwache! (Germany awake!). This cry, which Naziism was later to endow with bloody notoriety, was first coined by a Protestant clergyman, Adolf Stöcker, the court chaplain in Berlin, who became one of anti-Semitism's standard bearers. He came from a poor family in the German provinces, but swept to the heights of an ecclesiastical career. He took holy orders in Berlin where his church had massive congregations and he was promoted to court chaplain before he was forty, for there was use for him in the highest places. Stöcker had sociological interests and was at the head of the so-called *Stadtmission*, a Christian-Socialist movement, which worked among Berlin's teeming working classes. The government were on the look-out for a man who was in a position to split the Social Democrats or at least turn the workers' attention in another direction. So they watched indulgently when Stöcker founded his Christian-Socialist workers' party in 1879. Stöcker tried to square the circle. His party combined socialistic with conservative ideas and tried to lead the masses' discontent away from Marxist propaganda.

The attempt failed and was doomed to failure. The Berlin workers did not respond to Stöcker's call. He had to delete the word 'workers' from the party name. The Christian-Socialist party, as it was now called, gradually included a number of members of the Reichstag and the Diet, and also had quite a lot or supporters among the petty bourgeoisie, shopkeepers, artisans, shop assistants and officials. In other words the very class which had inherited their hostile attitude to the Jews from the guilds and corporations. Not for nothing did the same kind of people give Hitler their enthusiastic *Ja* half a century later.

Stöcker was undeniably a man of some stature. He was eloquent and ready-witted, a first-class debater and in addition a well-meaning zealous minister of the church. There is much in his social endeavours to demand our respect. But something inside him short-circuited when the conversation turned to the Jews. In them he saw the arch-enemy. He inveighed against them with impassioned venom from both pulpit and platform. It was Stöcker's agitation which put the Jewish problem on the agenda in the Reichstag and all the other German-speaking countries.

It is embarrassing and unpleasant to study the gibberish this minister pumped into his attentive congregation. The Jews were responsible for both capitalism and Marxist socialism; from above and below they were working to destroy the existing order. They boasted of having a universal mission. But where did one find their missionaries? On the Stock Exchange. One find day Nathan would disappear behind the figure of Shylock. Like the honest Christian Stöcker undoubtedly was, he naturally knew the words of St Paul: 'Here be neither Jews nor Greeks', and bowed to them. Consequently he did not agree with the new doctrine of war against an alien race, but recommended the ill-natured Jews to be con-

HEP! HEP!

verted and become good Christians. Nevertheless racial hatred shines through when he preaches that German blood contains the German soul, whereas 'modern Jewry is alien blood in the German body and it is of a destructive nature'. All the others can merge with the people they live among, except the Jew. His strict Semitism, inflexible ritual laws and hostility to the Christians is diametrically opposed to the German temperament. Stöcker is not ashamed of painting the devil on the wall when he describes the almighty Jewish International, full of ineradicable hatred of Christianity.

Adolf Stöcker had his academic counterpart in Professor Heinrich Treitschke, also a man in a high position—as I mentioned before he was the Prussian historiographer. More than anyone else the erudite professor personified the ideas which inspired Bismarck and the whole era of the Emperor Wilhelm. His lectures on German history were attended by a select public from Germany's highest aristocracy. Rightly so, for in them German nationalism was given a historical justification, equally convincing logically, temperamentally and for the wealth of knowledge displayed. Treitschke's religion was Germany, its temple Prussia; in its holy of holies the Hohenzollerns, monarchs by the grace of God, worshipped.

Wilhelm Marr's book found its way into the professor's study. In it Treitschke heard the 'people's voice' rise in warning. He undertook to give its ideas the best scientific expression he could. He did this in a book called *Ein Wort über unser Judentum* (A Word about our Jewry), but he also raised his voice on one of the most distinguished street corners for public German discussion, the *Preussiche Jahrbücher*, which he edited. This is what could be read in three papers:

'Year after year, a swarm of trouser-selling youngsters crowds over our eastern frontiers from the inexhaustible Polish cradle, youngsters whose children and grand-children will dominate Germany's Stock Exchanges and newspapers one fine day.'

And he goes on to describe how the new arrivals cannot become German and the Jews born locally *will* not, because they feel superior as a race to the German *goyim*, the heathens. With a sure sense of style Treitschke altered Heine's saying that 'Jewry is a misfortune' and gave it a quite different meaning:

'Die Juden sind unser Unglück! (The Jews are our misfortune!).

That was how Treitschke's fatal words went. In the not too distant future they were to re-echo from countless Nazi posters and be bellowed from the throats of the brown battalions' *Sprech-Chöre* (the SA men's choruses).

Of course the great historian was no vulgar anti-Semite. He considered that it was out of the question to annul emancipation; instead he claimed in increasingly strong words that the Jews must be prepared to become a hundred per cent German. There was no room in the German fatherland for any Jewish special nationality. And he pointed out firmly that the Jews had acquired their freedom, not as a people, but as a religious minority. If they wanted more, there was only one way open to them, the way out of Germany, for there was no place on German soil for double nationality.

With these sharp words Treitschke had gone to the roots of the German Jews' tragic problem, and he speared with his pen the eternally gnawing dilemma: the German Jews must choose between nation and religion, they must be either Germans or Jews. Naturally the same thing applied outside Germany's frontiers. The bloody issue of exile was laid bare.

Both Stöcker and Treitschke were answered. Another world famous historian, Theodor Mommsen, author of the celebrated *History of Rome*, wrote his *Auch ein Wort über unser Judentum* (Another Word about our Jewry), obviously directed straight at his colleague Treitschke, and repudiated his spiteful words. But Mommsen agreed with his colleague that it was the Jews' sacred duty, without reservation, to join the German people. In the ancient Roman Empire, the Jews had been, as he put it in his academic language, 'a ferment of cosmopolitanism and national decomposition', in other words a kind of bacillus which made national distinctions disappear. Mommsen did not mean to say by this that the Jews had had a disintegrating effect but that they had been a healthy uniting influence. The same thing could happen in the German empire, provided the Jews would go all the way and become Germans. Providence had seen that German metal needed a certain percentage of Israel for its casting. It was the same thing as Bismarck had said, but in different words. Mommsen had great hopes that it would turn out like that, and pointed to the rising number of mixed marriages between Germans and Jews.

More of Germany's greatest men besides Mommsen turned away from anti-Semitism. Nietzsche was one of them. To be sure he despised the Jews at first. For the slavish Christian morality stemmed from them, the morality he loathed with all his might. But he changed and learnt to value the Jews, even if he was never blind to typically Jewish inferior characteristics. Here is a quotation which shows both sides:

'Every nation, every individual has unpleasant, even dangerous characteristics and it would be cruel to demand that the Jews alone should be an exception to the rule. Even if these characteristics in their case are particularly frightening and dangerous—perhaps the young Stock Exchange Jew is mankind's most loathsome discovery—yet I wonder how much we ought to bear with a people who not without our guilt have had an unparalleled tale of woe and whom the world must thank for the noblest men, the brightest sages, the greatest of all books and the most effective moral law.'

And with an ironic smile he remarked on another occasion:

'It is a benefit to meet a Jew especially when one lives among Germans.'

Once a hole is made in a dam, it only takes seconds for the flood-wave to sweep all before it; it tears all obstacles to pieces, pushes them aside and pours forth in violent fury. That was the kind of horrifying drama a surprised world witnessed when budding German anti-Semitism suddenly threw off its academic cloak and the spectre of hatred for the Jews was revealed in all its hideous nakedness. Elemental passions were whipped up by unscrupulous agitators and given free rein. Old jealousies and resentments, envy and discontent combined with inferiority complexes and exploded. The prelude to the Nazi persecution of the Jews had its beginning in the years after 1880.

Eugen Dühring can rightly be called the grandfather of the Nazi ideology. Like so many anti-Semites he was a disappointed warped man who hammered away with morbid fury at the defenceless opponents he suspected of being guilty of his misfortune. He was a gifted philosophical thinker, but he had a pathological streak in his mind which made him see red if a Jew crossed his path. Dühring had been professor of philosophy at the University of Berlin, but was dismissed because of his anti-religious agitation. In addition two of his Jewish colleagues had voted for his dismissal. Dühring had always been a bitter critic of Christianity and he regarded it as a product of the Jewish spirit, i.e. of Jewry. No sooner did he hear of the Jewish professors' part in his dismissal than he threw in his lot wholly with the anti-Semites. The result of this curious marriage between a professor of philosophy and vulgar anti-Semitism was the appearance in 1881 of a book entitled *Die Judenfrage als Rassen-, Sitten und Kulturfrage* (The Jewish Question as a Problem of Race, Morals and Culture).

In this book people were informed that the Jew is the most insignificant twig on the Semites' racial tree. Even Tacitus understood this and abominated them. Of course this despicable element has never given the world anything of value. What the Jew calls his own he has appropriated from others. The Bible's view of the world is not only far below Hellenic culture, but it is even inferior to the German mythology of antiquity. The Jew is worthless in every field connected with the intellect, he has no feeling for science, is an inferior philosophical thinker, is not capable of creative work in mathematics or art, not even in music. Allegiance to and reverence for that which is lofty and great is unknown to him. Yet this incompetent people tries to exploit mankind. Dühring goes on as follows:

'It should be the Nordic people's duty to exterminate these parasites, as we exterminate snakes and beasts of prey.'

HEP! HEP!

Provisionally the state should exclude them from the press, schools and trade, mixed marriages should be subject to a high tax to prevent the misfortune of German blood becoming *verjudet*. But the final goal must be to subject this inferior race to a new Egyptian thralldom and degrade the Jews to the pariahs they are.

Dühring's book presaged the hurricane which was to wipe out German Jewry half a century later. But even when the book came out, a storm blew up; Marr's and Stöcker's agitation had left its traces. The Christian-Socialist party worked zealously against the Jews in the Reichstag and Diet, while the League of Anti-Semites infested the streets. Noisy meetings were held; people with a Jewish appearance were molested in restaurants and railway carriages. The movement spread rapidly among the students. In the *Verein deutscher Studenten* (Society of German Students) members promised not to associate with Jewish students; there was a bare empty space around them in the lecture halls. If they felt insulted and challenged their assailant to a duel, it was refused. A Jew was not worthy to meet a genuine German with weapon in hand. A great stir was caused when a Berlin clergyman refused to be sworn in by a Jewish judge. Stöcker defended his colleague, it was the outcome of justifiable feelings of conscience, he declared. Women's societies which boycotted Jewish shops shot up. It was by no means uncommon for a Jewish shopkeeper to find '*Jude. Deutsche, kauft nicht bei den Juden!* (Jew. Germans, do not buy from the Jews!) painted on the window when he opened his shop in the morning.

It did not take long for the commotion to degenerate into physical violence. There was good reason why the judge Eugen Richter had long ago shouted at the anti-Semitic agitators:

'Do not rouse the wild beast in mankind, for nothing will stop it.'

But the incendiary orators could not be cooled down. And the inevitable happened. The agitation was not satisfied with words but turned into action. One winter day the synagogue in Neustettin was burnt to the ground. A few days previously a travelling agitator, formerly a teacher—dismissed for what was cautiously called improper behaviour—had incited the

THE CHAINS ARE BROKEN

people to acts of violence. A judicial enquiry decided that the incendiary was a drunken blacksmith who had been egged on by the teacher. Two months later a well-known citizen of the town, a lawyer, attacked the editor of the town's Liberal newspaper, who was a Jew, in the open street. The lawyer called to people to help him and they did so willingly. When the Jew had been given a thorough beating-up the incensed mob continued, breaking the windows of Jewish houses and looting some shops. The example of Neustettin was infectious. Similar occurrences happened in one town after another. Richter had indeed uttered prophetic words. The wild beast cannot be stopped once it has acquired a taste for blood.

So we need not be surprised that the mediaeval cock-and-bull story about Jewish ritual murder cropped up again in modern Germany. Not once, but many times. The corpse of a five-year-old boy with his throat cut was found in the little Rhineland town of Xanten. The rumour spread that he had been murdered for religious reasons and that the Jews were behind the crime. The police arrested the town's Jewish butcher as a suspect. The whole of the anti-Semitic press gave the alarm. Throughout the empire meetings were held which addressed resolutions to the Minister of Justice asking for legal prosecution. There was a violent debate in the Reichstag. The case dragged on for twelve days; a host of witnesses were heard. At last the verdict was pronounced. The butcher was acquitted unanimously. But both he and many other Jewish families found themselves forced to move away from Xanten.

As late as 1900 a Christian schoolboy was found murdered in the Prussian town of Konitz, also with his throat cut. On top of this it was at Easter, always the classic time for ritual murder. It was said that Christian blood had to be baked in the unleavened Easter bread. But there were many sinister clues. The boy had been in love with the Jewish butcher's daughter. So the case was clear to the anti-Semitic yellow press and it squeezed the lemon to the last drop. One of the witnesses was convicted of perjury and the enquiry disclosed other scandalous conduct by the rabble. But nothing could silence them. They went on screaming. Disturbances took place which were so violent that troops had to be called in to restore order in the town.

But of course the anti-Semites were not satisfied with turning the street upside down. They had their representatives in both Reichstag and Diet, and made their voices heard there. In 1880 one of them, a clergyman again, said in the Bavarian Diet:

'If the honourable members want to help the starving population, they only need to pass a single short law. It would read: Every Jewish pedlar should be either shot or hanged.'

Such speeches were naturally pure foolishness, but they had a serious background. For the anti-Semites were well schooled in the methods of *Realpolitik*. Their big congresses were front-page news in the papers and in the winter of 1880-1881 they proceeded to direct action. They started a campaign to collect signatures from all over the empire for a petition which they hoped would produce a decision. In it they claimed that the government should proceed to limit Jewish immigration, that Jews should be removed from public office, that only Christian teachers should be appointed in schools and that special statistics about the Jews in Germany should be introduced. The whole anti-Semitic propaganda machine was set in motion; mass meetings were summoned in every German country and the text of the petition was distributed everywhere.

Naturally the Liberals did not let things slide. Their most distinguished counter-measure was a protest signed by seventy-six prominent German scholars—Mommsen *inter alia*—politicians, business men and civil servants. But there was also a violent scene in the Prussian Diet. The petition was a disappointment. In spite of endless propaganda only 300,000 signatures were collected and the whole commotion caused repercussions. At the election of 1881 the Conservative and anti-Semitic parties lost ground to the Liberals after an unusually bitter electoral campaign. There were no less than eight Jews sitting in the new Reichstag.

But the defeat did not stop the anti-Semites' agitation. They went to work wherever they saw an opportunity. They inveighed against Jewish immigration from Poland and actually achieved a number of expulsion orders; they agitated against Jewish ritual slaughtering, adopting the cruelty to animals platform. But as long as Bismarck was Chancellor, he managed to some extent to show the red light to the very worst excesses. It is true that he also protected the anti-Semites, because he could use them. The old Chancellor did not have an easy time of it when playing this tricky game. After his resignation he admitted in an interview that in their attempt to hold down the Liberals and later the Social Democrats by anti-Semitic agitation the Conservatives 'had caught hold of the wrong insecticide'.

The old Kaiser Wilhelm I was from the Junker caste and shared their dislike and loathing of the Jews. It was clearly partly out of consideration for him that Bismarck allowed anti-Semitism so much rope. On the other hand Friedrich, the new Emperor in 1888, was Liberal. He it was who stamped anti-Semitism as 'the nineteenth century's greatest disgrace'. But he only reigned for a few months. His son, Wilhelm II, was one of Houston Stewart Chamberlain's enthusiastic readers. And with that name we come to the climax of anti-Semitic ideology.

As his name implies, Houston Stewart Chamberlain had an English father, an admiral. But his mother was German and the son followed her. He lived in Austria and Germany where he became Richard Wagner's son-in-law. This had momentous consequences. The great composer was a forerunner of Naziism with its passionate admiration for Wotan. He looked on the Jews as an artistically impotent people who were merely parasites on German culture. And the Wagnerian operas represent German ideal figures with suggestive strength.

When the century ran out, Chamberlain wrote his epoch-making book *Die Grundlagen der neunzehnten Jahrhundert* (the Foundations of the Nineteenth Century). I wonder if he realized that with it he was laying the foundation of a disastrous part of twentieth century Germany? Nevertheless he did, for nothing has done as much as this book to create the popular conception of Jewish debasement and German

HEP! HEP!

pride. The author's brilliant stylistic talents, his extensive reading and most of all the book's explicit aims made it an unparalleled success. The book was read enthusiastically by millions; the Emperor himself read it aloud to his sons and demanded that it be introduced into the schools.

Chamberlain puts the racial problem in the front rank in his book. His vital thesis is that the race directs history. And there are two races, the long-skulled and the short-skulled. Being long-skulled is a sure racial sign and proof of superiority. It testifies to a longing for the light and all history's great personalities were long-skulled—and naturally blonde blue-eyed people. But the Jew is short-skulled; he belongs to the Semitic race, *homo syriacus*, of which *homo judaicus* is the lowest species. He is a bastard and even his existence a racially disgraceful crime against life's holy laws.

The whole history of the world tells of the conflict between the Aryans and the Semites, and begins at the moment when the Teutons make their appearance on the scene and seize the heritage of antiquity with hands which swell with power. China, India, Babylon, Judaea, Persia, Greece and Rome are merely a prelude. Only shameful laziness or lying is capable of seeing in the Teutons' entry into world history anything but the rescue of dying humanity from the eternal beast's claws.

But even Chamberlain could not deny that great men had lived before the Germans. Fortunately he has his ingenious explanation for this undeniable fact. There is no place on earth where the Germans have not travelled and they left their mark. In reality all the great men were Germans, in Hellas, Babylon and Egypt, indeed in the Mexico of the Aztecs and the Peru of the Incas! Also in Judaea. No one denies that Israel possessed mankind's supreme geniuses, David, Isaiah, Jesus and Paul. But people had quite forgotten the Amorites, Isaael's neighbours! And they were a people who came from the far North, tall, blond and blue-eyed. All Israel's great men were Amorites. In this way Chamberlain reaches harbour safely.

From the scientific point of view Chamberlain's look is obviously stuff and nonsense. It is full of distortions, misunderstandings and self-contradictions, a witches' brew of

THE CHAINS ARE BROKEN

half-truths and whole lies for which one would have to go far to find an equal. But it is written in a wonderful style and with a self-confidence which can easily have an imposing effect. Naturally we shake our heads when we think that this hotch-potch was actually read and believed to the extent it actually was. In addition among one of modern times' most cultured people, Bernard Shaw was tragically right in his bitter words that our age is just as credulous as the Middle Ages were.

One would have thought that Chamberlain had won the master's diploma for absurd ideas with his book. But no, in 1926 appeared the glaring forgery which goes under the name of the *Protocols of the Elders of Zion* and breaks all records. Not for nothing is it anti-Semitism's foremost canonical work. The book tells that in the year 929 before our era the wise King Solomon together with elders of Zion drafted a mighty plan for winning world dominion for the Jews. And the contents of the book are not, as its title implies, a series of protocols, but a speech which the chief of the Jewish world government makes to the elders of Zion in which he lets them into the secret of how far they have advanced in the accomplishment of this thousand-year-old dream.

Things look promising. 'The non-Jewish peoples are destroyed by alcohol and lewd living into which our agents have enticed them' and 'with the help of the press we have captured the gold, even if it cost streams of blood.' All the disasters in world history, including the world war, are staged by the Jews to weaken the other peoples. Now the last great battle confronts the Jews. The Jews would see to it that social dissatisfaction rose to the skies. At the right hour Europe's working masses would be put in the street on one and the same day. In their rage they would kill and slaughter step by step. And the Jews' great hour would have come.

The protocols were a great sensation. They made a triumphant procession round the world and were translated from one language to another. The remarkable thing is that they were taken seriously and actually believed in many places. Serious newspapers such as the *Morning Post* and the *Times* devoted long articles to them. So there is nothing to be surprised about when we find an old anti-Semite like Henry Ford also bursting into print. He was inspired by the protocols and used their material to write his own book *The International Jew*, which was read by the whole of America. The philosopher of Naziism, Alfred Rosenberg, also read the protocols; he published them in German and armed himself to write his *The Myth of the Twentieth Century*.

But the balloon burst. The protocols were revealed as a colossal forgery. The truth about them is as follows: In 1868 a Frenchman wrote a satire on Napoleon III. He had something to avenge. The police had kept him in prison for fifteen long months. So he wrote his book, which recounts conversations in Hell between Machiavelli and Montesquieu. Into this framework he wove the Emperor's plans to usurp world dominion. The anti-Semites dug up this forgotten book. Where the original had Napoleon, they wrote 'the Jews'. The result was the *Protocols of the Elders of Zion*.

We have to stop somewhere. There are whole libraries full of anti-Semitic literature. I have merely referred to some peaks in its long and bloody career. For it did become bloody. Not for nothing was Houston Stewart Chamberlain the first prominent personality who joined the National Socialist party in the twenties. Many times he heard the SA men's song:

> *Stoltz weht die Fahne im Wind*
> *wenn Judenblut vom Säbel rinnt.*
> The flag waves proudly in the wind
> when Jewish blood runs from our swords.

Today, when we can see events in perspective, it can be established that it was not Nazism which made people hate the Jews, but hatred of the Jews which turned people into Nazis. From the ideological point of view it was anti-Semitism which sold Germany to Nazism.

No one would have believed it, but the incredible happened. France became anti-Semitic. Never mind that for nearly a thousand years there had always existed in Germany lurking fear, irritation and dislike of the Jews which finally

THE CHAINS ARE BROKEN

burst into high flames. For Germany has always been the country of mass-psychosis. Or that sparks from the German conflagration flew off and caught fire in several European cities and countries, Vienna, Galicia, Hungary and Bohemia. After all they were subjugated nations with ancient ignorance and superstition hidden in corners. But it cried to heaven when France, the cradle of liberty and the citadel of reason, stood in the bright flames of anti-Semitism. We have come to the Dreyfus affair, the case which dragged on for years and revealed such scandals that it was on the point of overturning France's reputation and pushing Parliamentary government into the ditch.

France was beaten, knocked flat, split into factions. But longing for revenge for the lost war smouldered in everybody's minds. Wounded national feeling looked for a scapegoat and their gaze fell on the Jews. There were certainly not many of them, the majority being in Algeria, with only 100,000 in France itself. But most French Jews came from Alsace and Germany. Surely they were the tools of the archenemy? Internal political tensions also drove the sparks towards the Jews. The anti-Semites were reactionaries and clericals, i.e. opponents of the republic; they lampooned it as the Jewish republic. The Rothschilds were singled out as the real masters of the country. One of anti-Semitism's most celebrated writings came out in 1886; it was *La France Juive* (Jewish France), by Edouard Drumond, a book so evil and spiteful that it is hard to find its like, even in anti-Semitic company. This Edouard Drumond started his newspaper *La Libre Parole*, financed by the Jesuit Order, and it ate up every hateful attack concocted against both Jews and Protestants.

France stood with arms ordered, on perpetual guard against the enemy east of the Rhine. In September, 1894, one of the French counter-espionage's agents, a cleaning woman in the German Embassy at Paris, made a sinister find. From the wastepaper basket of the Military Attaché, Schwarzkoppen, she removed the paper which later became famous as the so-called *bordereau*. The word means register, catalogue. It contained a list of documents about French military top secrets which had been sold to Schwarzkoppen. There must obviously be a traitor who had access to such secrets, in other

HEP! HEP!

words an officer on the general staff. Suspicion fell on Captain Alfred Dreyfus. It should have seemed quite preposterous to pick on him. Dreyfus was thirty-five at the time. His family came from Alsace, but when the province was ceded to Germany, Dreyfus père moved to Paris with his wife and children. Alfred Dreyfus was rich and happily married to the daughter of a well-known millionaire. He had totally forgotten that he was of Jewish birth; he was full of French patriotism and thoughts of revenge. His military career had been brilliant. He was promoted from the artillery to the general staff, the stronghold of the French chauvinists. Dreyfus did not dream that he was surrounded by enemies there who were waiting for a favourable moment to strike him. For he was a Jew. When the rumour of the *bordereau* spread in the general staff, everyone realized that the culprit must be Dreyfus, the only Jew in this French nerve centre.

General Boisdeffre, chief of the general staff, had Dreyfus arrested; the charge was high treason. An officer of the general staff sold this fascinating titbit to *La Libre Parole*. The whole of the reactionary press flared up and started a massive campaign of anti-Jewish agitation. If one Jew was a traitor, they could all be the emperor's liegemen, it was said. Anyone who believed in Dreyfus's innocence, was stamped as being bought by Jewish gold. The Minister of War had considerable doubts about Dreyfus's guilt; all the evidence pointed away from him. But the Minister was caught between powerful groups in the Chambre des Deputés and lacked the courage to go against the stream. He brought Dreyfus before a court-martial. The verdict was based on the introduction of a *dossier general*, a collection of documents, among others a note written by Schwartzkoppen himself saying that with the help of a man who was known by the letter D he had laid hands on the plans of Nice's fortifications. Later it was disclosed that this note was a forgery made by the French Colonel Henry, the man who played a sinister role in the whole affair. But the court-martial found that D could be none other than Dreyfus. They found him guilty unanimously and sentenced him to cashiering, life imprisonment and deportation.

An enormous crowd thronged behind the railings on the

THE CHAINS ARE BROKEN

Champ de Mars on the day Dreyfus stood at attention facing a company of French infantrymen. The sentence was read aloud to him, but Dreyfus shouted at the judge in despair.

'You have sentenced an innocent man. Long live France, long live the army!'

And from the vast crowd came the deafening cry: 'A mort les Juifs!' (Death to the Jews!).

An officer stepped forward. He cut the epaulettes off the condemned man's shoulders, took his sword and broke it over his knee, while Dreyfus went on sobbing the words:

'I am innocent, innocent.'

The next day Dreyfus was sent off to Devil's Island, a sun-baked pestiferous island off French Guiana on the coast of South America, which is notorious for its fiendish climate. His wife begged for permission to accompany him, but was refused. All alone, cast off and despised by the people whose favour he had courted, he had to die slowly on this desert island, with the eternal hissing of the surf against the steep cliffs as the only sound to reach his ears. In fact he was buried alive. The only thing that kept the unfortunate man going was a faint desperate hope of seeing his name cleared one day.

It was to take two long years before light was lit in the darkness. The Intelligence Service acquired a new head, a Colonel Picquart. By chance he happened to go through the files on the Dreyfus case and discovered that Dreyfus simply could not have written either the *bordereau* or the famous note which had cost him so dear. But there was more to it than that. When he intercepted a despatch from the German Embassy in Paris Picquart came on the tracks of the real traitor, Major Esterhazy, an officer who was heavily in debt and had been selling his country's secrets for a long time for German money.

It was not as if Picquart was merely friendly disposed to the Jews. He was not activated by such motives. But he wanted to see justice done and reported the matter to his chief, a general. This was his answer:

'If you just keep quiet about the affair, no one will know anything about it.'

He was up against a blank wall. Not only here, but every-

where he tried to penetrate, to the generals, and even the Minister of War. The eternal refrain was:
'What difference can it make whether this Jew is left on Devil's Island or not?'
Picquart looked like becoming embarrassing. So he was removed from his post and sent to serve in Tunis. He was sure to get shot there. But Picquart was lucky and came home alive. The previously mentioned Colonel Henry, a close friend of Esterhazy's, was given his former post. He would be certain to shield and protect his friend.

In spite of all these attempts to suppress the truth, an avalanche was about to start. The Dreyfus family had not been idle; they engaged one of Paris's finest lawyers with the object of having the case brought up for re-trial. An eminent Jewish journalist, Bernhard Lazare, issued a pamphlet called *The Truth about the Dreyfus Affair* and pointed out all the inaccuracies of which the court-martial had been guilty. People began to listen. Deputies and journalists raised the case. It dawned on them that they were on the track of an appalling injustice for which France was responsible. They were such men as Georges Clemenceau, Aristide Briand and Anatole France, the last named with Jewish blood in his veins. The Dreyfus affair began to split the nation. Reaction and clericalism stood hand in hand against French liberalism.

During the years from 1896 to 1899 the Dreyfus affair grew to be the dominating problem in French politics. No one spoke about anything but the affair. There was no need to say which affair. The rehabilitation of the sentenced officer finally became the main conflict between republicans and anti-republicans, between humanism and chauvinism. As always in French politics ministries came and went in rapid succession. But the stumbling block was the same every time: *l'affaire*. Passions were whipped up; Dreyfusards opposed anti-Dreyfusards; the distinction even arose inside families and split them.

One thing the changing Ministers of War were agreed on. The army's honour must be protected. Of course they all realized that there were blots on its escutcheon, but they had to be covered up. If there was a re-trial, it would be impossible to protect Esterhazy. Lie after lie was told to prevent

THE CHAINS ARE BROKEN

the affair being re-opened. Officers and ministers were involved in it and forced to make false statements in the Chambre des Deputés or commit perjury in court. The anti-Semites started a rumour that Esterhazy was the innocent victim of a Jewish plot; he had only been dragged into the case to whitewash a Jew.

But the whole house of cards which were piled on top of one another had to collapse one day. It is a comforting thought that no lie can last for ever.

The lightning struck on June 13, 1898. The Parisian *l'Aurore,* Clemenceau's newspaper, published Emile Zola's article *J'accuse!* (I accuse!) in capital letters. It was an open letter to the President of the Republic Felix Faure. In fiery words the great author accused the minister of war, the generals and the court-martial of high treason against humanity and demonstrated point by point the long series of forgeries, lies and corruption which had grown up and become the Dreyfus affair. Zola wrote:

'My burning protest is a cry from the heart. Summon me before the courts, but let the inquiry take place in the light.'

He concludes prophetically:

'Truth is on the march. It will not be stopped.'

The article cost Zola dear. An avalanche of insults poured down on this courageous man. He was sentenced to a year's imprisonment for libel, but managed to seek asylum in England to continue the fight from there. There were big riots against the Jews in Bordeaux, Marseilles, Nantes and Lyons. But there was violence in Algeria. Blood flowed in streams in the Jewish districts in Algiers, Oran and Constantine. One election went against the republicans and large numbers of reactionaries took their seats in the Chambre des Deputés. There were rumours of a *coup d'état* which was to overthrow the republic.

That was the last straw. But suddenly the case took a sensational turn. Colonel Henry was revealed as the man who had forged the fateful document. The next morning he was

HEP! HEP!

found dead. He had cut his throat with his razor. Esterhazy escaped justice by fleeing the country.

Yet even now the power of reaction was not broken. It redoubled its effort, indeed one of its leaders, Déroulède, attempted a *coup d'état*. In February, 1899 France went to the polls to elect a new president. Waves of passion were whipped up throughout the country; the republic tottered on its foundations. But to the relief of everyone who loved France the election was won by Loubet, a supporter of the revision of the Dreyfus affair.

After five years' deportation Dreyfus returned to France and appeared before the Court of Cassation at Rennes. The eyes of the world were on the little town. All the big newspapers had their best men on the spot to cover the story. One of France's finest brains, the barrister Labori, as Dreyfus's defence counsel, inexorably recounted all the sins which had been committed against his client. The case seemed to be as good as over.

But the Moloch of war did not let its prey go so easily. It was still stronger than justice. To the astonishment of the whole world Dreyfus was not acquitted. He had to be content with having 'extenuating circumstances' added to his sentence and getting off with ten years' imprisonment. The next day the President of the Republic gave him a free pardon.

Dreyfus was a free man, but he was still branded a traitor. Of course he ought to have pursued his case to the bitter end, but he could not go on. He was a completely broken man. Dreyfus accepted the verdict and retired to his home.

Reaction made one last desperate attempt to exploit the passions it had aroused and come to power. It is the strange story of Jules Guérin, the secretary of the Anti-Semitic League, who stayed entrenched in his headquarters for a whole month and defied the siege of 5,000 troops of the regular army.

But other things were going on in France. The government made a deep incision and reached the root of reaction. It was the Jesuits and Dominicans, the zealous vanguard of the church, who always egged on the royalists, especially the army, to be disloyal to the republic. In 1901 the government

173

THE CHAINS ARE BROKEN

firmly put into effect a new educational act, which conclusively broke the church's power over the rising generation. In 1905 they went even further and abolished the connection between church and state which had existed since Napoleon's day.

Only then did the curtain go up on the last act of the drama of Alfred Dreyfus. In 1906 France's highest court set aside the verdict of the Court of Cassation and unanimously pronounced Dreyfus innocent. The Captain was promoted to Major and awarded the Legion of Honour. About the same time Colonel Picquart was made a general and a month later Minister of War in Clemenceau's government. Emile Zola was dead by this time. He did not live to see the triumph of the cause for which he had fought so valiantly. But his coffin was borne to a hero's grave in the Panthéon. After all those years French intellect finally exorcised the spectre of anti-Semitism.

Was der Jude glaubt ist einerlei,
in der Rasse liegt die Schweinerei.
It doesn't matter what the Jew believes,
filthiness is inherent in the race.

These oft-sung lines are the inscription on anti-Semitism's banner. But the idea contained in them is new in the history of hatred of the Jews. The Jew has felt the hostility of his non-Jewish neighbours ever since he has been in dispersion. He was the foreigner, he was different; people feared him. In fact he was a dangerous competitor, because of his ability and the remarkable solidarity there is between Jews. He never became one with his surroundings, but was always obstinately apart. It was bound to happen to people who had been driven out of every milieu where they could breathe freely. For many centuries they were shut in behind the wall. And the ghetto set its mark on them, even after they had left it. The Jew, people said, is watchful and sly, but also servile and cringing, provided he is not the exact opposite. That was how the world saw the image of the wandering Jew in all its horror.

But the blackest shadow over the Jew was religion. He be-

HEP! HEP!

longed to the people who had murdered Our Saviour. And that was not all. He continued to hate him and his church. No power could attract him into the saving arms of the church. So Christianity gave him the choice of baptism or death. And the Protestants were nearly as bad as the Catholics.

But at the end of the nineteenth century all that changed. Now it was no longer the Jew as heathen who aroused people's hatred, but the Jew as a Semite, from a foreign inferior race. This remarkable transformation of ideas has its natural explanation. The whole of Europe had simply entered on a new phase of its development. We need only look at Germany, the womb of anti-Semitism.

Right up to imperial times Germany had been proud of being 'a Christian nation'; it had been the Holy Alliance's great ideal. But as the century advanced, Christianity lost its power over the people who became more and more secularized. In its place—for people must always have something to believe in—came pride in the German victory, the pursuit of world dominion and a massive economic expansion. The image of the pale bleeding Galilaean faded to be replaced by the yellow-haired, blue-eyed and long-skulled Aryan who was Siegfried, Balder and Odin in one person. Germany stopped being Christian and became Aryan. That is the road from the first Reich, through the second and on to the third Reich.

As far back as history goes, we hear of men who believed in the power of blood and heritage. There is no end to the family trees we read. The ancient Greeks honoured their fathers and treasured their names in memory. The Jews did the same—the Old Testament teems with family trees. The word Semite comes from Shem, the one of Noah's three sons from whom the Jews consider they descend. But we find the same thing no matter where we look. In Spain *limpieza* means cleanness and signifies that a hidalgo's blood is free of Moorish and Jewish blood. The most distinguished families in America can trace their line back to the Pilgrim Fathers on the *Maypole*.

So it is an obvious thing also to be proud of the race one springs from. And the Nordic races were Aryans into the bargain. The word comes from Sanskrit and means noble. In

THE CHAINS ARE BROKEN

1808 the linguist A. W. Schlegel discovered that the Indo-European languages belong to the same family of languages and are distinct from the Semitic tongues. From there it was a short step to classifying the ancient peoples who spoke Indo-European in the same race. And it was given the name Aryan.

But modern anthropology is certain that this is incorrect. Even in those ancient times different races were intermixed and had merely adopted the Indo-European language. No one thinks of calling an American negro an Aryan, even if he does speak the same English language as the 'Aryan' Americans. In other words the expressions Aryan and Semitic only apply to language, not race. Anti-Semitism based on racial grounds belongs to a long outmoded stage of anthropology. No modern geneticist considers that the Jews belong to a special race. Such a race simply does not exist. Racial anti-Semitism has had its weapon knocked out of its hand long ago. No one need give it a serious thought.

But if the Jew does not belong to a special race, what is he? We have seen how rapidly the newly-freed prisoners of the ghetto reached the conclusion that they were just as good Germans, Englishmen and Frenchmen as those they lived among. They merely held some distinctive religious opinions. For Jewry is a religion, not a nation. But the man who reads the last chapter of this book about how Jewish self-consciousness awoke circa 1900, or has seen the Jews in their own country of Israel building up their fathers' land with proud strength, while they form a nation from Jewish emigrants from all over the world, realizes that assimilation is a disastrous error.

What is a Jew? The problem is so complicated that no one can give an answer which can be put in a nutshell. Jewry's heritage is a precious jewel, cut with many facets; each of them makes the light gleam with its own brilliance. The religious, popular, social and national elements are indissolubly fused together. During a development unparalleled by any other people which has lasted for millennia, Jewry was formed into something living, always vigorous and growing, which points to the solution of one of life's darkest, yet most promising riddles.

IX

POGROM

IN the nineteenth century a journey to Western Europe's Jews after visiting their East European friends was like passing from day to night. True enough, the Jews in the west saw more clouds than blue sky over their heads and icy blasts and drizzles made the day grey. But the sun had risen, although the morning took a long time to grow light. And the Jews sustained an indomitable hope that summer sunshine and mild breezes were on the way. In the east it was black gloomy night, and the stars were often hidden behind clouds.

In the Middle Ages the Polish kingdom had welcomed countless homeless Jews and opened the door to them. They thanked their benefactors by creating such a flourishing culture that Polish Jewry was called 'The Third Temple'. But the temple was destroyed by frightful catastrophes and the Polish Jews suffered indescribable misery at a time when their brothers in the west were fighting their way to emancipation. When the partition of Poland took place at the end of the eighteenth century and after the Congress of Vienna at the beginning of the nineteenth, Polish Jewry was also split and divided between the neighbouring countries. One part came under the Prussian crown, a considerable part, Galicia's Jews, fell to Austria, but most were allotted to the Tsar of Russia. There were Jews in many European countries, especially Roumania. But I limit myself to drawing the picture of the Russian Jews. From them the sidelights fall on the Galician and Roumanian Jews. But the picture emerges more clearly and sharply if we limit ourselves to looking at Russia.

THE CHAINS ARE BROKEN

When the nineteenth century entered its second and third decades, Russia had 2,000,000 Jews. Towards World War I, the figure had risen to 5,000,000 or 6,000,000, in spite of all the adversity they had to bear, which is described in this chapter. Thus almost half the world's Jewry were locked up behind Russia's frontiers. It was an ill fate which forced so many Jews under the Tsar's sceptre and his political knout. Russia was the most despotically ruled kingdom in Europe at the time. And what was worse, the Russian monarchs had feared the Jews since ancient times. About the time of the Reformation they had crushed sporadic movements tending to conversion to Jewry with sword and whip. To be sure Peter the Great had followed a slightly more tolerant course, but his daughter, the Empress Elizabeth, abhorred Jews. Once she received a deputation which recommended opening Russia to Jewish settlement, saying that the country would benefit financially as a result. But the Empress answered:

'I want neither advantage nor profit from the enemies of Christ.'

And now the Tsar suddenly had millions of these enemies of Christ inside his kingdom, apart from the equally unwelcome Roman Catholic Poles. The Tsar took measures.

As early as 1791 an imperial ukase was issued in which the Jews were simply shut up in the so-called residential or settlement area. In plain words it was a ghetto, even if on a gigantic scale. The Tsar laid down that the Jews in his empire might not travel or live outside ten Polish and fifteen Russian adjacent provinces. The regulations governing this were changed now and then with the passage of time. Sometimes they were relaxed a little and then tightened up again. But by and large they had the same purpose: the Russian people were to be protected against the Jews and their extortions. All these fiendish inventions were not unreasonably compared with the macabre leaden chamber which became a fraction smaller every day around the condemned prisoner. Only a few thousand, mainly highly cultured Jews and specialist workers, could obtain a pass which gave them the right to leave the ghetto—excuse me, the settlement area.

Day and night. Already we can begin to understand why that phrase was used to describe the difference between east and west. Or to use another metaphor, the flood tide in the west which swept the ghetto's walls away was broken when it washed against the Russian empire's dams far away in the east.

All this is concerned with superficial political and social conditions. However, there was another difference between west and east which cut even deeper into the Jewish mentality. For the same tidal wave which forced emancipation through in the west, bringing spiritual freedom and often assimilation with it, saw the loss of millennia for Jewry. But this wave stopped just as abruptly in front of the double wall Russia's Jews had built as a defence of their spiritual heritage: the Talmud and Hasidism, just as the storm of political emancipation broke against the Tsar's obstinacy. And anyone who has a feeling for what is deepest in the soul of Jewry will be tempted to change the two words I put at the head of this section: day and night in west and east. Perhaps from the other point of view one ought to say: night in the west and day in the east.

'The rich man lives in the west and Lazarus in the east,' says the proverb. Another tells of being as 'poor as a Polish Jew'. Yes, poverty is the first word that comes to mind when one has to write about the Russian Jews in the nineteenth century. In our modern welfare state we have absolutely no comparative basis for understanding the wretchedness they lived in permanently. Penury was no isolated phenomenon, it was a national evil, the normal state of affairs. One is tempted to call their poverty a natural function.

In the big cities the Jews huddled together in the holes in the slum districts, for such they were, in Cracow, Lodz, Lemberg, Odessa and Vilna. In dark poky rooms which resembled the cross-section of a sewer four families lived. Here a man rented not a flat, or even a room, but a corner of a room. Four families had to share one room; hundreds of children grew up in the courtyards. It was estimated that a house in which Jews lived contained four times as many people as it would have if Christians lived in it. It was no better in the country. Thousands of villages with their aimless lines of buildings were scattered over the settlement area. Their

THE CHAINS ARE BROKEN

names were not to be found on any large-scale map; only the inhabitants and their nearest neighbours knew what they were called. They were teeming with Jews. Here the sun shone on them on hot dusty summer days; when spring and autumn came they waded along bottomless slushy roads and in winter looked out over boundless blinding expanses of snow, while the crackling frost made the river's three-foot thick ice sing in its embrace. It was almost impossible to get through the winter. The cold crept in through the unsound walls, people crowded round the glowing stove as long as they had some fuel to put in it. If the fire went out, the only thing was for them to huddle together under a tattered blanket in bed in hopeless expectation that either spring or a merciful death from cold would save them. Provided that hunger typhus did not come first; it was a constant threat to the Jews in Russia, like a national epidemic.

Only the most despised callings were open to the Jews. Of course there were also men in Russia who did very well, and rose to the top with energy and initiative. There have always been such people in the Jewish masses. But for at least 99.9 per cent the only outlet was as second-hand dealers, pedlars, inn-keepers or craftsmen among their own people. It was almost impossible to earn the hard black bread for a perpetually growing family, not to mention the white sabbath bread, a little pickled fish with gherkins and a glass of schnapps with a lump of celery in it. For not everyone can live by selling old clothes or being publicans where there are more tradesmen than clients. Eccentrics grew up as rankly as toadstools in the hopeless gloom. There were *schlemihl, schlimazl, luftmensch, schnorrer* and many other types who gasped for air. Unless a man had the ingenuity to invent a couple of side-lines.

These side-lines are a chapter in themselves and novels have been written about what people hit upon. One became an official in the synagogue, another a cantor, if he was lucky enough to have the voice for it, others again collectors of alms, or simply beggars, for begging was a recognized calling. And a common feature of all these occupations was that people thought that they were far more interesting and enticing than ordinary banal jobs, and they employed unique industry and ingenuity to solve the problems they presented.

Let us make a lucky dip and hear about the man who acted as a marriage broker, or *shadkan* as he is called in Hebrew. Of course the parents firmly arranged the partner the children should have. And they called in the *shadkan*, when the time drew near. He was a classical figure in Jewish life. And a very important person, for the family's future depended on his good or bad advice. Many Yiddish stories were told about the *shadkan*. Here are some examples:

An old *shadkan* persuaded a young man to marry an exceptionally unfortunate girl. The prospective bridegroom did his best to get out of the affair.

'Do you want to make a fool of me? The girl is blind,' he began.

But the objection made no impression on him.

'Do you call that a fault? In my opinion it is an advantage. You can do what you want without her finding out.'

'All right, but she's dumb as well.'

'That is a virtue in a woman. You will never hear a sour word from her lips.'

'She is deaf.'

'Nothing could be better. You can scold her to your heart's desire and she won't hear anything.'

'She's hunch-backed too.'

At last the *shadkan* became impatient and said angrily:

'I honestly don't understand you. Can't you put up with the only tiny defect in the girl you are going to marry?'

Then there is the other *shadkan* who got the prospective bridegroom to go for a walk with the girl he recommended. Afterwards the young man complained:

'She's lame,' but received the consoling answer:

'Yes, but only when she walks.'

And there was the pedlar or *dorfgeher* as he was called in Yiddish. In his pack he carried everything which might impress the farmers on whose doors he knocked. Straw hats, leather goods, pocket-knives, shoes, silk ribbons, coral trinkets, images of the saints, snuff, almanacs, old newspapers, playing cards, love-philtres and charms. The pack hung on his back all the year round, summer and winter, in heat and cold. If people needed him, they let him into the room, if he was too persistent, they set the dog on him. The policeman alternatively employed his wit and his whip on him. Yet the pedlar was never tired, he raised his hoarse voice from morning till night, haggling or cheating a little if he could get away with it. But he went back home on Friday afternoon. He changed his clothes, had a bath, was affectionate to his wife and children—in short he was a human being until he became a pedlar again on Sunday evening.

The Russian Jews continued faithfully to breathe the same air as their fathers in the days of the 'Third Temple'. Their isolated ghetto culture was alive right up to our own time, indeed there are places in the world where it still blossoms. They wore ankle-length black caftans, with a large round cap of polecat tails, the so-called *strejmel*, and they had ringlets, or *pajes*. Women wore the *paryk* after marriage. Their small children went to the *heder*, the young men and women to the *yeshiva*. Books which did not deal with the Talmud or the Torah were strictly forbidden. The language was Yiddish. It was the common language of ninety-eight per cent of all the Jews in the settlement areas in Russia and Poland. In Lithuania the Jews did not even understand Polish. This vivid melting tongue gave life its own special tone. It is best suited for feelings—pain and joy, hope and longing—but it is also witty, with a blend of humour and melancholy, smiling through the tears. And the smile, which tends to be ironic, is forged in the midst of a chaotic desperate life in which the Jew with unshakable will power is trying to do the impossible, to establish harmony between the scanty light and the pitch black. Consequently he trains himself to laugh. The experience of generations has shown him that a smile can take the sting out of an unjust fate. It is really a pity not to tell the stories which follow in Yiddish, for that would give them the genuine note, but necessity unfortunately compels us to use our own language.

Moscow lay outside the settlement area and was naturally a forbidden city for the Jews. But forbidden fruit tastes best and there were some dare-devils who went to Moscow and tried to live underground. Some of them managed extremely well, earned money and went far. But they always had to be on the alert, for the police had orders to check the papers of people with a Jewish appearance. So it was essential to be ingenious. Out in the country villages people loved to relate how smart brains outwitted the police in Moscow.

Two Jews stood chatting on a street corner one day in Moscow. One of them had a passport, the other had not. They spotted a policeman. He was obviously interested in them and started to approach. They decided on their tactics in a flash. The man whose papers were in order began to run. It was clear that he had a bad conscience. The policeman ran after him. The Jew without a passport saw his chance and hurried off to safety. But it took the policeman a long time to catch up with the other one.

'May I see your papers,' he asked breathlessly.

The Jew produced them. Yes, they were in order.

'Why did you run away from me?' asked the policeman.

'I wasn't really running away from you. My doctor has given me some medicine and told me to run for a while every time I take it,' he explained innocently.

'But you must have seen that I was running after you. Why didn't you stop?'

'Oh,' exclaimed the Jew in surprise, 'I was sure that you had the same doctor as me.'

Here is another quick answer which the Tsar's Court Jester gave his majesty. The Jester had irritated the Tsar and was immediately condemned to death.

'But you have amused me so often,' said the Tsar, 'that you can choose the way you want to die.'

'Then I choose to die of old age.'

Gaiety dressed in rags. That is how we can characterize the disposition of the Russian Jews. Poverty, but not grey and hopeless. The smile indicates the balance in their nature. And an inherited faith gave this shabby proletariat the equilibrium to live a dignified life. A Yiddish author relates how a Russian Jew was bewildered when someone asked him how he managed to earn his daily bread for himself and his family. He merely stammered:

'How do I earn my daily bread? Well, there is a God who

THE CHAINS ARE BROKEN

does not desert his people. He looks after me and will go on doing so in the future.'

'All right, but what do you do? Have you got a job?' The answer came little by little:

'Eternal praise to God! As I stand here, by God's mercy I have one talent, a precious instrument, a beautiful voice. On holy days I am cantor in the synagogue. I am also the *mohel* who does circumcisions and you will not find my like for perforating the unleavened bread. Now and then I am a *shadkan*. Now I deal in alcohol, but let that stay between ourselves, and that puts butter on our bread. I also have a goat which gives milk and am lucky enough to have a rich relative whom I can also milk from time to time. Yes, I say that God is my father.'

In a situation like that we have the Russian Jew in poverty, laughter and faith. One never tires of dipping into all the charm of this popular Russian life. It was the nursery of a very brilliant literature. Solomon Abramaowitch described life in small towns with the pen of a Dickens. Solomon Rabinowitch, known as Sholem Aleichem, is a Yiddish Mark Twain. A Jewish theatrical life blossomed and assumed a notable position—and still maintains it. But best known by the rest of the world are the folk songs in Yiddish which are constantly sung and loved in many countries. These songs take their subjects from every corner of Jewish life, from God and the Messiah to unrequited love and fun in the market-place. We recognize them by something moving, tender and unexpected. If they are melancholy they become plaintive, but the sorrow is lightened by the lyric sweetness of the music. Let us catch a glimpse of Jewish wit by quoting some of the countless proverbs, in which generations stored their experiences and philosophy of life to hand them down to posterity:

'What is the heaviest thing in the world? An empty pocket.'

'Some people become taller by standing on other people's shoulders.'

POGROM

'What the eye does not see, the hand does not take.'

'The best thing about always telling the truth is that you do not need to go round remembering what you have said.'

'The man who thinks he sees everything is blind.'

'The sun goes down just as well without your help.'

'Words should be weighed, not counted.'

The saying 'No pockets in a shroud' is also Jewish.

The Russian Jews built two walls around them, the Talmud and Hasidism. Up in the north, especially in Lithuania, the orthodox Talmudists stood fast and would not tolerate heresy. Further south the Jews were Hasidists, they flocked to famous *zaddics* and often stuck up to their necks in superstition, in which delirious dreams were mingled with piety, one other method of finding consolation for the misery of the present. There were signs of conflict between these two schools; the Lithuanian Talmudists were not called *Mitnaggedim*, Protestants, for nothing, for they waged an incessant war against the Hasidists and vehemently scorned their belief in miracle-working rabbis. They told stories like this one:
'Every night my rabbi turns himself into the prophet Elias,' assured one of his enthusiastic disciples.
'Who told you that?' asked a sceptical listener.
'He told me so himself.'
'But are you sure he isn't lying?'
'How can you say such a thing? Do you believe that a man who turns himself into Elias every single night needs to lie?'
Incidentally it was in Lithuania that we find the most extraordinary occupation any Jew could hit upon. There were quite a number of men there who made their living by being sons-in-law. They were former students of the Talmud who married the daughters of rich men. For the daughter made a good match if she got a scholar. Erudition was always valued higher than wealth and the son-in-law received a livelihood

and could spend his life engaged in devout studies. But he had to stick strictly to the narrow path of orthodoxy. If he dared to listen to modern temptations and study profane literature in secret, his father-in-law demanded immediate divorce. I could write of several human tragedies of this kind when western ideas found their way into remote Lithuanian villages.

We round off this picture of Russian Jewish life with the following anecdote which puts their piety in a nutshell, in almost classical form:

A disciple asks his rabbi:

'What do you do before you pray?'

The answer was:

'I pray that I will be able to pray with all my heart.'

Nicholas I was Tsar of Russia from 1825 to 1855. During these three decades the autocratic ruler of all the Russians waged a thirty years' war against his Jewish subjects. Even in Jewish history no parallel is known to the savage policy he followed, which was intended to crush their spirit and powers of resistance, not even the celebrated bull of Pope Paul IV introducing the ghetto. Of the 1,200 ordinances concerning the Russian Jews issued during more than 200 years, from 1649 to 1881, half of them belong to this short epoch. The Jews did not call Nicholas I the Iron Tsar for nothing. It was to take a whole century before Nazism surpassed him with its modern technique of mass murder.

The new Tsar was able to wade in blood as soon as he ascended the throne. The dangerous Dekabrist uprising was put down with barbarous severity and Nicholas I's régime went on to rely on the police, censorship and espionage. With the same ruthlessness he steered his course towards what was always the autocrat's goal: one state, one religion, one language. That meant Russia, the Graeco-Russian church and the Russian language. All national, religious and linguistic minorities felt the weight of his knout. But no national element in Russia was as 'different' as the Jewish one.

The Jews had their own religion, their own language, indeed their clothing was distinct. Even their economic basis was something on its own. They huddled together in towns where they were only allowed to be small tradespeople and artisans, or out in the country innkeepers. Their life was deeply rooted in the Torah and the Talmud, and precisely demarcated by *Shulhan Aruk*. The slightest deviation from this heritage was sacrilege. They met siren calls and threats with contemptuous incomprehension and total rejection. As a result they had to endure a much bitterer lot than even the Poles, Letts and Esthonians. But Nicholas I did not know that he was embarking on an enterprise just as impossible as the one begun by Antiochus Epiphanes two thousand years before him. It was not in the Tsar's powers to turn the Jews into Russians, any more than he could make them into Hellenes. But with his desperate and fruitless Jewish policy he succeeded in causing the Russian Jews indescribable misery.

The Jews in Russia had never been deemed worthy of being soldiers before. Instead they paid a so-called recruiting tax. In 1827 there was a sudden volte-face. Tsar Nicholas discovered that the barracks was probably the best reformatory. In them 'the inner enemy', for he regarded the Jews as such, could be transformed into Russians in the most effective way. An imperial ukase ordered the Jewish *kahal* governments to provide a large fixed number of boys and young men to undergo national service of twenty-five years. These cantonists, as they were called, were supposed to be from twelve to twenty-five years old, but they were often taken at the age of eight and subjected to the strictest military discipline. Each individual *kahal* was made responsible for delivering the required quota. If they did not do so, the authorities conscripted the leaders of the *kahal*.

The unfortunate victims were marched away to distant provinces by brutal non-commissioned officers. Many of them succumbed to the hardships of the journey and found their grave in some nondescript roadside ditch. The survivors were condemned to a narrow existence of perpetual drill. But first and foremost they had to be forced to accept baptism. Pious popes preached and admonished, but received only a desperate shake of the head in answer. Then more brutal methods were used to cow the obstinate conscripts. They were beaten and starved. After tattoo they were ordered to stay kneeling all night. Anyone who fainted with fatigue had a bucket of water thrown over him so that he woke up and could continue. They were forced to eat pork or were given nothing but salted fish and then refused water to quench their thirst. They were forbidden to write home; letters from their parents were burnt unopened. Those who gave in and accepted baptism were immediately treated less severely, but the unbaptized were kept strictly isolated. In spite of this barbarous treatment there were some who survived and reached home after serving for a quarter of a century. They had strange stories to tell of the steadfastness and loyalty which many of the cantonists had demonstrated.

The talk often turned to a company where subtle torture finally forced all the soldiers to accept baptism. It was supposed to take place with great ceremony. A review of the troops was planned to take place simultaneously, carried out by His Highness the Tsar in person. The occasion was chosen to present the company to the Tsar and have the troops baptized. The soldiers were goose-stepped towards the river where the baptism was to take place. The bishop was ready in all his paraphernalia. Someone gave the order:

'Into the river!'

From the company came a unanimous:

'Very good!'

The soldiers kept their ranks and marched into the water in step until they disappeared. No one came back to the surface. They drowned rather than deny their faith.

Naturally the Iron Tsar attacked his Jews on more than one front. In 1835 all Jewish ordinances were collected in one big statute. It narrowed the settlement area and banished the Jews from the Black Sea towns and Kiev. Westwards they were forbidden to live within fifty versts of the frontier. The last order was a catastrophe. With one hour's notice thousands of Jewish families had to leave house and livelihood, and flee to the east. But the statute contained many provisions. The *kahals*' traditional self-government was removed. In the future they were merely to serve as an instrument for collecting taxes and recruiting cantonists. Jews were forbidden to have Christian domestic servants; Hebrew books were subject to censorship and Jews could no longer wear ringlets.

But there was more to come. Tsar Nicholas was a soldier. He knew that the man who wanted to win had to attack the enemy's strategic point. It goes without saying that the government realized that the centre of Jewry was the school with its instruction in the Talmud and the Torah. If the Tsar could 'Russianize' the schools, his goal would be reached. Sergius Uvarov, the Minister of Education, had information from Western Europe about the Jews' eagerness to share in European culture and the assimilation which often followed it. He decided to try the same methods in Russia.

One fine day the world witnessed the absolute monarch of all the Russians wielding the knout with one hand, yet giving the Jews gifts with the other. He offered them enlightenment. A new ukase decreed the establishment of new schools for Jews. Two seminaries were founded for educating Jewish teachers. I should add in parenthesis that the Jews were allowed to pay for all this themselves. A special educational tax was imposed on *kosher*, i.e. ritual butchering, meat and Sabbath candles.

Uvarov had made sure of Jewish collaborators, preferably young West Europeans who were enthusiastic apostles of enlightenment. The most distinguished was a young Bavarian Jew, Max Lilienthal, who travelled widely and persuaded the Jewish communities to send their children to the new government schools. He was banging his head against a wall. Everywhere the answer was:

'I wonder if you're sure what you're doing? All the government wants is to make us Christians.'

The Jewish masses would not be enticed. The Tsar was powerless against their passive resistance. The battle was lost; the new schools had virtually no pupils. Even during the reign of Nicholas I the authorities started to close the schools. The last one disappeared under his successor. Lilienthal himself realized that he had been used as a tool. A deeply disappointed man, he left Russia and went to America. We shall meet him again later in his new country.

In Western Europe Liberal circles had welcomed the Tsar's new educational policy as a fortunate omen of reforms and

THE CHAINS ARE BROKEN

had given him moral support. Their enthusiasm was short-lived. It was damped by a stream of telegrams which told of the harsh fate of the Jews along Russia's western frontier when they suddenly and unexpectedly had to leave their homes and the sorrow and anxiety induced by so brutal a law. The decision was taken to try and pacify the Tsar. We have already heard about Moses Montefiore, the celebrated English Jew. He was on good terms with the court of Queen Victoria. He went to St Petersburg with a personal letter from the Queen to the Tsar. He was received politely. Montefiore was even given permission to make a trip round the settlement area. Afterwards he presented the Tsar with a series of projected reforms and returned to London. But in Russia everything went on as before.

The Iron Tsar was not Nicholas I's only nickname. He was also proud of the fact that people called him 'the Gendarme of Europe'. The Tsar lived up to the name. In 1830 he crushed the revolt in Poland. In 1848 his troops put down the Hungarian rebellion, but his long arm even reached as far as Jerusalem. Under the pretext of protecting the Graeco-Russian church's interests in the holy places the Tsar found a pretext for interfering in Turkish politics. This sowed the seeds of the Crimean War.

And it meant the red light for Nicholas I. Outside Sebastopol 'General Fever' put a full stop to the Tsar. It happened at a lucky moment for his Jewish subjects. The Tsar was just thinking of striking them one more blow. He intended to have them separated into two categories: 'harmless' and 'harmful'. The second group would have had a rough time of it. But he never managed to put the plan into execution, and all the Russian Jews breathed more freely when death rid them of a modern Haman.

The new Tsar, Alexander II, was made of softer clay than his father. He was also more intelligent and less narrow-minded. But those who knew him well knew that in his innermost being lived the shifty vindictive despot. There is no doubt that his reign began with big reforms; it was he who abolished the Russian peasants' serfdom, to mention the most important example. But in his last years Alexander II repented of the reforming zeal of his youth and reaction's deep black shadow fell on it.

Immediately it seemed as if a new day was dawning for the Jews. The inhuman cantonist system vanished with a stroke of the pen and the oppressed people were given quite incredible reliefs. The settlement area was enlarged and certain categories of Jews received permission to settle in towns outside it; they were mainly merchants and university teachers. The government realized that Russia could use Jewish ability and capital. But of course it was only the chosen few who profited by the milder régime. The masses were bogged down in their usual poverty. And there were more and more and more of them. The early marriages bore fruit. Circa 1860, four million Jews lived under the Tsar's sceptre. And the invisible walls still stood immovably around the people. The Talmud and Hasidism flourished and formed the defences around the Jews' traditional life. The new conspicuous phenomenon, which it is customary to say characterises Russian Jewry at the close of the nineteenth century, remained on the surface. It never penetrated deep into the people, although Europe had a keen eye on it.

It was the *Haskalah* movement. We met the word *Haskalah* in connection with Moses Mendelssohn. It is Hebrew and means enlightenment. The movement's adherents called themselves *Maskilim*. In order to understand the importance of this new element, we must take a look at the conditions which produced it. As long as the Jew lived in the ghetto and was cut off from intercourse with life outside, the rabbi was the most distinguished man he knew and often the richest. It was part of his office to act as the ghetto's highest administrative and legal authority. It was the dearest dream of every young man to be a rabbi and the study of the Talmud was the way to become one. But Moses Mendelssohn summoned up new visions when he breached the ghetto walls and pointed to life in the world outside. From that time onwards great numbers of young Jews sought enlightenment, i.e. *Haskalah*. There was method in the fact that name was Hebrew. The somewhat vague goal of the *Maskilim* was to modernize Jewry without breaking completely with tradition. So they regarded the language of the Bible as their most dis-

THE CHAINS ARE BROKEN

tinguished instrument. They devoted all their energies to re-creating and modernizing, in other words to giving it new life and with the help of the ancient language turning the people's gaze far back to a heroic past. Then something new and great could grow up. Consequently the books they wrote and the periodicals they issued were all in Hebrew.

In Russia it was the young forward-looking Jews who looked to the German *Haskalah* with expectation and tried to transplant it among their own people. There *Haskalah* came to designate those who rejected the time-honoured isolation of the Jews from their surroundings and devoted themselves to mastering both European and Russian culture. The Torah and the Talmud could no longer be the only subjects for study, the horizon had to be extended until it embraced the whole of modern literature. So they embarked on what they liked to call the battle between light and dark, and formed a strong opposition wherever they met isolation, narrow-mindedness and formalism among their own people. 'Against stultification and superstition, for enlightenment and progress,' was the motto under which they criticized and ridiculed both Talmudic hair-splitting and Hasidic ignorance and superstition.

The Talmudists and Hasidists fought back and branded *Maskilim* as *Apikoresim*, heretics. Not without reason. For the first *Maskilim* were one-sided and overdid their reformative zeal. They certainly went too far in their fight against superstition and formalism. Several of them were tempted to go so far to meet the modern age that they sacrificed the most precious part of their Jewish heritage. For the sake of the future they forgot the past and tore down more than they built up, with the result that they lost the people's confidence. Without that they could not achieve anything. It took the pogroms to open their eyes and show them that they had gone astray. Most of them turned back to their people when evil days set in.

But there were other *Maskilim* who ended up as revolutionaries. They met Christian comrades in the universities, which were now open to Jewish students. They were the years when young university men discovered the Europe outside Russia. New radical and socialist ideas took root and flourished among them. With the motto 'To the people' they went among workers and farmers to live with the poor. They organized revolutionary groups among these classes. The police began to keep a watchful eye on them.

Haskalah naturally had an inspiring effect and produced new poets. Isaac Baer Levinsohn, Juda Leib Gordon and Shalom Jacob Abramovitch are some of the best known names. Abramovitch is usually known by the name of Mendele Moker Seforim, which means Mendele the bookseller. He was not satisfied with writing exclusively in Hebrew, which would only bring him into contact with a minority, so he wrote his satirical and moving novels in both Hebrew and Yiddish. He was much loved, known by his countless admirers as 'Grandfather' and can rightly be called the founder of modern Hebrew and Yiddish literature. But Gordon was the poet who crystallized *Haskalah's* programme in his famous words: 'Be a universal man in the street, but a Jew at home,' and wrote the movement's battle-song:

> Rise up my people, you have slept long enough!
> Rise up open your eyes.
> What evil has befallen you
> that you tarry so long?
> The sun has long risen above the earth,
> and everyone is up and about.
> You are the only one still abed,
> huddled up, with closed eyes.

Gordon's development was typical of *Haskalah*. In his youth he fought doughtily against orthodox obscurantism with his sharp pen as a dangerous weapon. The government had a suspicion that he harboured revolutionary tendencies and banished him from St Petersburg. During the last ten years of his life he had boxed the entire compass. He annoyed his critics and ended as a zealous defender of what he had previously attacked. It could be said of him that he burnt what he worshipped and worshipped what he burnt. Gordon ended up among the Zionists and has a dearly loved name in Israel where many towns have named streets after him.

The Polish uprising in 1863 marked an epoch in Alexander

THE CHAINS ARE BROKEN

II's reign. This dangerous revolt frightened him and the Liberal Tsar turned into a reactionary. Wherever there is civil war, the Jews always seem to be between the devil and the deep blue sea. It was also the case in Poland. Both Poles and Russians wooed and desired their assistance. Warsaw's Jews had proud memories of the Koskiusko uprising in 1794 when Berek Yoselovich recruited a Jewish regiment of light cavalry which defended the suburb of Praha against Suvarov's attack. Stories are still told about the bravery with which they fought. The Jewish legionaries upheld Jewish tradition in the middle of the siege; they ate kosher food exclusively and during the assault they made sure of receiving rabbinical dispensation to fight on the Sabbath. The regiment fell almost to the last man. Only Berek and a handful of soldiers survived. In 1863 there was also a strong movement among the Jews in Poland, but the Russians rapidly crushed the revolt and took brutal measures of reprisal which affected the Jews as well. The year 1863 brought Jewish hopes of a milder régime to an abrupt halt. The government tightened the noose round the Jews' necks again.

A sizeable number of young Jews responded by joining revolutionary groups: no one could expect anything else. After all they belonged to the most brutally oppressed national minority in Russia. And in their veins flowed the same blood as had flowed in the veins of the ancient prophets. A programme which promised liberty, equality and fraternity struck sparks in their minds. Agitation by the underground was violent; now the socialists called themselves Nihilists. They met force with force. Pitiless oppression by the police was met by assassination; 'the red terror' defied 'the white terror'.

Alexander II was one of its victims. After a long mental struggle he had finally decided to make concessions to the opposition. On March 13, 1881, he signed the decree which was the first step on the road to a constitutional state of affairs in Russia. Encouraged by having taken this decision, which was still secret, the Tsar drove to a parade. The police had tracked down a conspiracy which was preparing an assassination and they advised the Tsar to stay indoors. He refused and drove out in his carriage. Nihilists were posted along the whole route; the Tsar did not have a chance. The first bomb missed its target, but killed some of his retinue. The Tsar got out of his carriage to inquire after the wounded. Then the second bomb exploded almost at his feet. His mutilated body was carried to the Winter Palace where he died a few minutes later.

This bloody deed brought catastrophe on the Russian Jews. The government made them the scapegoat. The legal enquiry decided quite rightly that a young Jewess, Hessja Helfmann, had been a member of the terrorist group which carried out the assassination, although admittedly she only held a minor post. But a great fuss was made about it. With the big St Petersburg newspaper *Nowoje Wremja*—the name means new times—at the head, the press branded the Jews as responsible for the Tsar's murder. The Jews were behind the Nihilists.

Alexander III, married to the Danish Princess Dagmar, ascended his father's throne, which had so suddenly become vacant. The new Tsar was a real 'old Russian', just as simple in character as his father had been ambivalent, a zealous supporter of the right doctrine, i.e. that of the Graeco-Russian church, an excellent father, thrifty, conscientious and industrious, but with a deeply reactionary outlook. His first act of government was to repeal the ukase his father had signed a few minutes before his death. All Alexander III knew about the five or six million Jews of whom he was absolute monarch was what their enemies had taught him. That his father's 'favours' had sharpened their competition with the Christians, that they bored their way into industry, railway construction, banking and academic callings. During the war against Turkey in 1878 some Jews had been mixed up in a scandal about supplies to the army. Following the old principle 'One Jew uses bribery, all Jews are corrupt', the Tsar listened to the reactionary accusers and *Nowoje Wremja's* battle-cry 'Beware, Jews on the march!' re-echoed in his mind.

The Tsar's chief adviser was the head of the synod of the holy church. Konstantin Pobjedonoszef was a man whose faithfulness to his convictions was beyond doubt. On top of that he was the most reactionary man in Russia. In his view the only salvation for Russia was for the Graeco-Russian Church to reign supreme. There he ran up against the Jews. Pobjedonoszef knew that it was impossible to assimilate them. What was the answer then? With cynical frankness he pronounced that the solution of Russia's Jewish problem was only possible by forcing a third of them to flee, while the second must be coerced to the baptismal font and the remainder could die of starvation. But starving people to death takes time. Why not speed matters up by simply massacring the Jews? Incredible as it sounds, this became the Russian government's policy. We are confronted with the pogroms.

Pogrom is a Russian word which means destruction. In every modern language it stands as the noun describing mass-persecution of the Jews, either organized or at least viewed sympathetically by the authorities. Of course it was never admitted that the pogroms in Russia were inspired or organized from above, but the regularity with which they exploded tells its own story. Immediately after the new Tsar's ascension to the throne secret envoys from St Petersburg reached Odessa, Kiev and several southern Russian towns to organize, in collaboration with the local authorities, 'the spontaneous outbreak of mass indignation against the Jews', and the police were ordered to remain passive up to a certain point.

The first thunderbolt struck in Jelizavetgrad (Elizabethstown), with its 1,500 Jews. The night after the fourth day in Easter Week—pogroms often picked Easter—an incensed mob stormed the Jewish district. The rabble threw themselves on the Jews who were still out in the streets, they attacked houses and broke in, killing, raping the women and plundering to their hearts' content. In two days the Jewish streets were turned into a howling jungle where all the evil passions had free rein. All that could be seen were broken windows, doors torn from their hinges, streets full of furniture and everywhere could be heard hoarse cries and weeping and wailing. The police looked on without lifting a finger. The rioters realized that they had a free hand. Farmers from the surrounding country poured into the town to take their share

POGROM

of the booty. Not until the third day did the police and some troops intervene and restore order.

But the pogrom in Jelizavetgrad was only planned as a prelude. The sparks from the bonfire spread systematically. They first caught hold in the country villages. These appalling scenes were repeated in nearly a hundred of them. A few weeks later it was the turn of 'the mother of Russian cities', the Ukraine's ancient capital of Kiev, the city where Jews had lived since the grey dawn of history and been pioneers of culture and enlightenment. Here the police showed the Jews the consideration of warning them in advance. But as so often both before and since they could not believe that something evil was going to happen to *them*. Those who remained were to regret their optimism bitterly. It seems to be almost a rule that Jews can never paint the future black enough; reality always turns out more sombre than even their worst forebodings.

One Sunday morning the streets in Podol—that was the name of the Jewish district of Kiev—rang with shrieks and cries and laughter, while youths, workers and artisans went berserk. Twenty women were raped, several men were killed or wounded. The synagogue was securely locked, but the door was broken in. The Torah scrolls were pulled out, torn to pieces and trampled in the dust. The Christian inhabitants of Podol hastily put images of the saints in their windows and painted crosses on their doors to avoid Armageddon. During the looting Cossacks patrolled the streets; they confined themselves to looking on inquisitively; a few generals rode past and inspected the progress of the operation. The storm raged for three days. Then at last the soldiers advanced and put the drunken rabble to flight with the butts of their rifles. But from that day onwards the peasants began to talk about 'pogrom duty'. They had realized that they pleased their little Tsar if they killed Jews. When horrors are repeated *ad infinitum*, the mind is deadened so that they are liable to become a habit. That is true of the pogroms. I am simply forced to limit myself to naming the places where they struck. There were Odessa and a great number of towns in Podolia and Volhynia; they even went as far as Warsaw. But one place stands out above all the others; it was Balta, a town

THE CHAINS ARE BROKEN

in Podolia. Many Jews lived there and they hit back, so that the mob could not overpower them. But the chief of police came to its help. He had a bridge cut off so that an individual sector of the town was isolated. In it the 5,000 rioters were able to break the Jews' resistance. It was impossible for the great majority of the Jews to come to their brothers' assistance. They stood helplessly watching what happened on the other side of the river. The rabble had stormed a spirit merchant's and drunk themselves into a state of courage. Every passion was unleashed. The Jews were murdered in scores. One had a nail hammered through his skull; another writhed with his eyes put out, but no one gave him the *coup de grace*; children were spitted on knives, women were first raped and then their breasts were cut off.

Balta put a full stop to pogroms in this first period. But when the 'hot' pogroms faded away, the 'cold' ones began. The government had the audacity to claim that the Jews themselves were guilty of the pogroms. As a punishment they issued the so-called May Laws of 1882. They were invented by the Minister of the Interior, Count Ignatiev, who was dismissed for swindling very soon afterwards. But his laws, which were called provisional, proved more stable than their originator. They were allowed to remain in force until there was no longer a Tsar in Russia. By the May Laws the Jews in the settlement area were forbidden to live in the country. Suddenly they had to leave house and home and make their way to the already overcrowded towns. It did not improve matters when towns of 15-20,000 inhabitants were classified as villages, which meant that the Jews had to leave them too. The result was that several towns eventually had a population which was eighty per cent Jewish.

The 'cold' pogroms grew rankly during the years under Alexander III and his son, Nicholas II, Russia's last Tsar. By unscrupulous methods the new decrees barred the Jews from almost every possibility of making a living and reduced them to a hungry, shabby proletariat. The 'cold' pogroms' most evil product was the *numerus clausus*, the locked number, which put a ceiling on the numbers of Jewish university students. The ceiling was low. Inside the settlement area where the Jews numbered from thirty to eighty per cent of

POGROM

the population, only ten per cent were entitled to higher education. Outside the settlement area the number was microscopic; three per cent in Moscow and St Petersburg. Female students could only live in a town if they produced proof, the so-called yellow ticket, that they were registered in a brothel. In the middle of the icy winter of 1891 thousands of Jewish students were banished from Moscow.

The inevitable result of *numerus clausus* was that the Jewish students who were able to went away from their homeland and received their education at free European universities. But when they returned home again after having taken an examination all paths were barred to them. For example the government forbade Jewish jurists to establish themselves as lawyers.

The age of bloody pogroms was not over. On Easter Day, 1903, tragedy struck Kishinew, the capital of Bessarabia. The savagery of the pogrom there surpassed everything which had so far been seen. The police disarmed the Jewish sentries and let the mob go wild. When a Jewish deputation on the second day of the pogrom made an urgent request for protection, the chief of police answered:

'I have not received instructions from the capital yet.'

The Minister of the Interior, the notorious von Plehwe, was behind the Kishinew pogrom. The following year he was murdered by the Nihilists.

The events in Kishinew at long last tore the blindfold from the eyes of the people in the free world. With horror and revulsion they read news stories from Russia and learnt of the Russian Jews' misery. Of course people had been conscious of what was going on long before this. But not until 1903 did they realize the extent of the infamous activity of which the Tsar's government was guilty. In London questions were asked in the House of Commons and big protest meetings were held all over the world. But the only tangible result of the commotion was that England and America opened their doors even wider to refugees from Russia.

A new severe crisis happened two years after Kishinew. The Jews were permitted to pay a handsome part of the bill for Russia's humiliating defeat in the war against Japan.

THE CHAINS ARE BROKEN

After 'the bloody Sunday' in January, 1905, when 100,000 workers in Saint Petersburgh demonstrated by walking in procession to the Tsar and were met by rifle fire, the revolutionary ferment rose to bursting point. Once again the government tried to lead the erupting volcano away from themselves to the Jews. The 'black hundreds'—organized terrorist bands—embarked on new pogroms. The Jews were to blame for the defeat. They must be killed. The black terrorists murdered in hundreds of towns; 300 Jews were killed in Odessa alone and thousands were mutilated.

When the government was forced to give in to public opinion at long last and introduce the shadow of a constitution, the Jews elected twelve members to the first Duma, in spite of subtle intimidation of the voters. The Duma's life was short. The counter-revolution was victorious and dissolved the Duma. Right up to World War I the history of the Russian Jews was one long drawn-out saga of oppression and degradation. No chains were broken in Russia.

Yet the Russian Jews tore at the chains which bound them till the iron rang. And some of them managed to escape from them. Many turned to socialism to find salvation. It was inevitable that young lively Jews came to hate the Tsar and all his works, and all his being like the evil one himself. They became revolutionaries. The most daring of them joined groups in favour of direct action. And as the rotten Tsardom gradually crumbled into dust, the great socialistic experiment which took its place, the Soviet régime, included a disproportionately large number of Jews among its pioneers. It could not be otherwise. Today they have all disappeared. The revolution suffered the fate to which all revolutions seem to be subject; it devoured its own children.

The more moderate socialists—and they were the great majority—founded their own socialist organization, known as the Bund, after a conference in Vilna in 1897. The name is an abbreviation of the Jewish Workers' General Confederation in Lithuania, Poland and Russia. The Bund adopted a very antagonistic position towards Zionism; it preferred Yiddish to Hebrew and aimed at forming a future for the Jewish people in a liberated Russia.

POGROM

'How can you bear your fates?'

Theodor Herzl asked this question in amazement when he travelled through the settlement area in 1903 and met his cowed fellow Jews. The answer was that a national awakening pierced and reached the innermost being of even this tormented people, far deeper than any political considerations could penetrate. The Russian Jews were ripe to be proved a nation. One of them expressed it in these words:

'The Jews do not constitute even four per cent of the Russian people, but they are one hundred per cent their own people.'

As always the national renaissance set its mark on literature. Great poets appeared and interpreted the unconscious longings in people's minds. Chaim Nahman Bialik is the greatest Jewish poet since the days of Jehuda Halevi, and Asher Ginzberg, better known as Abad Ha'am, who was a man of the people, ranks by his side. Both of them finally reached Palestine.

Here we come to the renaissance of the Jewish people in its Zionist form. The sparks were lit far away from Russia, but it was among the Russian Jews that they really caught fire. In Russia the inflammable material was waiting for them. With the advent of Zionism the Jewish people broke their chains and took their destiny into their own hands. For two thousand years they had been on the passive receiving end of events. Now at last they were controlling them and very actively too. But Zionism deserves a chapter of its own.

Proportionately the Zionists were a minority among the Russian Jews. The great majority, who in the long run could not tolerate the oppression they were subjected to, emigrated to America. The government put no obstacles in their way. After all it was part of their programme to force one-third of these parasites to disappear from the soil of holy Russia. 'The western frontiers were open to the Jews,' St Petersburg proclaimed. And the Jews flocked to the crossing places. Their only wish was to escape from this hell. In 1905 and 1906 alone 25,000 Jews disappeared from Russia.

They left their chains behind them.

X

EXODUS

TEARS streamed down the old man's cheeks and into his long white beard. Eleven of his twelve children were saying goodbye before boarding the river boat which was to take them to Rotterdam. There the big emigrants' ship to carry them across the sea to America was waiting. One by one, the eldest first, the youngest last, sons and daughters went into their father's arms and kissed the wrinkled tear-stained face. Then followed his sons-in-law and daughters-in-law and finally fourteen grandchildren, the youngest only two months old. The father was eighty-three; he knew that this was the long farewell; he was seeing his family for the last time. He himself was too old for the long journey. He stayed behind with the only one of his twelve children who opted to remain in Germany. Thirty-six times he laid his hand in blessing on the travellers' heads and watched them walk up the gangway into the ship.

The old father was not the only one who stood on the quay and said goodbye. Ebenhausen is a small German town near Stuttgart. Ninety-two of the town's 500 Jewish inhabitants emigrated on that June day in 1836. The quay was teeming with people; all the town's Jews and many Christians waved goodbye. Not an eye was dry, everyone wept and sighed when the boat put off from the jetty and was slowly carried away downstream by the current. Tear-stained eyes followed it until a bend in the river took the boat out of sight.

This farewell at Ebenhausen was only one of thousands of similar scenes. Jewish emigrants flowed from every German state. It was during the years when the reaction following

EXODUS

the Congress of Vienna and later the unsuccessful revolution of 1848 caught the Jews in its toils, barred them from spheres with financial potentialities, intervened in their right to marriage and forbade them to travel to one town or settle in another. They saw no other way out than leaving Germany.

The Jews were not the only ones who left their old homes. Millions of Europe's oppressed poverty-stricken minorities said goodbye and sought salvation in America. Irish, Italians, Germans and Poles formed a mighty stream of immigrants across the sea. But the Jews had by far the worst of it and therefore they were the great majority in relation to their total numbers. Between 1880 and 1914 America opened its doors to a total of twenty-two million European emigrants. Between two and three million of them were Jews. But they formed only the vanguard of the mightiest exodus the world has ever seen.

'Exodus' is both Latin and Greek; it means departure. The Greek translation of the Septuagint puts Exodus as the title of the Second Book of Moses. It is more apt than the old Hebrew title: *Shemot*, names, for the book does describe the departure from Egypt and Pharaoh's tyranny. It was not the first Exodus. That happened four thousand years ago when the Lord ordered Abraham:

'Get thee out of thy country, and from thy kindred, and from thy father's house, unto a land that I will shew thee.'

Exodus became an oft-repeated title in Jewish life. During millennia of long wandering Israel had to leave other Pharaohs than the Egyptian ones. The Jews left Palestine, Babylon, England, France, Isabella's Spain, the Crusaders' Germany and Poland under Chmelnickij's terror. But the mightiest exodus belongs to modern times. First the German, and then on a vastly greater scale, the Russian exodus.

Far back in the nineteenth century America erected the gigantic Statue of Liberty outside its eastern port of entry in New York. She raises her torch to heaven and bids the oppressed and persecuted from the old world welcome to the new. The inscription on the bronze plaque in the base celebrates in a sonnet the right of storm-tossed and homeless people to breathe freely again. It was no coincidence that it was written by a Jewish poetess, Emma Lazarus. For here

THE CHAINS ARE BROKEN

millions of Jewish refugees found their haven and a new homeland.

America was the land of liberty. It was also the realm of great possibilities. The Sephardic Jews were the first of their people to find their way to the new world. They were few in number, but had done well and made use of their opportunities. Many of them were now in big business and had become rich men. One of them was Mordecai Manuel Noah, a remarkable visionary and a bit of a braggart. Noah was diplomat, poet and jurist as well; for a time he was mayor of New York, at another period he was American consul in Tunis. He conceived the fantastic idea of creating an asylum for his homeless people in America and bought an island in the river Niagara. Here the Jewish people were to settle and rise again under American protection; he himself wanted to be 'judge in Israel'. Of course he knew perfectly well that the little island, which he called Ararat, could not possibly hold all the Jews. But the plan was that it should only be the preparatory school for the people's ultimate settlement in Palestine. The idea was the great sensation of the year. The American newspapers described it in long articles; everyone was talking about Ararat. But the idea never got any further than its theatrical introductory phase. Soon afterwards it faded into oblivion.

In the course of a few years the number of German Jewish immigrants far exceeded that of the Sephardim. These Ashkenazic Jews came at a lucky hour. It was the period of America's great expansion. Louisiana was added to the States; there was room for everyone who had the courage to accept hard work and adventure. In those years America needed men more than money; the frontiers were pushed steadily westwards. Just as Israel's people struggled through the wilderness of Sinai to the promised land, German Jews were pioneers in pushing deep into the new world's endless prairies. When the rumour of gold in California swept through the country, they took part in the great gold rush. On the Day of Atonement, Yom Kippur, in 1849, they held their first service in a tent in San Francisco. They attracted attention wherever they went; the Puritan inhabitants of

EXODUS

America had never seen a Jew before. When the first Jew came to Cincinnati, an old Quaker woman was anxious to see 'one of God's chosen people'. She walked round him for a long time and considered the spectacle. At last she burst out: 'You are no different from other men!'

The settlers could use the Jews. A pedlar was naturally welcome at every farm. He came bringing both goods and news. More than one great fortune was founded in this modest way.

The first German Jews in America were provincials; they came from small towns in Baden, Würtemberg, Bavaria, East Schlesia and Pomerania—people like those we saw boarding ship at Ebenhausen. The same stamp was on them, they were hard workers and conservative in their faith; they clung together in their *Landmannschaften* (country associations) and spoke German to each other. The stream of refugees after the revolution of 1848 was of a quite different type. They came from towns and consisted of intellectuals with revolutionary political opinions. And they brought the ideas of Reformed Jewry with them. One of their rabbis was Max Lilienthal, who left Russia after his unsuccessful collaboration with the Tsar in the government schools.

From that time America became the citadel of Reformed Jewry. Magnificent synagogues were built which held reformed services. They were held on both Saturday and Sunday, prayers were abbreviated and were always in English, not Hebrew; there were organ music and mixed choirs, men and women sat together and the service asserted 'Israel's mission' among the people and denied the possibility of national revival. But in America these radical ideas never provoked the same violent reactions as those we saw in Germany. In the free air of the new world everyone could imbibe divergent opinions without suffering for it.

Even in those days America's Jews were starting to become a force. During the Civil War most of the Jews were on the side of the Northern States; they supplied no less than 700 officers, eight of them generals. Judah P. Benjamin was a minister in Jefferson's cabinet. It is also to the credit of the Jews that the American government decided to stand firm in a long-drawn-out diplomatic crisis featuring Switzerland. It took an abnormally long time in that country before the Jews acquired equal civilian status. The Swiss government adopted the offensive attitude that American Jews who visited Switzerland were subject to the same restrictions as her own. America replied by appointing a Jew as consul in Zurich. The conflict lasted twenty-five years; not until 1875 did Switzerland give her Jews full emancipation.

After the German emigrants came the Russian. And it was the invasion of Russian Jews which set the decisive stamp on American Jewry. The flood began as early as the middle of the 1840's. The Jews fled from Russia to prevent their sons from becoming cantonists. These *Hinter-Berliner* (Behind-Berliners) as the German Jews called them—they travelled via Berlin—were a quite new type. They were desperately poor, far more so than their German predecessors, and happily adopted the callings the Germans had long since outgrown. They also brought their traditional Russo-Polish Jewry with them. For all their poverty they hastened to open both *heder* and *yeshivah*, and summoned rabbis from their home country. They spoke Yiddish and observed the Sabbath and holidays strictly; they only married among themselves—mixed marriages were shunned like the plague. People with this outlook naturally became a bulwark of the traditional Jewish faith; they made many a dying spark of ancient Jewry flare up again. The stream became a veritable tidal wave after the pogroms at the beginning of the 1890's. From those days of mass flight it can be said that Jewish America arose from Russia's ruins. But when millions of penniless unemployed refugees suddenly storm forward, many are trampled underfoot. And the birth of the new Jewish centre in America meant severe wounds and a sea of tears. European railway stations and New York's harbour were the stages for these birth pangs. Emigrants flocked there in swarms; they pushed their way through the crowd in unruly mobs. All their wealth was contained in a bundle on their backs; the children clung to their fathers' caftans and their mothers' skirts. Hatred and hunger drove them from one end of the world to the other. What on earth awaited them in America? They did not reach their goal simply by landing in New York.

EXODUS

There they were stopped by strict uniformed policemen and officials who were ready to investigate and medically examine every single one of them. If they did not pass the control-point satisfactorily, they were siphoned off and given orders to return to Europe on the next ship. If they got through successfully, they were pushed into the icy, crowded transit barracks at Castle Gardens in the harbour. There they had to stay until work and housing was found for them in the great city. They were foreigners, they did not understand the language. Their only hope was a life of toil and trouble.

As a matter of course America's Jews applied all their energies to helping these unfortunates, who after all were their fellows. Hias—the name is an abbreviation of Hebrew Immigrant Aid Society—welcomed them and looked after them during their first hard period. It advised about jobs, found housing and trained unskilled persons. There were idealists with great plans among the new immigrants. They founded a society, Olam, the eternal people. Their aim was to go back to the land. For millennia the way to the land had been barred to the Jewish farming people, who were always forced to live in narrow streets in big towns. But in America there was virgin soil waiting for plough and harrow. With extremely generous help from many quarters these young Jews established agricultural settlements far out in the west. But the project failed. Floods, droughts and storms were too doughty opponents for these people whose only equipment was their enthusiasm.

By far the most stayed in New York, the city in which they had landed from Europe. But populous centres also grew up in other big cities: Chicago, Baltimore, Cleveland, Boston and Philadelphia. New York eventually housed an enormous number of Jews. In 1872 there were twenty-nine Jewish communities in New York, in 1886 the number had risen to 300. In 1925 the Jewish population in that city alone was almost two million, one-third of the total. Today it is even higher. Never before in Jewish history have so many been gathered in one place.

The great majority of the new immigrants became factory workers, especially in the textile, cigarette and fur industries. The employer was often a Jew who had started at the bottom and worked his way up, but that did not prevent him from exploiting his friends in the most heartless way. Many Jewish workers were victims of the sweat-shop system. The supply of manpower was so vast that wages could be kept to a minimum. But earning them called for 12-15 hours' work a day. In addition the work was monotonous, dull and tiring. In the clothing factories some employees did nothing but make button-holes all day long, others sewed them, while still others put the buttons on. Men from the liberal professions had no easier a time of it. It was almost impossible for doctors, engineers and journalists to find work in their own professions. These intellectuals had to accept manual labour, often of the hardest kind, for which they had never been trained. One of them, many years later, tells of his ordeal during his first spell in America:

'I was a navvy, day-labourer on a farm, ticket collector, bank clerk, street cleaner, sanitary inspector, teacher and employee on a small weekly until at last I got the job I was trained for. I was lucky enough to become a journalist on a big daily.'

In contrast to the 'old' Jewish families, both Sephardic and Ashkenazic, whose prosperity was demonstrated by big houses in distinguished streets, the Russian immigrants crowded together in the East River side of the metropolis. Like London's East End, but on a much vaster scale, it became the home of a remarkable alien world. The masses were packed in over-populated tenement houses with dark cramped rooms, lacking the most elementary forms of sanitation. It finally became a veritable ghetto where whole streets, indeed whole districts, hummed with Yiddish and street signs, newspapers and weeklies were written in Hebrew or Yiddish. Life bubbled and seethed; there was hunger and hard work. The efforts of all the relief institutions were but a drop in the ocean.

But this was only the beginning. These people knew that their misery was an interim period, the lowest rung of the ladder leading up to the light. Hope made life bearable. In Russia they had been the victims of a destiny without hope. In America they had to fight for existence. It was a hard fight, but they survived it. As the years went by they adapted

EXODUS

themselves to the new conditions, learnt the language, got used to the work and victory was in sight. Later, millionaires could tell their children about this phase of their lives. World famous business houses were begun in basement shops in a gloomy side-street. The rumours of such successes spurred on young new arrivals to try their luck too.

The sinister sweat-shop system of the factories did not flourish for long. The credit for its abolishment belongs to the Jewish working-class movement in America. Its beginnings were uncertain and fumbling; its leaders were young revolutionaries who had suffered for their convictions in Russia, but were often men of ideas rather than men of action. It took a long time to convince the working masses of the need to organize and close their ranks. All they knew was the primitive life in Polish and Russian villages. But as the battle for higher wages, shorter hours and better working conditions in the factories advanced step by step, the Jewish workers learnt the art. Today they are members of the more conservative American Federation of Labour. The fiery socialistic philosophy lost its grip on them and it was not long before the Jewish workers also began to cast their votes for one of the two great parties which dominate the political scene in the new world.

The Russian Jews became Americanized. The poor cowed *Nebbich* Jew, a favourite Jewish expression for poor devil, over whose head the sword of Damocles had hung in Russia and who used to shiver like an aspen if a policeman appeared in his street, became a free American citizen. After five years' stay in the country, the law of the United States turned the thralls into Americans with full civil rights. It was a remarkable metamorphosis to watch, both outwardly and inwardly. The patriarchal head of the family in a small Lithuanian or Polish town hung his ankle-length caftan in the wardrobe and exchanged it for a blue workman's blouse, his beard was cut off, his ear ringlets disappeared, the women gave up the *paryk*, which tradition ordered them to wear from their marriage day onward, and let their hair grow again. Liberty and progress straightened the backs of the former slaves of Tsarist despotism.

But invisible bonds continued to link them to the place

they came from. Letters frequently crossed the sea so that they could continue to follow every little incident in the street where they were born and lived until they left Russia. Dollar was piled on dollar. The goal was only reached when they could send the boat ticket to their father and mother in Russia, so that they too could come to America and end their days in the bosom of the family.

Many of the new American citizens did not renounce their past. They remained individuals in the middle of modern bustling New York. Of course they hastened to learn English —they were forced to—but at home and among friends they spoke Yiddish. And in the new world new blooms unfolded from this remarkably vivid language. A great Yiddish literature and drama experienced another summer, equally as colourful as the one at home in Poland and Russia.

Their faith was traditional Jewry. Of course there were some who, taking exaggerated pleasure in everything new, threw it overboard and, as Jews often go to excesses, held dances on Yom Kippur. But for the general run of the people the synagogue was the centre of their life. People from the same *Landsleit*—to use a Yiddish word for *Landmannschaft* derived from *Landsleute* (fellow countrymen)—people from Kovno, Vilna and Kishinew built their own synagogues with all the usual life around them: the divine service, education, philanthropy and other social institutions. It was the stream from Russia which summoned up new life in Jewish orthodoxy and made it a partner with equal rights with the reformists in America. The orthodox Jews formed strong associations and founded both Talmudic schools and theological seminaries.

They are a great source of strength in American Jewry. Their concentration in individual towns, especially New York, has made them a political factor of importance. The politicians are literally forced to take Jewish opinion into consideration if they do not want to lose a disastrous number of votes. And the remarkable combination of old Sephardic and new Ashkenazic Jews, the vast stream of Russian and, under Nazi persecution, fresh German refugees, has turned America into a melting-pot in which a brand-new Jewish conglomeration is being forged today. There are centrifugal forces among the American Jews. It cannot be otherwise with people of such varied origins, cultural backgrounds, economic status and religious beliefs. Consequently all attempts to form a common organization or *kehilla* have proved in vain.

There are also external difficulties to contend with. America has acquired its Jewish problem like every other country where Jews settle in large numbers. Anti-Semitic tendencies are observable. The Klu-Klux-Klan detests both Jews and negroes, and does them as much harm as it can. The automobile magnate Henry Ford was also one of the vulgar anti-Semites. He disseminated furious anti-Jewish propaganda and used the *Protocols of the Elders of Zion* as a weapon. Suddenly he repented and made public penance. But the anti-Semites have also made use of practical political methods; by putting the brake on further immigration by European Jews, for example. The results are noticeable.

But America has grown steadily stronger in the midst of these inward and outward tensions. In spite of all the assimilation, which has naturally set its mark on the new world, the greatest Jewish centre in the world has written world history.

Without the American Jews Zionism would never have become the vital factor it eventually did.

XI

ZION

'A mort les Juifs!' (Death to the Jews!). Like a hoarse snarling yell a single voice began to scream the old French cry of hate. Scarcely had it died away when a whole chorus took it up. As sparks in a powder keg send the whole cargo sailing into the air, the roar rose and rolled liked waves through the hazy wintry air above the Champs de Mars in Paris.

'A mort les Juifs!'

The packed crowds behind the cordon of soldiers had become a horrifying spectacle; they had turned into thousands of open mouths which went on and on rhythmically shouting their vile slogan at a lone figure in the centre of the square. Even the Lieutenant who carried out the degradation kept himself at a distance from Alfred Dreyfus as he broke his sword across his knee and contemptuously threw the bits on the ground. As an echo to the tinkling sound the cry came again:

'A mort les Juifs!'

Les Juifs, the Jews? Yes, but there was only one there. So why all Jews? It is an old story. One Jew has sinned—or more accurately one Jew has been sentenced. But the sentence strikes them all with the force of a thunderbolt.

The idea became a needle which bored deep into the mind of one of those who stood watching the macabre drama. This sharp needle hit a nerve centre. The pain flashed piercingly through his brain so that he began to tremble and shake as if subjected to some sudden vile torture attacking unexpectedly from an ambush. This malevolent cry also applied to him. He was one of the Jews these screaming savages wished in hell.

ZION

A mist closed over his eyes, the figures out in the square and all the open mouths faded away. He had to make a violent effort to pull himself together. He stood in the middle of a group of journalists who were to report on the celebrated affair for their newspapers. Exerting all his great willpower he managed to collect himself and note down all the details of the degradation. His despatch to the *Neue Freie Presse* in Vienna was objective, measured and accurate.

Theodor Herzl—that was the journalist's name—was tall and slim, his face was built up of delicate pale features, eyes which were now dreamy, now clever and observant. An air of *grandezza* surrounded him, as if he was a Spanish grandee. But a huge square jet black beard which framed his face and flowed down over his chest made one think of old Assyrian kings as we know their portaits from the statues of antiquity.

When he had drafted his telegram to Vienna and sent a messenger to the telegraph office, Herzl rose from his desk and went to the window. Down in the street life streamed by, colourful, vivid, teeming. He loved this street and the whole of Paris's exciting atmosphere and bustle. But today he saw nothing of what usually pleased him. Slowly a well-known picture appeared and took hazy shape. He was no longer in Paris nor even in France on January 5, 1895. Instead he was whirled more than three thousand years backwards to ancient Egypt. Herzl saw Moses, the people's deliverer, before his very eyes. *His* people's. Pharaoh's slave master was whipping a Jewish thrall who lay screaming under the lash. Moses was seized with furious anger. Like a lynx which springs on its prey, Moses was on the miscreant and killed him with a single blow. He breathed his last with the death rattle in his throat.

Moses came from the palace. He had never felt the yoke of bondage or cried out under the lash. Yet he felt as if the slave master's whip had actually struck him. Herzl himself had come a long way from that; he was the proud, free-born European. But at this moment the fact welled up that in his innermost being he was a Jew. France was Egypt, Dreyfus the whipped slave. Who was he? Was it possible that he was the deliverer who would lead Israel out of the land of bondage?

THE CHAINS ARE BROKEN

During these momentous minutes the power which governs the fate of men and peoples in its strong hands led Theodor Herzl towards his *Teshuvah* (conversion).

Like Moses in Pharaoh's palace, Theodor Herzl had lived in a milieu which was far removed from traditional Jewry. His cradle stood in Budapest, the capital of Hungary, Europe's frontier land between east and west since the grey dawn of history. There he was born on May 2, 1860. The story ran in the family that his father's stock came from Spain and they proudly considered themselves among Israel's nobility. Jacob Herzl was a Jew on whom assimilation and Europeanization had set their mark. Once he was a banker, later a broker. He lost his fortune in a crash, but like the energetic, industrious man he was, he began again from the beginning and became extremely prosperous.

His mother, Jeanette Diamant, was known both for her exceptional beauty and her gay wit. Like her husband she moved away from Jewry, read German literature and was eagerly engrossed in everything which was fashionable with the *gojim*. Her dream was to turn her handsome talented son into a German or Austrian, an emancipated European. But more than that, he was to be a great man. It was undoubtedly the women in these old Jewish families who acquired decisive influence and consciously led those they loved as far away as they could from the life the people had been faithful to for countless generations. Perhaps she was ashamed of giving up the old customs completely, but she would have been even more ashamed of emphasizing them. And this mother who idolized her son and was a dominating personality, tied him to her by such a bond that throughout his life he was instinctively on his guard against other women. She was largely responsible for his marriage being the opposite of a success.

So we can understand that the son from this home never visited a *heder* and was only a pupil in a modern German-Jewish school for a brief period. At the age of fourteen he entered the Evangelisches Gymnasium, became a student and moved to Vienna where he matriculated at the University. His family went with him.

ZION

His student life was carefree and happy. Young Herzl received plenty of money from his father. Behind him was a home which followed him admiringly; his studies went amazingly easily and the student had an open mind to all the impressions the metropolis offered him. Herzl could write and soon started to work as a free-lance journalist for the *Neue Freie Presse*. We have already mentioned that it was owned by Jewish capital and was one of Central Europe's most influential newspapers. It was to give Herzl his daily bread for the rest of his life. Even in his student days he was a writer to be reckoned with. He wrote *feuilletons*, which were popular at the time, corresponding roughly to serial novels. He soon busied himself with plans for writing for the stage. He never actually became a creative writer, but he was an industrious and productive man of letters. Most of his plays, which had long runs and played to full houses, have sunk into oblivion. Had it not been for his later achievements, no one would stage them again. But in the days when the world was young, success smiled on him. He seemed to be made for it, this good-looking young man, whose person was dominated by peace and harmony, and behaved with the natural self-assuredness otherwise only found as the fortunate heritage of old aristocratic families.

But it was not a true balance. Even at that time he felt the needle point prick the vulnerable place. Suddenly and unexpectedly the *Judenschmerz* no Jew in dispersion escapes awoke. It had even happened in school when a teacher said one day that 'idolaters' Mohammedans and Jews are heathens'. In burning indignation the boy rose from his desk, ran home and made his father move him to another school. In Vienna he joined the student society Albia in which he enjoyed himself greatly. One fine day the general assembly decided that in future Jews could not be accepted as members. Those who had already slipped inside the walls could remain, but no more would be tolerated. Then the glamour was gone for Herzl. He resigned in protest. We sense something deep down in the young aesthete's subconscious. He felt totally alien to the Jewish nature; he did not know it and was not interested in it. But without his knowing it, it lived concealed inside him and continued to do so. No one can escape his own shadow.

At first there were only faint ripples on the smooth gleaming surface of the water. Everything went well for him. He became Doctor of Law, he married and had children. The *Neue Freie Presse* offered him the important post of Paris correspondent at the monthly salary of one thousand gold francs—a princely sum in those days. They were his happiest, most carefree days. Herzl lived alone. His wife and he never learned to understand one another. She went on living in Vienna with the children. Herzl plunged into his new work, he was content to be the successful German author in Paris, breathing in the cosmopolitan atmosphere of the city where he felt at home.

Until the Dreyfus affair came as brutal awakening.

Teshuvah is Hebrew and means conversion. It is one of the key-words in both the Old Testament and later Jewish literature. Herzy himself described the transformation he underwent during the months following Dreyfus's degradation as his *Teshuvah*.

It is an old theological saying that the first step in conversion is called enlightenment. A man realizes that he is on the wrong track; he stops, goes back to the point where he deviated from the right way and takes it again. This was also true in Herzl's case. He felt as if a veil had been torn from his eyes. Theodor Herzl was typical of the assimilated Jew of the last half of the nineteenth century, full of optimistic faith in progress and the improvement of human nature. A steadily progressive enlightenment would make humanity look on Dühring and his fellow anti-Semites' writings as relics of the murky gloom of the Middle Ages. The Jews of course were perfectly normal people. Apart from certain inherited religious attitudes they did not differ from other Europeans. In the course of a generation or two they would become incorporated with their non-Jewish fellow citizens and the union would be total. Herzl himself had gone through the process. He had no positive relation to the Jewish faith. French positivism was the philosophy of his youth; it filled

ZION

the vacuum where his fathers' faith would normally have grown.

That was what Theodor Herzl had believed. And now the dream burst like a soap bubble and the stinging water made his eyes smart. Brutal reality, quite different from all his bright dreams, stared him in the face, cold and bitter.

'A mort les Juifs!'

He had to hear this hoarse cry in Paris, in the centre of his beloved France, the motherland of the revolution, the cradle of human rights and liberty. The evil slogan was aimed at Dreyfus, but not only him; it affected every single Jew. Herzl himself felt the hatred strike him in the face. In other words they could become as assimilated as they liked, but they still remained Jews. Alien, despised, persecuted.

This sudden awakening threw Herzl into a violent crisis, a feverish state fluctuating between excitement and deep melancholy. His friends saw him rambling through the Bois de Boulogne and wandering through the streets of Paris without noticing who went past because he had tears in his eyes. He spent the evenings at the Opera, listening to Wagner's works.

We can follow his crisis day by day in a diary he kept during those fateful months. There are passages in his entries where we can still, more than sixty years later, literally hear how he groaned under the scourge of anti-Semitism and the false world he had lived in. Despairing visions loomed up. He finds himself wishing that he was a member of the Prussian knighthood; he saw visions of himself as a doge in Venice, governing a brilliant hierarchy with Hungarian Jews as Hussars. But Herzl's origin breaks through steadily and strongly:

'My Jewishness has been immaterial to me. Yet all the time it lay there under the threshold of my consciousness, *unter den Schwelle meines Bewusstseins.*

'No one dreamed of seeking the promised land where it actually is. And yet it is so near. For it is in ourselves.'

His *Teshuvah* is proceeding apace. Herzl is finally finding himself. Jewry cannot be merely a question of religion, it is also a people. But a people cannot exist without a state. He was going to create the Jewish state.

THE CHAINS ARE BROKEN

The breakthrough has taken place; something new and epoch-making was born in the world.

'I believe that my personal life is at an end. World history has begun.'

On June 13, 1895, Herzl began the first draft of *Der Judenstaat*.

A Jewish state. Around the turn of the century it was an unexpected and shocking idea. Hardly had Herzl begun to ventilate his new conception to individual friends when he felt a cold wind of consternation and criticism blowing in his face. The first people he spoke to were on the verge of tears; deeply worried about their friend's mental health, they were sure he was insane.

At the time a certain Baron Maurice Hirsch lived in Paris. Like Herzl, he was a Hungarian Jew and had made a colossal fortune by building railways for the Turkish government. But he gave away everything he had in grandiose gifts for the relief of Russian, Hungarian and other down-trodden Jews. We find his name among the Russian refugees in New York; he started an enterprise which attempted the massive Jewish colonization of Argentina and he sacrificed millions of pounds to his philanthropy. Herzl sought out the Baron and had an hour's conversation with him during which he tried to win him over to his plan. But the two men did not hit it off. The past met the future and the gap was too wide to be bridged. When Herzl had gone, the Baron was furious. What did this young visionary imagine? Was a journalist to come and teach the great philanthropist that the tragedy was far too great to be alleviated by charity? Had he not dared to say that the Baron was merely creating more beggars?

Herzl also wrote to the Rothschilds and spoke at the Maccabees' club in London. There at last he found growing understanding and sympathy. But for a long time he felt alone. Only one man understood him straight away, the eminent psychiatrist and author Max Nordau. In the middle of his crisis Herzl resigned from his post in Paris and went home to Vienna.

But nothing could stop the work. Herzl finished writing

ZION

Der Judenstaat. It was done in a state of burning inspiration, 'standing, walking, lying, in the street, at table, and in the middle of the night the book rouses me from sleep'. During his poetic frenzy Heine thought he heard the sound of eagle's wings above his head. Herzl had the same feeling. Or more accurately he was like Isaiah, who felt the seraph press the glowing coal against his lips and said:

'Here am I; send me.'

When the book was completed, new difficulties arose. No publisher dared to publish such a controversial book. At last Herzl found a firm of 'outsiders'. They left the financial risk to Herzl and took a chance on a *succès de scandale*. *Der Judenstaat* appeared in February, 1896.

'The idea I shall put forward in this book is age-old; the idea of re-establishing the Jewish state. This slumbering idea was aroused by the outcry aimed at the Jews the world over.'

Those are the book's first words. Then Herzl analyses the Jewish problem and anti-Semitism. Assimilation does not solve the problem, because in spite of all their honourable attempts to merge with their fellow-citizens the Jews remain Jews and the European people are traditionally anti-Jewish. Herzl's conclusion ends with the decisive words:

'*Wir sind ein Volk, ein Volk!* (We are a people, a people!).

So no one but the Jews themselves can solve the Jewish problem. They must do so as a unit, making a combined effort. The issue of the Jews is 'neither economic nor religious, it is a national problem. To solve it, it must be turned into a universal problem and placed before the great powers as such.' Herzl wanted a charter, a guarantee, with international legal effect, which would assure the Jews who did not want assimilation a homeland they could go to. With prophetic foresight he conceived the idea, a generation before the League of Nations, of a 'Council of Cultural States', which, in collaboration with the Jews, was to organize the great exodus and the journey home the Jewish people have dreamt of for millennia. He was a determined opponent of gradual infiltration or piecemeal colonization, of the kind favoured by the Rothschilds and Hirschs. No, the Jews ought to enter their new country in large organized groups.

THE CHAINS ARE BROKEN

In the first great exile, by the rivers of Babylon, the prophet Ezekiel dreamed of reconstructing the nation in Jerusalem. Far away in the future he saw visions of the new temple. Like an architect, he drew and described a detailed plan of it. Herzl was a modern Ezekiel. He worked out his plan for the new state, overflowing with ideas about every detail: the constitution, the legislation, language, flag, army —in fact everything which constitutes a modern state.

It was no Utopia. 'The Jews who really want it shall have their state and deserve to win it.' The book closes with great visions:

'I believe that a generation of wonderful Jews will grow up from the soil. The Maccabees will be reborn. At long last we shall live as free men on our own territory and die peacefully in our own homes. The world will be freed by our freedom, enriched by our richness and aggrandized by our greatness. And what we try to create for our own prosperity will have a powerful life-enhancing influence on the well-being of all mankind.'

One shot in the mountain starts the avalanche which sweeps down with invincible force. *Der Judenstaat* was such a shot. The book set massive accumulated forces in motion. It sounds like a paradox, but it is a fact, that when Herzl fired his pistol he had no idea of the vast pile of snow which lay up on the mountain side, merely waiting for the signal to slide.

Hitherto Herzl had been the assimilated Jew. He knew very little about his own people. It is possible that his strength actually lay in this limitation. In any case he said that if he had read the books about the Jewish renaissance which German and Russian Jews had written before him, he would have remained silent and *Der Judenstaat* would never have been written. If that had happened, the course of history would have been changed. Not until the book made an impression far in the east did Herzl discover his predecessors' achievements. Russian and Polish Jews rallied round the ideas he voiced, then a whole world began to listen.

A generation before Herzl, a German Jew had fired *his*

pistol shot. The only answer to it was an echo. The avalanche had not snowed up sufficiently. Consequently Moses Hess remained a voice in the wilderness. But this remarkable man was nevertheless a pioneer of both modern socialism and Zionism; his tragic fate was a portent of the new events which were afoot.

Moses Hess was born in Berlin in 1812. His father was a well-to-do sugar merchant who brought up his son in the traditional Jewish faith. When he finished school young Moses Hess studied at the university in his home town. There he absorbed modern radical ideas and began to develop his character in a way which led to a break with his home. His excitable restless mind never left him in peace. Hess roamed all over Europe and at the same time went through all the phases of contemporary thought: Spinoza's ideas, Hegelianism, Communism and Socialism. For forty years he collaborated with revolutionary periodicals.

Moses Hess was one of the fathers of modern socialism, the first man to proclaim the social revolution, 'the last revolution of all' as he called it. His historical importance lies in the fact that he initiated Karl Marx into the ideas of Communism. Later he broke with Marx and joined Lassalle. Marx was too materialistic for him, he turned socialism 'into a question of the stomach'. To Hess its basis was ethical. It was not in vain that he had in him something of the old prophets' spirit, with their awareness of the eternal conflict between right and wrong. In Parisian revolutionary circles Hess was nicknamed 'the Communist rabbi'.

If we take a look at his home life, we get a remarkable picture of this eccentric man. He married a whore, not because he was in love with her, but because he wanted to make restitution for the wrong the community had done her. The dangerous experiment was successful. The two of them lived in harmony and domestic bliss. His wife, who was not Jewish, loved and idolized her husband, and patiently shared his poverty.

But even this emancipated spirit had his share of *Judenschmerz*. The first warning shot was the Damascus affair, which completely unmanned him. But he really felt it personally when in a moment of enthusiastic German

THE CHAINS ARE BROKEN

patriotism he composed a melody for the *Wacht am Rhein* and sent it to the author of the song. The score came back with an anti-Semitic slogan scrawled on the back of the envelope. There came a time when forgotten memories of his Jewish childhood with its feasts and prayers was revived. This made Moses Hess slowly move towards his *Teshuvah*. Hess was given the decisive impetus by the Italian struggle for liberty between 1859 and 1861, a period when Europe seethed with nationalism. Moses Hess became Jewry's Mazzini. He became conscious of his Jewishness and raised his voice to rouse all his people.

He did so with his classic book *Rom und Jerusalem*. This was published in 1802, the fruit of a long period of growth. It consists of twelve epistles with notes and an epilogue, but in reality it is a confession. The very first sentence shows that:

'Here I am again among my people after twenty years in the wilderness.'

These were words which many a Jew was to repeat as if they were his own. Moses Hess said in plain language that Jewry is *a people*. Yet if that was true. Europe had given the Jews their emancipation on false premises. It had believed in the reformed Jews who claimed that Jewry is a religion. He attacks this belief with bitter words. The reformists have only 'brought emptiness and broken whole branches off the people's tree'. With a shameless lack of pride they had persuaded the Jews to conceal themselves among the different peoples, imitate them and disappear into them. *Ubi bene, ibi patria*, where it's good, there's your fatherland, was their cheap catch-phrase. But no, cries Hess, 'The Jews are a people destined to rise again on a level with all the other nations'. It may easily be that Heine was right when he said that Jewry is a misfortune. But no Jew escapes his innate 'misfortune' by accepting baptism, for no one can escape their destiny. The Jews must bear their *Ol Malkut Shamajim*, the yoke of heaven, until the end.

But, Moses Hess continues, Jewry is invincible; no one can destroy it. It merely has to win its freedom. And that can never happen so long as the Jews live in dispersion. 'Jewry can never be reborn in exile. In exile reforms and philan-

ZION

thropy only tempt it to apostasy, but no reformer or tyrant is ever going to succeed.' There is only one place on earth where the Jewish people can develop their national entity: on the banks of the river Jordan.

He expected that help would come from France. During the very same years France executed the Suez Canal project. This meant that she had a foot in the Middle East and would be interested in its future development. Under France's powerful pinions perhaps the Jews could build their homeland from Suez to Jerusalem, from Jordan to the sea, says Hess. Which Jews were destined for the task? It would be hopeless to expect anything from the Western Jews. They were already too bound up with European culture. Whereas the future lay in Eastern Europe's Jewish population. There faith and tradition had kept the national soul sound. The Russian and Polish Jews hide the key to the Jewish renaissance.

Moses Hess's book was a failure; no one listened to the heart-cry which issued from its pages. Hess died in Paris in 1875, unknown and poor. During his tormented confused life he only managed to become one of the prophets who are without honour in their own country while they live. Only today is it possible for anyone to see what sort of an ideologist Moses Hess was—a pioneer in the history of socialism and the first visionary in the history of Zionism. Herzl says that 'the Jewish people have never fostered a greater spirit than the forgotten and despised Moses Hess since Spinoza's day.

Although Hess did not know it, during the same years the pious rabbi Hirsch Kalischer from Thorn in East Prussia had been engrossed with the same ideas. The strange thing is that it was precisely an orthodox man who did so. For the old orthodox Jewry is passively oriental in its relation to God and the world. It dreams of the age of the Messiah but it would be a great sin against God to take matters into its own hands and try to realize its hopes. Kalischer dared to take exactly the opposite direction to this weak submissive attitude. He said that the Saviour the prophets had foretold would only come if the Jews themselves helped. Therefore the colonization of Palestine should be started immediately.

THE CHAINS ARE BROKEN

Kalischer was not content with talking. He summoned a rabbinical conference and it had practical results. The first agricultural school in Palestine, Mikweh Israel, just outside present-day Tel Aviv, is the fruit of Kalischer's efforts.

There were also growing signs of interest in the idea of Zionism in Germany. But it was the Russian Jews who constituted the avalanche which Herzl set in motion.

'I thank and praise God's name because He has opened my eyes. He has sent pogroms to my town and they have woken me from sleep.'

It was a Yiddish poet in Russia who sang like that in 1881 during the bloody wave of pogroms. He was not the only one who awoke. The soil was ready among Russia's Jewish masses. The first seed of Zionism was sown and it grew.

Moses Leib Lillienblum's development followed the same paths as the poet Gordon. While he was still in his twenties, he hammered away to his heart's content at the 'obscurantists', the orthodox. In his thirties he almost foundered in the frivilous revolutionary circles of Odessa. When he reached forty, the pogroms swept over Russia and he rejected everything he had previously believed. The hope of the Haskalah movement of finding liberty and a future in Russia vanished as an illusion. Lillienblum stamps it as 'invention of weak brains and weak hearts'. Here again we follow a modern Jew who becomes conscious of his Jewishness. In fiery words he claims that the Jews can never bury or forget their unique history. That would mean national death and 'a nation cannot die voluntarily'. It was the Europeans, the Romans who drove the Jews out of their own country. So they must give it back to them. He took a severely critical attitude of the Jews who went to America. They were putting themselves on the same level as the gipsies. The only future for the people lay in Palestine.

The poet Perez Smolenskin had to leave Russia and settle in Vienna. But his inner career resembles Lillienblum's. In his periodical *Hashakar* (The Dawn), he fought vigorously against assimilation, considering the Hebrew language and the colonization as the dual foundations the Jewish renaissance should be built on. He was also the man who founded the first society of Jewish students who supported the same ideas. Its name was *Kadimah*, which means eastwards or forward. Smolenksin died young. Nathan Birnbaum succeeded him as the leading Jewish personality in Vienna. He it was who coined the word Zionism. It is as recent as that.

But it was the Odessa doctor Leo Pinsker who formulated the new ideas most clearly and concisely for Russia's Jews. He too had been one of the *Maskilim* and looked forward to a future of assimilation. The result of Pinsker's *Teshuvah* was the book *Autoemancipation*. It appeared in 1882, immediately after the pogroms. When Herzl read it many years later, he declared he would never have written his *Judenstaat* if he had known *Autoemancipation*. Everything was already said in it, and said with a calm logic and elegance of style which constantly keeps this book in the front rank of classical works on Zionism.

Pinsker asserts that Jewry is sick, and as a doctor he makes the diagnosis. As long as the Jews are in exile, they form no living nation, only the shadow of a people, a restless vagrant spectre, which healthy people refuse to approach in revulsion. And the Jews allow themselves to be trodden underfoot, indeed they have learnt to kiss the feet which have trampled them in the dust. Pinsker sums up the Jews' helpless and humiliating position in these words:

'We do not count as a people among the other peoples and we have no voice in the councils of nations, not even in matters which concern us personally. Our fatherland is an alien land, our unity a joke, our common lot the hatred of others, our weapon humility, our defence flight, our originality adaptability and our future in the tomorrow. What a despicable role for a people which once had its Maccabees.'

But the doctor pointed out the way to a cure. The Jews must free themselves by their own strength, in other words, *autoemancipation*. They must find a territory in Palestine or America—the place was immaterial to Pinsker at the time—with room for the homeless millions. This land must be guaranteed to the Jews by international help so that the people could settle there and live and develop in freedom.

Pinsker was not a voice in the wilderness, like Hess before him. The blood spilt in the pogroms had fertilized the soil for his ideas. A group of twenty-five young students from the University of Kharkov travelled round the Jewish communities and recruited 400 enthusiastic young men and women, who pledged themselves in writing to emigrate and settle as pioneers in Palestine. As a motto they chose the words of Isaiah: 'Beth Jacob Leku Venelka' ('O house of Jacob come ye, and let us walk in the light of the Lord.') The movement's name was formed of the initial Hebrew letters and became world-famous as *Bilu*. But even before Pinsker's book came out, *Hibbat Zion*, which means love for Zion, was founded. The members called themselves *Hoveve Zion*, Zion's lovers. Its goal was the same as *Bilu's*. These associations became the nurseries for practical Zionism and something effective happened. A broad gushing stream of Russians went westwards over the sea to America, but a little gurgling brook headed for the ancient Jewish land of Palestine. It was the one with a future ahead of it.

The first *Aliyah* began as early as 1882. *Aliyah* literally means ascent; the word is used specifically in the Book of Psalms in the Old Testament of the ascent to Jerusalem and the holy temple high up in Judaea's mountains. So there is something emotional and religious in the Zionist terminology when it uses a word like *Aliyah* for immigration into Palestine.

The only equipment the first colonists took with them was their faith and enthusiasm. The reality which met them when they began to transform themselves into farmers was want, toil and sickness. They were entirely ignorant of the difficulties they had to overcome in order to cultivate a country which had lain fallow and neglected for more than a thousand years. Palestine simply was not the promised land they had dreamt of by a warm stove in Bertitchev or Kiev, a land flowing with milk and honey, as they had read in the Bible. No, their eyes saw nothing but stony ground, sanddunes, empty deserts or bottomless swamps where millions of mosquitoes swarmed. How could they break the hard soil

ZION

or procure water for irrigation with their bare fists, for they had no other tools, and still live in a harsh unfamiliar climate? Many of them succumbed; they were victims of malaria or lost courage and gave up. If it had not been for the princely generosity of Baron Edmond de Rothschild the experiment would have collapsed. He sent them aid so that they just managed to get by. Small Jewish localities found their way onto the map of Palestine: Rishon le-Zion, the first in Zion, Petah Tikvah, the gate of hope, Rosh Pinnah, cornerstone, to name only a few of them. These first colonists have been given the honorary title of 'the Jewish Pilgrim Fathers' after the English Pilgrim Fathers who founded the colonies in America which were the kernel of the USA. Few as they were, they formed the vanguard of an army which was to follow and win their fathers' land for their sons.

We are in Palestine, the country which was known as 'Jews' Land' in Danish schoolbooks when I was a boy. For there the Jews had lived and experienced their classical great period until catastrophe overcame them in antiquity, broke the back of their state and drove the people out on their long wandering through two thousand years of dispersion. Yet they never forgot Zion, and the idea of re-establishing the people in the ancient country which came to Theodor Herzl as a revelation was really nothing new. There is good reason for the old saying that a chip of Jerusalem's broken walls has stuck fast in the heart of every Jew. It torments them and keeps the wound open. Zion lay hidden in the daily prayers, and the law ordered the people in dispersion, too, to celebrate the wine harvest, just as in their lost home country. A propos of this Disraeli said that a people which continues to celebrate the wine harvest, even though it has no grapes to harvest, will get its vineyard back one day.

'If I forget thee, O Jerusalem, let my right hand forget her cunning.' This immortal verse from the Psalms could stand as the title for the whole of Israel's long wandering. Every day threads from Zion were spun to every corner of the dispersion. As when Jehuda Halevi, with passionate love, sang his troubadour's song to the Holy City:

THE CHAINS ARE BROKEN

'All Spain's beauty is but emptiness
compared with finding the dust of the fallen sanctuary.'

The poet actually did make the long trip to Jerusalem and met his death outside the gates of the Holy City. Great men like Abraham ibn Ezra and Moses Maimonides longed to go there. They both did visit the country and Maimonides found his grave at Tiberias on the shores of Lake Genesareth. Nahmanides also took his place in the ranks of those who, during their last years, wanted to breathe the air of the country 'which makes men wise.' These great men were followed by countless lesser-known figures. Great numbers of Jews ended their days in Jerusalem and lie buried on the slopes of the Mount of Olives. Statesmen also made practical political plans for the country. In the sixteenth century Joseph Nasi was made a present of Tiberias by the sultan and devoted much of his efforts to laying the foundation of the newly-created Jewish kingdom. We have also heard in an earlier chapter about Napoleon's plans and Mordechai Manuel Noah's Ararat project.

The dream of Israel back home again in Jerusalem also caught on outside the Jewish people. It flared up in Cromwell's England and the great evangelical revivals of the nineteenth century poured fresh oil into the lamp. The revivalists passionately awaited Christ's second coming, but the prerequisite for that, according to the prevailing Christian belief, was the Jews' conversion to Christianity and their return to the Holy Land. One of the most distinguished men in the revivalist movement, the Earl of Shaftesbury, wore a ring on his right hand with the inscription: 'Pray for the peace of Jerusalem.' During the years after the Damascus affair the Middle East came on the agenda in English political debates and Shaftesbury was a keen advocate of settling the Jews in their ancient country. In a speech in the House of Lords he said that it was not an artificial experiment, but nature, history. When the Suez problem flared up, Disraeli expressed similar ideas and the eccentric mystic Laurence Oliphant caused a stir when he went to Constantinople to persuade the sultan to give the Jews the title to Palestine.

But Theodor Herzl did not discover all this until his

ZION

Judenstaat swept the country like a gale and lit the fire afresh. This time it was not to be extinguished.

Herzl wrote the following words in a letter to the Baron de Hirsch:

'Do you know from what elements the German empire arose? From dreams, songs, fantasies and a black, red and yellow flag. Bismarck only needed to shake the tree which the visionaries had planted. Then the fruit rained down on him.'

The same thing happened to Zionism and the Jewish state. Millennia of longing, hope and prayers, the dreams of devout readers of the Bible and the Talmud, the Cabbalists' castles in the air and the pogrom victims' blood had finally borne fruit.

But Theodor Herzl was the man who shook the tree at the right moment. His greatness did not lie in his originality, for the idea he had was an age-old one, but he had the ability to put it forward in modern language, melt it down into a plan and force the world to listen. Herzl was a genius. Not as a poet or philosopher, but because of his talents as a politician, agitator and organizer, with his indefatigable energy and profound knowledge of people. The theoretician is seldom the man to take practical action. Marx conceived the idea of Communism, but it took Lenin to put it into practice. We are perfectly justified in saying that Herzl was his own Lenin. When he published his *Judenstaat* at the age of thirty-five, not a single Jew had heard of him. Eight years later he died and every single Jew felt that he had lost his king. In his funeral oration Max Nordau said of him:

'Herzl was a born statesman. Without a state, without an organized people, without a single one of the means of coercion which normally go hand in hand with practical politics, he founded a state.'

Der Judenstaat made itself heard as soon as it lay on the booksellers' counters. The chaplain at the British Embassy in Vienna, a pious visionary of Oliphant's type, had calculated that the prophets pointed to 1896 as the year when the Jews

THE CHAINS ARE BROKEN

should get their country back. This same clergyman had been tutor to the Archduke of Baden. He went to him and opened the door for Herzl to the first of the many monarchs to whom he submitted his plan. Simultaneously a notorious anti-Semitic writer announced that he greeted Herzl's plan with satisfaction. If it was carried out in practice, Europe would be freed of its Jews. But the Western European Jews received *Der Judenstaat* sceptically. Herzl saw many raised eyebrows and cool smiles. One of the French Rothschilds said:

'A Jewish state in Palestine? Wonderful, so long as I become its ambassador in Paris.'

Baron de Hirsch was not the only man who turned a deaf ear to 'this dangerous seer'. Large Jewish organizations also rejected him. There were several orthodox rabbis who proclaimed him dangerous because he would not wait patiently for God's intervention, which alone could give Israel back her country. Herzl called them 'protest rabbis'. Often he remembered the account in the Talmud of the Jews who would not follow Moses out of the land of Egypt. They had adopted Egyptian names, painted their walls in the Egyptian manner and lived comfortably in fine houses with splashing fountains in the garden.

But in spite of all the critical voices Herzl immediately had a presentiment that he had touched the vital nerve of his people.

'The call you have made to the Jewish people in your *Judenstaat* finds powerful echoes in thousands of your fellow-Jews' hearts.'

Those were the words of a telegram Herzl received from Jewish students in Vienna, Graz and Czernowitz. So youth backed him up. The Kadimah groups also rallied round him. New communications containing enthusiastic support continued to reach him.

'I meet with approval in Russia, Galicia, Rumania, Bulgaria and Hungary,' he noted in his diary.

'The young university students say that the idea is taken very seriously in England.'

On journeys he was fêted in Sofia and London's East End.

ZION

People claimed that now he should act, and Herzl did so.

First of all he had to have a mandate to be able to act on behalf of the Jews. So he immediately convened a congress, the first of the Zionist congresses. It suffered severe birth pangs. Indignant opposition tried to destroy it before it could meet. What had this man Herzl hit on? All Zionism's predecessors had gone on tiptoe. But he struck the big drum and wanted the Jewish question debated in the full light of day, with the whole world as an audience. It was unheard of. And might it not jeopardize the Jews' newly-won emancipation? The German rabbis put every possible obstacle in the way of the congress. Munich was fixed as the venue. But the Jewish congregation in the city at once hired all the halls available on the very day the congress was to be held. At the last moment it had to be transferred to Basle. So from August 25 to 27, 1897, Basle was the seat of the Zionist congress.

It made history. It was the Basle congress which accepted Zionism's official programme.

'Zionism aims at the creation of an internationally guaranteed home for the Jewish people in Palestine.'

The congress consisted of 204 delegates from an equal number of Jewish communities. In addition there were 300 observers and journalists. *Hoveve Zion,* Zion's lovers, only joined in hesitantly. They were the people who lived most deeply in the traditional Jewish sense: they were dreamers and philosophers, expert in the Torah and the Talmud. They were not sure what this sudden shooting star in the western sky might bear on its shield. For the first time in history since Jerusalem's walls crumbled to dust under the hammer blows of the Roman legions, the Jewish people stood on the world stage united.

From the moment that a veteran Rumanian Zionist, a rabbi, chanted the old *Sheiyana* prayer which says 'Praised be the Lord who has led us to this day', they all felt as one. Deeply moved, the delegates fell weeping into each other's arms. As the river of speakers progressed, the divided streams flowed together to form a mighty flood. Afterwards Herzl was quite entitled to write in his diary:

'If I was to sum up the results of this congress in a few words—words which I am cautious enough not to pronounce

THE CHAINS ARE BROKEN

publicly—I would say: I founded the Jewish state in Basle. If I said it aloud today, I would meet with general derision, but in five years, or at the most fifty years, everyone will be able to see it.'
Herzl was right almost to the day.

Herzl lived for eight more years after he had set the work in motion. Without paying the least attention to the heart disease which was to put him into an untimely grave, Herzl hurled himself into an indefatigable struggle to realize the vision he had seen. Before his time *Bilu* and *Hoveve Zion* had colonized Palestine on a small scale and planted their scattered settlers who fought for their lives. Herzl never learnt to value this practical Zionism at its true worth; disparagingly, he called it 'infiltration drop by drop'. His contribution was political Zionism. Herzl viewed the Jewish problem in a world perspective.

So he practised foreign politics, and it is fantastic to see this hitherto unknown journalist accepted by the world's great powers as the plenipotentiary of a people numbering twelve to fourteen millions, scattered all over the world, always split into factions which fought with each other, and many of which were coolly critical of Herzl's majestic idea or opposed it. When he succeeded in spite of this, he could thank his cleverness and charm for it. And also the myth Christianity itself had created of a powerful wealthy Jewry led by a hidden secret world government.

Herzl turned boldly to the monarchs and statesmen he considered as key figures. To name some of the many: the Archduke of Baden, the Grand Vizier of Constantinople, King Ferdinand of Bulgaria, Emperor Wilhelm II, Joseph Chamberlain and a circle of British statesmen, the King of Italy and Pope Pius in Rome. He appeared before the crowned heads of Europe like a sovereign, this king of dreams and hope which have survived all other crowns and dynasties.

It was most important of all to win the ageing Sultan Abdul Hamid, the ruler of Palestine. During these very years the Turks carried out their notorious massacres in Armenia. Abdul Hamid existed as the fossilized symbol of a dying epoch; there was blood on his hands. But Herzl could not do

ZION

without him. In 1901 the Sultan received Herzl for several discussions. Herzl requested a charter for the Jews which would give them the right to the mass colonization of Palestine. In return he offered that the Jews would save Turkey from the bankruptcy which otherwise stared the country in the face. He made an impression on the Sultan.

'This Herzl is like a prophet, a spokesman for his people,' said Abdul Hamid after one audience. 'He has clever eyes and talks cleverly. Jesus must have looked like that.'

There are jokes about Herzl saying that he asked for a country and got a tie-pin and a decoration instead. It is in fact true that nothing came of the negotiations. But even if he never achieved tangible results either in Constantinople or the many other places he visited, his diplomatic activity made an impression. European statesmen took him seriously. From that moment Zionism was a factor in European politics.

In the midst of Herzl's busy life of travel, Zionism's great organization was built up. Its parliament was the congress which was held every year at first, but later every other year. Representatives from many countries met at these congresses, especially from the East European lands where Zionism had its stronghold and where most of the colonists were recruited. Every Jew who paid his *shekel* had a vote in the congress. The word *shekel* was taken from an old Jewish coin. The everyday leadership and organization was taken care of by an executive committee which functioned as Zionism's shadow government. Banks and big foundations were set up; Keren Kayemet le-Israel was established as early as 1901. The name means Israel's eternal foundation and is usually abbreviated to KKL. Its task was to buy land in Palestine, land which could never belong to individuals, but was owned by the whole people. Much later came Keren Hayesod, the basic fund, which looked after practical colonization. The Jewish people, hitherto stagnant and passively suffering, felt new blood flowing through their veins. Zionist clubs and societies shot up; new newspapers and periodicals were started. There was a political renaissance with heated debates, agitation and intrigues. The Jewish people were waking up and preparing to take their place among the nations as an independent state.

THE CHAINS ARE BROKEN

A group of spokesmen grew up round Herzl. We have already named Max Nordau. In addition to him there was the businessman David Wolffsohn. These two men became Herzl's political heirs. More colourful personalities were Menahem Usrischkin, one of the old *Hoveve Zion* hands, a pioneer of practical Zionism, Ahad Ha'am who aroused national feeling and the poet Chaim Nahman Bialik. Even in those early years people began to listen to the clever words of a young student. He was Chaim Weizmann, who was to become the wise leader of Zionism and later the first president of Israel.

In 1902 it suddenly looked as if political Zionism would produce results. Its ideas had met with a response from British statesmen. They began to see their duty to help the Russian Jews out of the hell of the pogroms. The English government solemnly offered to give the Jews self-government over a strip of land on the north side of the Sinai peninsula. Unfortunately the plan proved impractical. It would have been impossible to procure enough water to cultivate the desert. The following year England had a new suggestion. This time they proposed Uganda in British East Africa. The plan caused the first great uproar among the Zionists. It happened at a congress in Basle.

Herzl was in favour of the Uganda project.

'Of course Africa is not Palestine and can never become Zion,' he admitted. But the need in Russia was so enormous that the Jews ought to say yes. Max Nordau called Uganda a *Nachtasyl*, an overnight refuge away from the Tsar's knout and pogroms. But the Western Europeans did not know the Eastern Jews. A stormy opposition party was formed. The Russian Jews could never dream of giving up the land of their fathers, the one place on earth where the people could rise again. The congress was on the verge of disintegration; Zionism's days seemed to be numbered. A fanatic actually tried to murder Nordau. The delegates overcame the crisis by the skin of their teeth. They decided to postpone the final decision. Two years later the Uganda plan vanished into oblivion.

During these conflicts Herzl's lifeblood ebbed away. He died on July 3, 1904.

ZION

'Hail Palestine,' he said, 'I have shed my blood for my people.'

When the state of Israel was founded, Theodor Herzl's coffin was taken to Jerusalem. It is buried in Mount Herzl on the outskirts of the Holy City.

For centuries the people had not known a sorrow like that which struck the Jews after they received the news of Herzl's death. In Russia the Jews called him Hamelek Herzl, King Herzl. He had indeed been a regal figure to his people. When he spoke at the first Basle congress, someone said of him:

'He is like a branch of David's house, risen from the dead, clad in legend, fantasy and beauty.'

In the course of eight short years Herzl had made the scattered split people into a unit. He revived their national consciousness and placed the Jewish question on the agenda of debates by the world powers. It has never been deleted since.

'Zionism is our *Kiddush Ha-Shem*, the hallowing of the ineffable name of God, in life and death.'

That is how one of today's most profound Jewish minds, Professor Hugo Bergmann in Jerusalem, has expressed it.

The remarkable thing is that this Western European, who scarcely knew that he was a Jew, became the *new Jew*. The type had been in the melting pot for a long time. Mendelssohn's walk to Berlin, his break with the ghetto, was the first step. These new Jews groped their way forward uncertainly. The *Maskilin*, the enlightened in Russia, gave their strong support to them. But they were few in number and were never understood by the masses.

Herzl woke up and saw that he was a Jew, and he became the chosen instrument for recreating Jewry's national self-consciousness. In his person ancient dream and longings became flesh and blood, and stepped out onto the world's stage. With all his great past living in his mind, the new Jew stands foursquare on the earth, energetic, bold and strong.

But it was Theodor Herzl who gave him the vision when he pointed to Zion, the mountain which hides the soul of millions, and cried:

'If you *want* it, it is no fairy tale.'

THE CHAINS ARE BROKEN

A not too distant future was to show that his people had the will-power which turns dreams into reality.

THE END

For Product Safety Concerns and Information please contact our EU
representative GPSR@taylorandfrancis.com
Taylor & Francis Verlag GmbH, Kaufingerstraße 24, 80331 München, Germany

www.ingramcontent.com/pod-product-compliance
Lightning Source LLC
Chambersburg PA
CBHW061442300426
44114CB00014B/1799